W9-BPE-026

"Everything the New Zealand-bound cyclist needs to know, all in one package. The volume will pay for itself many times over, simply in time and money saved on research. And no one should hit the Kiwi-land roads without this book tucked into their panniers."

————Michael McCoy, Program Director, Bikecentennial; author, *Mountain Bike Adventures in the Northern Rockies*

"Bruce Ringer makes me pine for the green valleys and wide-open spaces of my homeland. His tantalizing descriptions sit well beside candid facts about weather, terrain, safety . . . Like me, readers will want to pack their spandex biking pants, and head for New Zealand."

————Maggie Kerrigan, New Zealand Tourist & Publicity Office, Los Angeles

Cycle Touring in New Zealand

Including Both the North and South Islands

■

Bruce Ringer

The Mountaineers/Seattle

THE MOUNTAINEERS: Organized 1906 "... *to explore, study, preserve, and enjoy the natural beauty of the Northwest.*"

3   2   1   0   9
5   4   3   2   1

Published by The Mountaineers
306 Second Avenue West, Seattle, Washington 98119
Published simultaneously in Canada by Douglas & McIntyre, Ltd.,
1615 Venables Street, Vancouver, B.C. V5L 2H1
Published simultaneously in New Zealand by Hodder and Stoughton, Ltd.,
46 View Road, Glenfield, Auckland, New Zealand

Manufactured in the United States of America
Cover design by Betty Watson
Book design and layout by Barbara Bash
Maps by the author
All photos by the author unless otherwise credited
Cover photograph: On the road to Mount Cook (Photo by Richard Oddy, courtesy NZ Pedaltours)
Frontispiece: Abandoned cycle shop, Outram, Otago
Pages 10-11: Dutch cyclist peeling a peach near Cromwell, Central Otago
Page 51: Hills above Manai, near Coromandel (Photo by Richard Oddy)
Page 199: Lake Wakatipu near Queenstown (Photo by Richard Oddy)

Map licence 1989/55. Crown copyright reserved,
New Zealand Department of Survey and Land Information

Library of Congress Cataloging in Publication Data

Ringer, Bruce, 1952–
    Cycle touring in New Zealand : including both the North and South islands / Bruce Ringer.
        p.   cm.
    Includes bibliographical references.
    ISBN 0-89886-182-9
    1. Bicycle touring--New Zealand--Guide-books. 2. New Zealand--Description and travel--1981– --Guide-books. I. Title.
GV1046.N45R56   1989   89-38348
796.6'0993--dc20   CIP

CONTENTS

ACKNOWLEDGEMENTS

The following people have been of especial assistance in preparing this guidebook: my wife, Lynne Ringer; my father, Bill Ringer; and my agent, Ray Richards. I am also grateful for advice and assistance from Heike Bank, Eugen Schmitz, Madelaine Johannson, Karen Lawson, John Fraser, and a host of (unfortunately anonymous) cyclists encountered while on tour; and for hospitality provided by Bob and Robyn Lawrence, Suskia and Peter Wood, Peter Roy, John and Isobel Fraser, Dr Jim Begg, and Mark Sogge and Cecily Stern. Several people have kindly provided photographs for this book: their names are given alongside the appropriate shots.

A COUNTRY MADE FOR CYCLE TOURING

Why cycle tour in New Zealand? For New Zealanders, perhaps a sense of adventure and self-discovery is enough, simply because it is there. Overseas visitors come because of its varied and unspoiled scenery, its mild climate, and its good open roads. Just as important, they come because the water is safe, the food is different yet familiar, and the people speak English and are helpful and hospitable to strangers.

New Zealand is, in short, a country made for cycle touring.

This book is designed to help visitors to New Zealand come prepared to enjoy their stay to the utmost. It will also help New Zealand cyclists discover or rediscover their own country.

Part I gives essential background on New Zealand itself and practical advice on what equipment to bring, how to get around, and where to stay: everything necessary to plan a trip. Parts II and III describe thirteen tours which, together, take the cyclist from the tip of the North Island to the tip of the South Island and back again.

Not every road in the country is covered (that would be impossible in a book light enough to carry in a handlebar bag) but the most interesting and picturesque regions certainly are. A cyclist who follows the tours described here can be confident of seeing much of the best New Zealand has to offer.

Each tour is divided into daily itineraries. In most cases, these "days" are between 80 km and 100 km in length and connect towns or localities which have organized campgrounds. This guidebook is flexible, however: with the information given, cycle tourists can easily modify these tours to suit individual needs.

The symbol ■ is used to indicate a side trip or an alternative route. Alternative routes have a similar ■ at the end of the description indicating the end of the alternative route.

Terrain and road conditions are described, also the type of scenery to expect, and points of historical interest along the way. Accommodation is also noted, with precise directions given to the most conveniently-situated campgrounds at the end of each day's ride. The location of shops in isolated regions is also given. Wherever possible, routes follow safe and scenic alternatives to busy main roads. When directions refer to points of the compass, these are approximate only; also, distances are usually rounded off to the nearest half-kilometre.

Cyclists should be warned that New Zealand is a hilly country. Major hills along the routes described are generally noted in this guide, along with their heights and distances. But, without letting the book grow unreasonably long, it has been impossible to list every individual bump and rise. Some stretches of country can only be described in such general terms—and in ascending order of difficulty—as undulating, rolling and hilly.

Some routes have been described as easy, others as strenuous. I have been as objective as possible, but definitions involving effort are by nature imprecise. Cyclists' perceptions of the same route can vary widely from one day to the next, according to wind and weather, load and fitness, and other factors. Rolling country can seem easy one day but laborious the next, after a hard night out; and even undulating country can seem uphill against the wind. Make allowances according to your physical condition, and the weather. But be assured that, however difficult the road, it will be made easier by the breathtaking scenery through which it passes.

Cycle Touring in New Zealand is largely self-contained, but other useful information sources are listed following the tours.

Information as given was compiled in 1989. Some prices, timetables, opening hours, and road conditions may have changed since, and cyclists should verify these if a tight schedule or budget matters. The author would be glad to hear of any other changes or additions that readers feel would be helpful.

Good cycling and happy cycling!

Bruce Ringer

Auckland
New Zealand

A NOTE ABOUT SAFETY

Safety is an important concern in all outdoor activities. No guidebook can alert you to every hazard or anticipate the limitations of every reader, so the descriptions in this book are not representations that a particular trip is safe for your party. When you take a trip, you assume responsibility for your own safety. Some of the trips described in this book may require no more than normal cycling precautions; on others, more attention to safety may be required due to terrain, traffic, weather, the capabilities of your party, or other factors. Keeping informed on current conditions and exercising common sense are the keys to a safe, enjoyable outing.

The Publisher

KEY TO TOURING MAPS

⊕	WANGANUI	Cities (ppn. 20,000+)
⊙	Matamata	Major towns (5,000+)
○	Russell	Towns (1,000+)
○	Waipu	Small towns (ca. 500+)
○	Opoutere	Villages and localities
	Waikato River	Geographical features
▲		Youth Hostels
△		Campgrounds
△		Campsites
▬▬▬		Recommended routes
═══		Side-trips and excursions
───		Other roads (selected)
②		State Highways/Provincial State Highways

PART I

GETTING ACQUAINTED WITH NEW ZEALAND

THE LAND AND PEOPLE

New Zealand is a green and mountainous land consisting of two main islands and a number of lesser ones in the southwest Pacific. It was first settled by migrants from Eastern Polynesia as long ago as the eighth century A.D. Their descendants, the Maori, developed an impressive tribal culture, warlike and politically fragmented, and stone age in technology, but rich in social organization, mythology, and arts such as carving. The Maori numbered perhaps 200,000 at the time of first contact with Europeans.

The first European navigator to touch on New Zealand was a Dutchman, Abel Tasman, in 1642. He was followed more than a century later by an Englishman, James Cook, who charted the coastline in 1769. The first Europeans to settle in New Zealand were sealers and whalers; missionaries, farmers and traders followed.

The British Crown assumed sovereignty of New Zealand in 1840, by proclamation and by virtue of the Treaty of Waitangi, signed by the Queen's representative and a number of Maori chiefs.

Widespread European settlement followed. Disputes over land led to war from 1844 to 1847 and 1860 to 1881, followed in some areas by widespread confiscation of Maori land. European settlers, mostly from England, Scotland and Ireland, soon came to outnumber the Maori, who declined in numbers and self-confidence.

New Zealand rapidly became self-governing in internal affairs, and became independent in 1907. It remained, however, part of the British Empire, and is today a member of the British Commonwealth. It has long been a parliamentary democracy and has traditional links with Western nations such as Great Britain (once known as the "mother country"), the United States, and Australia. Until recently it was a military ally of the United States under the Anzus agreement, but this alliance has lapsed with New Zealand's recent adoption of a nuclear-free policy.

New Zealand has a sparse population by overseas standards. Its 268,112 square kilometres (roughly the same size as Great Britain or West Germany) are home to slightly more than 3.3 million people. New Zealand has the image of a bucolic, pastoral nation; in fact, most New Zealanders live in the cities and larger towns. Rural New Zealand is declining in numbers of people, if not in numbers of sheep—more than 67 million at the last count.

Milford Sound with Mitre Peak in the background (Photo by Richard Oddy, courtesy NZ Pedaltours)

About nine percent of New Zealanders today are Maori, descendants of the original inhabitants. More than 85 percent are pakeha, mostly of British descent, but with significant numbers of Dutch, Yugoslavs and other Europeans. Of the remainder, the largest group is that of relatively recent immigrants from Samoa, the Cook Islands, Tonga, Niue and other Pacific Islands. There are also small numbers of other ethnic groups, notably Chinese, Indians and Vietnamese.

The dominant culture is European-derived. The major language is English, and most people are at least nominally Christian. Cultural influences from Britain, Australia and the United States prevail. With few exceptions, New Zealand writers, artists and musicians have adopted and adapted overseas models. There is, however, a growing interest amongst Maori people in reviving their own art, language and culture, and Pacific Island groups have preserved many of their own traditions.

New Zealand has long been one of the world's most prosperous nations. It was also one of the first countries to develop a comprehensive welfare state, priding itself on its egalitarian society. Recent years, however, have seen a decline in relative prosperity with long-term inflation, increasing unemployment, and consequent social unease.

Whatever stresses New Zealand's society faces today, its scenery remains varied and magnificent, with a diversity of landforms and landscapes usually found only in much larger areas: mountains, downlands, plains, river valleys, thermal regions, forests, wetlands, tussock lands. The landscape has been greatly modified since the days of first settlement, but is green and unspoiled to the passing eye, with large tracts of forest preserved in national and regional parks. Outside the main cities, the pace of life is slow, and the people are generally welcoming and hospitable to visitors.

HOW TO GET THERE

In three simple words: come by air. It is surprisingly difficult to get to New Zealand by sea. Occasional cruise ships call at Auckland, but there are no regular passenger services.

In the United States there are daily flights from San Francisco and Los Angeles to Auckland, via either Honolulu or Tahiti. The main carriers are Air New Zealand, Continental and United. UTA French Airlines also flies from Los Angeles via Tahiti.

Canadian Pacific links Auckland with Vancouver and Toronto via Nadi and Honolulu. From Australia, both Air New Zealand and Qantas fly direct from Sydney, Melbourne and Brisbane to Auckland, Wellington and Christchurch. Qantas also flies direct from Cairns and Townsville to Auckland.

Pacific connections with Auckland include Cook Islands Airways from Raratonga, Polynesian Airlines from Apia (Western Samoa) and Tonga, UTA from Noumea and Tahiti, Air Pacific from Nadi, and Air Nauru from Nauru. Aerolinas flies once weekly from Buenos Aires in Argentina to Auckland. Japan Airlines connects Auckland with Tokyo; Garuda Indonesia connects Auckland with Jakarta; and Singapore Airlines connects Auckland with Singapore.

From London, Air New Zealand flies via Hong Kong, Singapore

and Los Angeles; Continental and United both fly via Los Angeles; British Airways flies via Sydney. Lufthansa flies from Frankfurt via Singapore. Various other carriers connect London, Amsterdam, Rome, Athens, etc. with Air New Zealand flights from Hong Kong and Singapore.

Fares vary according to season and competition. As of mid-1989, standard midseason economy class return fares (round trip) were: Los Angeles–Auckland $1370 (U.S.); London–Auckland, £1385; Sydney–Auckland, $518 (Australian). Whatever the standard fare, it is easy to do better by shopping around.

Cyclists should bring their bicycles with them as personal luggage on the plane. The alternatives are to send them separately as air freight, which is expensive, or as sea freight, which is slow and unreliable. With sea freight, besides, it is necessary to organize and pay an agent to see the bikes through customs at the New Zealand end, and to pay storage charges.

Airlines generally like to see bicycles in bike bags or boxed, although some take them with just the pedals removed or turned inwards and the chain covered. Most carriers are fairly relaxed about weight allowance, but it is a good idea to take small heavy items on board in the handlebar bag. If stopping over en route to New Zealand, it is necessary to check the bike in and out of customs, and perhaps find somewhere to store it for the duration of the stop-over.

WHEN TO COME: THE WEATHER

Exactly when cyclists come to New Zealand and how long they stay will depend on the timing of their vacations and the state of their pocket books, but the state of the weather will also be a major factor.

New Zealand's climate is generally mild, but ranges from subtropical in the far north, to subantarctic in the far south. Most weather comes from the west. The standard pattern throughout the year is for anticyclones bringing six or seven days of settled weather to be succeeded by low pressure systems bringing stronger winds, clouds, and sometimes rain for shorter periods, followed by more anticyclones, and so on. However, there are wide regional and seasonal variations on this basic pattern.

In broad terms, the midsummer months of December, January and February are warm and sometimes hot while the midwinter months of June, July and August are cool and sometimes cold. Spring and autumn are mild. Extremes of temperature are rare at

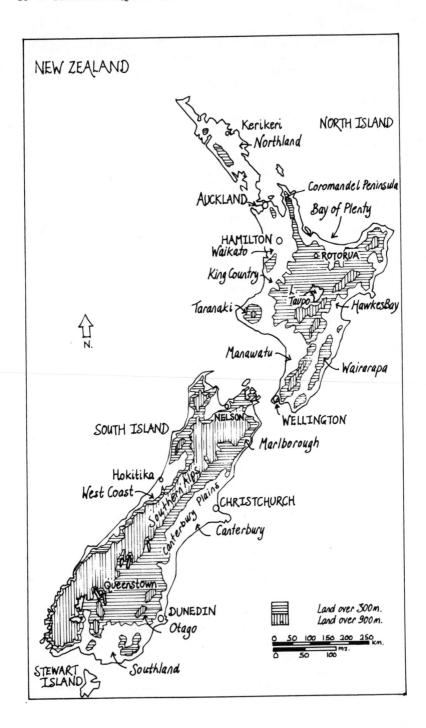

any season, as is snow in winter, except in the mountains. However, in all seasons, carry rainwear.

There are some regional differences in climate. As a general rule, the north is warmer than the south, coastal areas are warmer than the interior, and the west is wetter than the east.

In the North Island, Auckland and Northland have warm, humid summers and mild winters; the Bay of Plenty is similar but sunnier and drier; Taranaki is similar but wetter. In these regions, the heat of summer is tempered by sea breezes in coastal areas, frosts are uncommon in winter, and snow is almost unknown.

Hawkes Bay and the Wairarapa region have warm dry summers and mild wet winters. The southern part of the North Island, around Cook Strait, is somewhat cooler. The high country of the central North Island is cold and wet in winter, when snow often occurs.

In the South Island, Marlborough and Nelson have climates similar to Hawkes Bay, but colder winters. Canterbury is more extreme, with warm to hot summers and cold winters. Over the other side of the Southern Alps, the West Coast is mild and damp all year but, perhaps surprisingly, more rain falls in summer than in winter. To the south, the interior of Otago is semi-arid, with extremes of heat in summer and cold in winter. Southland and the coastal Otago region are relatively cool all year. The Southern Alps can be cold at any time of year. Snow is common in the mountains in winter, and often falls in the foothills, and there is permanent snow on the high peaks.

TABLE 1
NEW ZEALAND'S CLIMATE (ANNUAL AVERAGES)

	Rain-fall (mm)	Days of rain	Hours of bright sun-shine	Days of ground frost	Mean daily temp. Jan. C.	Mean daily temp. July C.	Annual extreme temp. C. max.	min.
Kerikeri	1682	135	2004	24.9	18.9	10.8	34.3	−2.0
Auckland	1185	140	2102	4.2	19.4	10.9	32.4	−0.1
Rotorua	1491	123	—	56.9	17.6	7.5	29.8	−5.7
Wellington	1240	125	2019	15	16.4	8.2	31.1	−1.9
Nelson	986	99	2397	89.7	17.2	6.5	36.3	−6.6
Christchurch	666	87	1974	88.7	16.6	5.9	41.6	−7.1
Hokitika	2783	168	1846	56.4	15.3	7.2	27.5	−3.2
Queenstown	805	92	1921	140.7	15.8	3.7	34.1	−7.8
Dunedin	784	120	1676	77.7	15	6.4	34.5	−8.0

Reproduced with permission of the N.Z. Meteorological Service

Since New Zealand's climate is highly subject to maritime influences, strong, unpredictable winds are common. Although these can pose difficulties for cyclists, they are also responsible for the country's largely unpolluted skies.

It is impossible to plan a trip to avoid unfavourable winds entirely, but the following observations may be some help. The general trend of weather is from west to east. Southwesterlies are the prevailing wind over much of the country, particularly the northern half of the North Island and the West Coast and southern coasts of the South Island. Local exceptions are the coastal region around Gisborne, where northwesterlies prevail, and the vicinity of Cook Strait, where strong winds, often gale-force, are common from all directions but especially from the northwest. Canterbury sees a mild annual predominance of southwesterlies, but strong northwesterlies are common inland in summer. Along the coast, as well, an easterly to northeasterly sea breeze often sets in towards the end of the day.

On the whole, winds are stronger towards the south of the country than the north, but strongest around Cook Strait. The Spring Equinox is the windiest time of year over much of the country. Auckland and Northland, for instance, rarely escape one or two short periods of northeasterly gales between September and November. Conversely, the Autumn Equinox is generally the calmest time of year.

The extreme variability of New Zealand's climate must be stressed again. Prevailing winds are rarely the rule anywhere for more than a third of the total days in any given year, and wind direction can switch from one day to the next, and even during the day.

In addition, every few years, warming of surface waters in the Eastern Pacific—a phenomenon called El Niño—disrupts weather patterns in New Zealand, leading to a cool and windy summer. It is best to avoid touring New Zealand during an El Niño summer. If El Niño is active, postpone your trip until autumn, or come another year.

When to tour, then? Most New Zealand cycle tourists get on the road between late December and the end of February, partly because this is the warmest time of year, but mostly because their holidays fall at that time. It is, however, possible to plan a satisfying tour with reasonable confidence in the weather any time from October through April.

Hardy cyclists can tour in winter too. However, the daylight hours are short (in midwinter it is dark by 5.30 P.M. in the north and 4.30 P.M. in the south); the nights are cold, especially away from the coast; and the mountain passes are occasionally closed by snow.

I like to tour the North Island best in January and February, when the long evenings make for pleasant camping and, if near a beach, the swimming is good. The South Island is best in March and April, when the holiday crowds have gone, the weather is crisp but settled, and the trees have their autumn colours out.

ENTRANCE FORMALITIES

Visitors to New Zealand must have a passport valid for six months or more beyond their intended departure date from New Zealand, plus a confirmed onward or return ticket, plus proof of adequate funds for the duration of their stay. They must also have an entry permit, except in the cases outlined below.

Citizens of Australia and citizens of Commonwealth countries who have right of permanent residence in Australia and who are arriving direct from Australia do not need a permit. United States citizens, Japanese citizens, and holders of French passports issued in Tahiti or New Caledonia do not need a permit for stays of less than thirty days. Citizens of Finland, Iceland, Malta and West Germany do not need a permit for stays of less than three months. Citizens of the United Kingdom, Eire, Belgium, Canada, Denmark, France, Luxemburg, Monaco, the Netherlands, Norway, Sweden and Switzerland do not need a permit for stays of less than six months. All other visitors must have permits for stays of any duration.

Permits can be obtained from New Zealand diplomatic posts overseas. In the United States, the New Zealand embassy is in Washington, D.C., but there are also consulates in New York, San Francisco, Los Angeles and Honolulu. In Canada, New Zealand has representatives in Ottawa and Vancouver; in Australia, in Canberra, Adelaide, Brisbane, Melbourne, Sydney and Perth; in Japan, in Tokyo and Osaka. Other countries with permanent New Zealand diplomatic posts include the United Kingdom, Austria, Belgium (also serves Denmark), France, West Germany, Italy, the Netherlands (also serves Norway and Sweden), Switzerland, Malaysia, Singapore, Western Samoa, Tonga, the Cook Islands, and New Caledonia (also serves Tahiti). Where New Zealand is not represented, contact the nearest British diplomatic post.

Once in New Zealand, visitors who want to stay longer will find that extensions of permits for up to a year are readily granted if proof can be given of adequate funds. Apply to the nearest office of the Immigration Department (generally housed with the Labour Department).

Work permits are harder to get. Applicants must supply the Immigration Department with a signed letter from their prospective employer giving a full description of the job, the period of employment proposed, and an undertaking that the job has been advertised, preferably throughout New Zealand, and cannot be filled by a New Zealand citizen or permanent resident. A nonrefundable fee of $80.00 is also required by the Immigration Department. Processing of applications takes a minimum of two weeks, usually longer. Approval is unlikely to be given for unskilled work, but could be given if the job requires a specialized skill or a qualification in short supply.

There is no customs duty on personal effects brought into New Zealand and not intended for resale. Bikes are not registered with Customs so selling an imported bike before leaving the country poses no problems other than the risk of not getting the desired price.

Because of the risk of spreading animal diseases in an agricultural country, the importation of animals (live or dead), meats and processed meats, saddles, animal rugs, eggs and egg products, seeds, plants, vegetables, fruit, soil, wooden packing cases and crates, straw, hay, etc. is forbidden. Cyclists should try to ensure bicycles, shoes and camping equipment are clean before getting on the plane. The importation of firearms is also forbidden, and possession of narcotics in any amount is illegal.

Vaccinations are not necessary, unless coming direct from an area where an epidemic is current.

MONEY AND BUDGET

Currency

The New Zealand dollar is a decimal currency. Some coins of the old pre-1967 decimal currency—mostly shillings and sixpences—are still circulating. Shillings are accepted as ten-cent pieces and sixpences as five-cent pieces. Australian and Pacific Island coins are also in circulation. Most, but not all, shopkeepers accept them as of the same value as New Zealand coins of equivalent size.

Prices in this book are given in New Zealand dollars, unless specified otherwise. This is a floating currency, so the exchange rate varies from day to day. Over the last few years, the New Zealand dollar has traded as low as $0.48 U.S. and as high as $0.75 U.S. As a very rough rule of thumb, halve the amount in New

Zealand dollars to give the equivalent in United States dollars. Current exchange rates within New Zealand are posted in the larger banks and are published daily in the major city papers.

For security, sensible travellers carry travellers cheques. United States dollars are probably the wisest choice, but Australian dollars, pounds sterling, and deutschmarks are all widely accepted. Banks give better rates than hotels, shops and travel agents. There is no black market or unofficial exchange rate.

The bank of Auckland International Airport is open for the arrival of all overseas flights. All banks in the cities and larger towns have offices with overseas departments, but all branches of all banks will change travellers cheques in the major currencies. Normal bank hours are 9.30 A.M. to 4.30 P.M., weekdays only.

Major credit cards such as American Express, Visa and Diners Club are widely accepted, although cash is more useful in small towns and rural areas, and is essential for minor transactions.

New Zealand dollars are virtually worthless outside New Zealand. Change them back before departure, leaving only enough to pay the airport departure tax, currently $15.00.

Budgeting

Cyclists, like other travellers, will naturally work out their own budgets according to their styles of travel; however, the sample list

TABLE 2
TYPICAL PRICES

motel room, two star, two people, one night	$50.00 minimum
youth hostel, single bed, one night	$8.00–$12.00
campsite, one night	$4.00–$8.00
meal, average restaurant, food only	$29.00 minimum
bottle white wine (bottle store)	$8.00 minimum
takeaway fish-and-chips, one person	$2.50
takeaway hamburger	$2.50
500 g pack cheese from supermarket	$3.50
loaf whole grain bread	$1.60
litre milk	$0.75
1 kg apples	$1.00–$3.00
250 g bar dark chocolate	$2.10
1 bicycle tire, medium quality	$24.00
1 inner tube	$9.00
repair broken spoke, cluster side	$10.00
movie ticket, central city	$6.60 minimum
train, Auckland to Wellington, full-fare	$68.00–$78.00
bus, Auckland to Whangarei, full-fare	$26.00

of prices given on the previous page may be some help. As elsewhere in this book, **prices are given in New Zealand dollars,** and are
valid for mid-1989. Add 5 percent + per year for inflation.

COMMUNICATIONS ────────────────

Postal services
In recent years, the number of postal outlets throughout New
Zealand has been substantially reduced. However, all cities and
major suburban centres still have Post Offices, as do most rural
towns of (say) 750 people or more. A few smaller towns also retain
their Post Offices, some combined with the local store. Standard
Post Office hours are 9.00 A.M. to 5.00 P.M. Poste restante mail can
be addressed to the recipient c/o any Post Office, and will be held
for up to one month. In cities, it will go to the Central Post Office
unless otherwise specified.

Telephone services
Public phone booths are common in the cities, and most small
towns have at least one as well. Post Offices also have telephone
cubicles. Larger Post Offices carry telephone directories for the
whole country; otherwise, call directory service. In Auckland dial
100 for local numbers, 102 for numbers elsewhere in New Zealand,
and 0172 for international numbers. There is an extra charge for
directory service.
Local calls from private phones are free. Public pay phones take
10c, 20c and 50c coins. There are plans to introduce credit card pay
phones, with cards available at dairies and news agents. Direct
dialling is possible over most of the country. Locality prefixes are
listed in the front of all phone books, otherwise call the operator.
Long-distance calls are cheapest in off-peak hours, that is, after
6.00 P.M. weekdays and during weekends. Main Post Offices have
facilities to make monitored international calls.

UNDERSTANDING NEW ZEALANDERS ────────────

The Language
Most New Zealanders speak English as their first language.
Maori is also an official language, but is much less widely spoken.
The New Zealand accent may be unfamiliar to foreigners, but only
a few words and phrases are likely to cause difficulties to English-
speaking visitors. However, it may be advisable to learn the words
listed in Table 3, many of which are used where appropriate in
this book.

TABLE 3
GLOSSARY OF COMMON NEW ZEALAND ENGLISH WORDS

Word	Equivalent Words
aerogramme	airmail letter
bach (pronounced 'batch')	weekend cottage
bike	bicycle, but also motorcycle
bush	native forest
caravan	house trailer, mobile home
chemist's, chemist shop	pharmacy, dispensary
crib (Otago and Southland only)	weekend cottage (see bach)
cycleway	bike path
dairy, corner dairy	neighbourhood store, selling newspapers, basic foodstuffs and sweets
footpath	sidewalk, paved walkway
garage	service station, gas station
gas	industrial/natural gas (sometimes gasoline)
jandals, thongs	light rubber sandals
licensed hotel	hotel serving alcoholic beverages
metal (as in "loose metal")	gravel
milkbar	ice cream parlour
motorcamp	commercial campground with full facilities
motor-mower	power mower
motorway	freeway, expressway
off-license	bottle store
parka	rainproof jacket with hood
petrol	gasoline
petrol station	service station, gas station
phone box	phone booth
pub	bar
sandfly	gnat
scrub	low brush
seal (as in "tarseal")	blacktop, macadam
sealed road	paved road
takeaway bar	fast-food restaurants, places serving food to go
takeaways	food to go
taxi rank	taxi stand
track	trail
tramp (as in "go tramping")	hike (usually in bush or mountains)
tussock lands	vegetation consisting of widely spaced clumps (tussocks) of grass, bunchgrasslands

An amusing and informative book which translates New Zealand English for Americans is Louis S. Leland's *A Personal Kiwi-Yankee Dictionary* (Dunedin, McIndoe, 1980).

Most Maori are fluent in English, but a few basic words and phrases might be useful. The Maori language is written phonetically and vowels have roughly the same values as in Spanish and Italian.

TABLE 4: GLOSSARY OF COMMON MAORI WORDS AND EXPRESSIONS

kia ora	hello
tena koe	greetings (to one person)
tena korua	greetings (two people)
tena koutou	greetings (more than two)
haere mai	welcome
ka pai	good
kino	bad
ehoa	friend
haere ra	goodbye
e noho ra	goodbye
ae	yes
kahore	no
marae	meeting place, ancestral home
pa	earth fortification, usually on a hill-top
pakeha	white person, person of European descent
tangi	funeral, grieving
tangata whenua	people of the land, original inhabitants

Many place names are Maori names, and a little knowledge of Maori suggests what topography to expect.

awa	river
maunga	mountain
manga	stream
papa	flat
roto	lake
wai	water

Aotearoa, the Maori name for New Zealand, is commonly defined as "the Land of the Long White Cloud."

Measurements
In New Zealand, weights, distances and measures are officially given in metric terms. In conversation, however, the old nonmetric

terms of miles, pounds, and the like are still frequently used.

1 mile = 1.6 kilometres (k)
1 kilometre (k) = 0.6 miles or 1093 yards
1 foot = .30 metres (m)
1 metre (m) = 3.28 feet
1 inch = 2.54 centimetres (cm)
1 centimetre (cm) = .39 inch
1 pound = 0.45 kilograms (kg)
1 kilogram = 2.2 pounds
1 litre = 0.22 gallons
1 gallon = 4.55 litres (l)

Dates

When in New Zealand, write the date the New Zealand way, that is, day/month/year, or get into the habit of writing the month as a word. To New Zealanders, 2/10/87 is the 2nd of October *not* the 10th of February 1987.

FOR FURTHER INFORMATION ────────────

For further information about New Zealand, contact the nearest branch of the New Zealand Tourist and Publicity Department. Overseas offices are as follows:

UNITED STATES

- 10960 Wilshire Building, Suite 1530, Los Angeles, CA 90024 Phone: (213) 477-8241
- Citicorp Center, Suite 810, 1 Sansome Street, San Francisco, CA 94104 Phone: (415) 788-7404
- 630 Fifth Avenue, Suite 530, New York, NY 10011 Phone: (212) 698-4680

UNITED KINGDOM

- New Zealand House, Haymarket, London SW1 Phone: 9308422

CANADA

- New Zealand Consulate, Suite 1260, IBM Tower, 701 West Georgia Street, Vancouver, BC V7Y 1B6 Phone: (604) 684-2117

AUSTRALIA

- Standard Chartered Centre, 26 Flinders Street, Adelaide, SA 5000 Phone: 2310700
- 288 Edward Street, Brisbane, QLD 4001 Phone: 2213722
- 330 Collins Street, Melbourne, V1C 3001 Phone: 676621
- 16 St. Georges Terrace, Perth, WA 6000 Phone: 3257055
- 115 Pitt Street, Sydney, NSW 2001 Phone: 2336633

JAPAN

- New Zealand Embassy Annex, Second Floor, Toho Twin Tower Building, Chiyoda-ku, Tokyo 100 Phone: 03-5089981
- New Zealand Consulate General, Daiwa Bank Semba Building, 4-21 Minamisemba 4-Chome, Minami-ku, Osaka 542 Phone: 06-2432756

WEST GERMANY

- Kaiserhofstrasse 7, 6000 Frankfurt-am Main 1 Phone: 69-288189

SINGAPORE

- New Zealand High Commission, 13 Nassim Road, Singapore 1025 Phone: 2359966

HONG KONG

- 3414 Connaught Centre, Connaught Road, Hong Kong Phone: 5-255044

There are also New Zealand Tourist and Publicity Department agents in Buenos Aires, Brunei, Jakarta, Kuala Lumpur, Manila and Bangkok.

Within New Zealand, the Tourist and Publicity Department has office in Auckland (99 Queen Street), Rotorua (67 Fenton Street), Wellington (26 Mercer Street), Christchurch (Cathedral Square), Queenstown (41 Shotover Street) and Dunedin (131 Prince's Street).

All cities and larger towns also have their own public relations offices or visitors centres. Addresses in the four main centres are: Auckland Visitors Bureau, Aotea Square; Wellington Public Relations Office, Mercer Street; Canterbury Information Centre, 75

Worcester Street, Christchurch; Otago Visitors Centre, the Octagon, Dunedin.

For in-depth information on New Zealand on the spot, try the main public library of any of the larger cities, most of which have comprehensive reference collections of New Zealand books, periodicals and maps. Information and staff assistance are free, except for photocopying.

For questions purely about cycling, contact Southern Cyclist Inc. at Box 5890, Auckland. This is a voluntary organization dedicated to the promotion of cycling in New Zealand. If writing from overseas, enclose return postage in international reply coupons or cash.

On the road to Mount Cook (Photo by Richard Oddy, courtesy NZ Pedaltours)

ON THE ROAD

WHAT TO BRING

If coming from overseas, bring bike, touring bags, bike accessories, tools and camping equipment. Good quality equipment is available in New Zealand but, like most kinds of manufactured and imported goods, is relatively expensive.

When selecting a bike, keep in mind that New Zealand is very hilly and that in some areas the roads are quite rough. The right bike to bring is probably a specialist touring bike with a long wheelbase (say 41 inches/104 cm or more). The long wheelbase gives a smoother and more comfortable ride than the shorter racing frame. Buy the best frame affordable.

Twenty-seven-inch wheels are preferable to 26-inch, which have a higher rolling resistance. Use 27¼-inch tires, however, not 27⅛-inch. These give a more comfortable ride, handle better in gravel, and lessen the possibility of broken spokes. For gears, fit a wide-range freewheel cluster and a wide-range chainwheel. Try to get a bottom gear as low as 27 inches (example: 53/33 chainwheel and 14/16/20/26/32 sprockets): there are a lot of steep hills to climb.

Some cyclists may want to bring their mountain bikes to New Zealand. These are coming into fashion here, but are not yet as commonly used by New Zealand cyclists as are traditional touring bikes; but standard parts are available in specialist bike shops, at least in the main centres.

Mountain bikes, being more stable and lower-geared then touring bikes, are an excellent choice for cyclists who intend to do a lot of gravel riding. Because of their smaller wheel size and higher rolling resistance, however, they are slower on sealed surfaces.

Cyclists who possess only one bike will presumably want to bring it, whatever its type. For those who have a choice, however, I suggest assessing the amount of gravel riding planned. If this is less than (say) a third of the total distance, bring a touring bike; if more, bring a mountain bike.

There are any number of roads and tracks in New Zealand suitable for mountain bikes (some cyclists would say it is a mountain bike paradise). They are banned, however, from National Parks, except on designated roads.

Keep gear to a minimum. Many tourists start off with too much gear and quickly pay for it. In my opinion, cyclists who cannot lift their fully loaded bikes with one hand are carrying too much weight. When packing, make out a list of what to take, then go through it and cross out debatable items, then go through it again and cross out some more.

A checklist of gear for a summer cyclist-camper is given below. Many of the items are superfluous and can be picked up for temporary use when needed. Cyclists who do not intend to camp, or who do not mind roughing it, can travel very much lighter.

BIKE ACCESSORIES
bike tools (see below)
pump
saddlebags
handlebar bag
bike helmet
lights
bike flag
luminescent vest/sash
water bottle & bottle-cage

DOCUMENTS
passport
plane tickets
travellers cheques
bankcard
insurance documents
wallet/purse
money belt

CLOTHING
waterproof jacket/parka
waterproof hat
woollen jersey/sweater
army-style cotton shirt/swandri
  shirt
rugby jersey (genuine, not
  designer)
T-shirt/sweatshirt
underwear
dark long trousers
bike shorts
touring shoes
light sandals/jandals
socks
bike booties
 sunglasses

CAMPING EQUIPMENT
lightweight tent
sleeping bag
sleeping sheet
sleeping pad
lightweight stove
aluminium pot/billy
aluminium plate
knife, fork, spoon
cup
matches/lighter
pocket flashlight

MISCELLANEA
aerogrammes/envelopes
notebook
pen
camera and film
first-aid kit
sunscreen
moisturizer
insect repellent
needle and thread
shampoo
soap
shaving gear
comb
guidebook
map(s)
watch
toilet paper
hand towel
playing cards
portable chess set

Cyclists who intend to do some tramping (hiking) will also need suitable lightweight boots, thick socks, and perhaps an inner-frame pack.

BIKE MAINTENANCE

Most tools and standard spare parts are available in New Zealand, at least in the better bike shops in the cities. Spares and replacements for rare and highly expensive equipment, however, may be difficult or impossible to find. Keep this in mind when setting up a bike. I have known tourists to wait weeks for replacement parts for "state-of-the-art" equipment to arrive from the States.

The standard tire size in New Zealand is 27 inches. Specialist bike shops in the cities also stock 700 mm tires.

Most towns over 5,000 people have at least one bike shop, although this may be combined with a business which also sells motor-mowers or toys. In smaller towns, it is often possible to get emergency help or borrow tools from the proprietor of the local garage or service station.

Nonetheless, since trouble usually strikes unexpectedly and miles from anywhere, all cyclists should be able to do basic repairs and maintenance. Practise before setting off on the big trip. Once the basics have been grasped, there is no need to carry a bicycle maintenance book. The best guides are intelligence and common sense.

BASIC TOOLS AND PARTS TO CARRY ARE:
adjustable spanner (wrench)
allen key (allen wrench)
spoke key (spoke wrench)
tire irons/teaspoons
spare tube
puncture kit
pump
spare spokes

OPTIONAL ITEMS ARE:
spare tire
oil
pliers
chainlink breaker
spare cables
brake pads
grease
screwdriver
freewheel remover

ROAD CONDITIONS

Most New Zealanders own cars, and New Zealand has developed a wide network of roads to serve them. Main highways between the cities are mostly well surfaced and well maintained but the condition of minor roads varies widely. Main highways are often referred to as State Highways and are numbered consecutively: S.H. 1, S.H. 2 etc. Some maps and guides distinguish between State Highways (S.H.) and the lesser Provincial State Highways (P.S.H.): this book does not make that distinction.

Signposting in New Zealand is generally good. Even the smallest rural roads are signposted, with distances between towns and villages given in kilometres. All streets in towns and villages are signposted. Arterial routes through the larger cities, however, can be hard to follow.

Most roads are tarsealed (tarseal = blacktop). Concrete surfaces are rare, and cobblestones are almost unknown. A number of

East Cape road block! (Photo by Richard Oddy, courtesy NZ Pedaltours)

minor rural roads, however, and some remote stretches of national highway, are still unsealed. These are called gravel roads or, sometimes, 'metal' or 'loose metal' roads.

The condition of gravel roads very widely. Some are well graded and easy to ride on. Others are a bone-shaking and spoke-breaking experience. The same road, in fact, can change from one day to the next. If a gravel road has not been graded for some time, traffic will have formed ruts that a cyclist can follow quite easily. If the road has been graded recently, however, the uncompacted gravel will have spread across the road, and the cyclist will have to push through it. Corrugations form on the corners of heavily travelled gravel roads in summer, and dust can be a problem.

This may sound like hard going, but the techniques of riding on gravel are in fact easily learned, and necessary to reach some of New Zealand's more isolated regions and most beautiful countryside. When riding on gravel, accept that progress will be slower than on tarseal because of increased rolling resistance and reduced stability. (It might help to loosen the toeclips while gaining confidence.) Keep the weight on your bike as low as possible. Use the lower gears. Do not get up too much speed downhill—there is always the risk of hitting a patch of loose gravel. When going into gravel at speed, keep the wheels straight, especially the front wheel. When braking, favour the rear brake—locking the front wheel will result in a spill. Use 27¼-inch tires in preference to 27⅛-inch. Low tire pressure, padded handlebars, and cycling gloves can all help cushion shocks. Wear your helmet.

Mountain bikes, of course, are ideal for gravel roads, but strong, well-designed touring bikes, properly loaded, are almost as good.

ROAD SAFETY

Bicycles are largely classed as vehicles in New Zealand, and can go almost anywhere cars can go. The one exception is motorways, which carry fast-moving traffic and are strictly forbidden to cyclists and pedestrians alike. In Auckland, this includes the Harbour Bridge, the new Tamaki Bridge, and the new Mangere Bridge. (Mangere Bridge has a cycleway underpass).

New Zealand's road rules are outlined in the *New Zealand Road Code*, which is available for $3.00 from offices of the Ministry of Transport or from larger bookstores. This publication is also available for reference in any public library.

The three main rules to remember are: (1) ride on the left; (2) left-turning traffic gives way to everything on the right; and (3) at night, cyclists must have an effective white front light and red rear light and reflector. Bicycles manufactured since 1 January 1988 must also have effective front and rear brakes, and reflectors mounted on the pedals.

New Zealand drivers are often aggressive towards one another and unsympathetic towards cyclists. Cycle defensively. Wear a good cycle helmet and a luminescent vest or sash, however short the trip. A flag will also increase visibility, and may keep some drivers away for fear of scratching their cars.

There are few cycle paths in the cities or on approaches to towns, except perhaps in Christchurch. Plan a route along quiet suburban streets in preference to arterial routes wherever practical. Obstructions to watch out for especially are glass on the edges of the road, and drainage traps close to the gutter. These can catch a bike's wheel and throw the rider.

Watch out also for suburban buses. The drivers have a nasty habit of pulling out from stops without noticing passing cyclists. Cyclists should never let traffic or timidity squeeze them too close to a line of parked cars. If anyone opens a door, a cyclist passing too close could be knocked down, or pushed into the traffic flow.

In the countryside, one feature American cyclists might miss is wide shoulders alongside the road. Relatively few New Zealand roads have these. As mentioned before, New Zealand is a hilly country. Roads in steep hill-country tend to be narrow and winding. Keep as far to the left as possible, particularly on blind corners, since vehicles often take corners tucked close to the edge. On particularly bad roads, it may be safer to walk the bike, crossing to the outside edge of tight corners as pedestrians do.

One final feature should be mentioned—roundabouts. These are circular intersections with an island in the middle and roads radiating off like the spokes of a wheel. They may seem chaotic to drivers and cyclists unused to them, but in fact allow traffic to flow freely through busy intersections without the need for traffic lights. Traffic entering the roundabouts gives way to traffic already on the roundabout. When circulating, watch out for cars exiting from the roundabout which could cut in front, and signal clearly at all times.

All this advice should help you have a safe trip!

MAPS

New Zealand is well covered by maps. The maps in this guide can be supplemented with the ones described below.

Public relations offices provide city maps free or for a small charge. Various commercial firms also publish maps of the main cities; these maps are available from bookstores and stationers. The easiest city maps to carry around are those put out by New Zealand Minimaps.

The ARA (Auckland Regional Authority) has also published bike maps of the Auckland isthmus. Because of the undeveloped nature of cycle facilities in Auckland, the main feature of these maps is the colour-coding of routes *unsuitable* for cyclists. They are available from the Auckland Visitor's Bureau and from some bike shops. The Christchurch City Council has published a much more comprehensive and helpful bike map covering the Christchurch urban area. This map is available from both the Council itself and the Canterbury Information Centre.

For touring, the most detailed maps are the topographical series issued by the Department of Lands and Survey (now the Department of Survey and Land Information). The NZMS (New Zealand Map Series) 265 covers New Zealand in two sheets, which will be adequate for many tourists; there is also a two-sheet touring series. More detailed are NZMS 242 (1:500,000), which covers the country in four sheets, and NZMS 262 (1:250,000), which covers the country in eight. These large maps are unwieldy to handle on a bike, but can be cut into manageable parts. NZMS series are on sale at offices of the Department, government bookshops, and some commercial bookshops. For detailed coverage of a limited area, consult the relevant sheets of NZMS 260 (1:50,000) at a main city library.

New Zealand's automobile associations (AA) also issue some very useful regional touring maps. These are available from AA offices, and are usually free to AA members and members of associations with reciprocal rights.

Cyclists who prefer to carry a book of maps rather than individual sheets could buy the AA's *Road Atlas of New Zealand* ($10.95 to members, $12.95 to non-members), which includes useful maps of the larger towns. It is available both from AA offices and commercial bookshops. Shell Oil also issues a book of road maps, *Shell Road Maps of New Zealand*, which is available from some of its petrol stations.

OTHER WAYS OF GETTING AROUND

Purists who must pedal every inch of the way without compromise can ignore this section. Cyclists who only have a short holiday, however, and would like to save some time by taking a

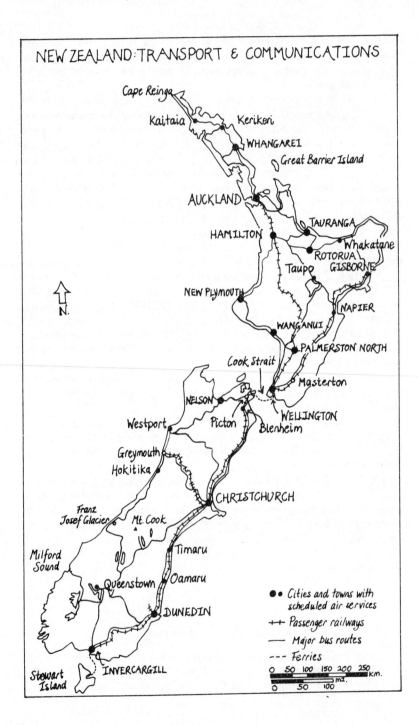

train or bus or plane some of the way, or even by renting a car, can read on.

Railways

Long-distance passenger services in New Zealand are few but potentially useful. Currently there are daily services between Auckland and Wellington, Wellington and Gisborne, Picton and Christchurch, Christchurch and Greymouth and, on six days a week (not Sundays), between Christchurch and Invercargill. The following schedules are correct at the time of writing, as elsewhere in this book, but cyclists intending to take a train should also check with any Railways Corporation office.

The *Silver Fern* leaves Auckland at 8.30 A.M. to arrive in Wellington at 6.40 P.M., and leaves Wellington at 8.20 A.M. to arrive in Auckland at 6.30 P.M. Stops, including request stops, are made at Papakura, Hamilton, Taumarunui, Ohakune, Waiouru, Taihape, Marton, Feilding, Palmerston North, Levin, Paraparaumu and Porirua.

The nighttime *Northerner* leaves Auckland at 9.15 P.M. and arrives in Wellington at 8.30 A.M., and leaves Wellington at 8.45 P.M. to reach Auckland at 8.15 A.M. Stops are as for the *Silver Fern* plus Pukekohe, Huntly, Te Awamutu, Te Kuiti, National Park and Otaki.

Tray lunches are available on the *Silver Fern* but it is cheaper to take one's own food. Morning and afternoon teas are complimentary, but the *Northerner* no longer has a sleeping car.

The Wellington to Gisborne service leaves Wellington at 8.45 A.M. and arrives at Gisborne at 6.50 P.M. The reverse journey takes from 9.35 A.M. to 7.35 P.M. Major stops include Palmerston North, Napier and Wairoa.

The Picton to Christchurch service via the Kaikoura Coast links with the boat-ferry across Cook Strait. The train leaves Picton at 2.10 P.M. and arrives in Christchurch at 7.55 P.M. Stops include Blenheim, Seddon, Kaikoura, Scargill, Waipara and Rangiora. In the opposite direction, the train leaves Christchurch at 7.45 A.M. and arrives in Picton at 1.40 P.M.

The *Tranz-Alpine Express* crosses the Southern Alps to Greymouth via Arthurs Pass daily, leaving Christchurch at 7.30 A.M. and arriving in Greymouth at 12.45 P.M., and leaving Greymouth at 1.15 P.M. and arriving in Christchurch at 6.40 P.M.

The *Southerner* leaves Christchurch for Invercargill at 8.50 A.M., arriving at 6.30 P.M., and leaves Invercargill for Christchurch at 8.55 A.M., arriving at 6.20 P.M. Stops include Ashburton, Timaru, Oamaru, Palmerston, Dunedin, Milton, Balclutha and Gore.

Fares are reasonable. The full fare for the longest trip, Auckland to Wellington, via the *Northerner*, is $68.00; via the *Silver Fern*, $78.00. It is possible to save 25 to 30 percent by leaving on a Tuesday, Wednesday, Thursday or Saturday and paying at least seven days in advance. Bikes can be taken on all these services, except on the *Silver Fern*, as accompanied luggage (despatch it via the parcels office at the station before 4.30 P.M.). The current charge for bicycles is $14.00, but may be reduced. Bicycles can also be sent ahead on any service as freight, but they must be boxed. Groups should check about carriage several days ahead.

Suburban trains

Suburban trains in Auckland run weekdays only (not weekends or public holidays) west to Waitakere and south to Papakura. Suburban trains in Wellington run north to Paraparaumu, Johnsonville and Upper Hutt. Some services in Wellington are replaced by buses on Sundays. There is also a service several times a day between Wellington and Masterton.

These trains offer a quick escape from the suburban sprawl and, in the case of the Masterton service, an easy way through the Rimutaka Mountains. Bikes are carried free in Auckland and for the equivalent of an adult fare in Wellington. Space is limited. Avoid rush hours, and load the bike into the luggage compartment yourself. This is sometimes difficult if the bike is fully loaded; be prepared to remove the panniers if necessary.

Note that the suburban lines in Auckland are under threat of closure. Please check with the Auckland Visitor's Bureau or local office of the Railways Corporation before planning a trip involving these trains.

Buses

The Railways Corporation Road Services Division operates New Zealand's most extensive network of long-distance bus services. Other major carriers are Newmans and Mt Cook. Long-distance buses are marginally cheaper than trains for the same distance.

If space is available buses take bikes as a passenger's luggage, for an extra charge. Otherwise they are sent separately as freight. Bikes need not be boxed, but should be packed to avoid damaging other passengers' luggage—pedals removed or turned inwards, handlebars turned sideways, chain and derailleur covered. If service is frequent, as between Auckland and Rotorua, a bicycle will arrive the same day as despatched. If service is infrequent, it is a good idea to send the bike in advance.

Air

Scheduled flights serve almost all the cities and major provincial centres: Auckland, Kaitaia, Whangarei, Hamilton, Tauranga, Whakatane, Rotorua, Gisborne, Taupo, New Plymouth, Napier, Wanganui, Palmerston North, Wellington, Nelson, Blenheim, Westport, Hokitika, Christchurch, Timaru, Oamaru, Dunedin and Invercargill. There are also tourist and charter flights to such destinations as the Bay of Islands, Great Barrier Island and Stewart Island. Air New Zealand and Ansett are the major carriers, but there are also several third-tier carriers. Fares are expensive by overseas standards; for instance, the full one-way fare from Auckland to Wellington is $162.80. Savings of up to 45 percent on certain flights can be made by asking for a thrifty fare and booking at least three days ahead, or up to 25 percent with City Saver fares, which are available on some flights right up to boarding time. Student standbys are also available.

Bikes are taken as a passenger's luggage if packed as described above for buses. Most carriers and booking clerks are relaxed about weight restrictions.

Ferries

The local Auckland ferries to Devonport, Birkenhead and Waiheke Island all take bikes for a charge. The Wellington to Picton inter-island ferry takes bicycles for an extra $12.00. (This charge is under review.) The ferry leaves Wellington daily at 8.00 A.M. (not Mondays and Tuesdays), 10.00 A.M., 4.00 P.M., and 6.40 P.M. (not Sundays). Timetables may be altered during holiday weekends. The crossing takes three hours. Wheel the bike on, secure it with ropes provided on the vehicle deck, and take all valuables above deck.

Rental cars

Renting a car or van can save time if not money on long hauls. A group could consider renting a car for the whole trip, using it to carry luggage and taking turns to drive. To hire a rental car, drivers must be 21 years or over and have a New Zealand driver's license, or a current license issued in Australia, Canada, Fiji, Holland, South Africa, Switzerland, the United Kingdom, the United States or West Germany, or an international license valid for at least three months.

Renting from a large firm with agencies throughout New Zealand sometimes costs more than from smaller firms, but offers the advantage of dropping the vehicle off en route without paying a relocation fee. Several specialist firms supply campervans equipped with beds and cooking facilities.

Rental firms will provide roof racks if asked. Bicycle racks that fit on tow-bars at the rear of cars must be purchased separately. Single racks cost $45.00 and double racks cost $70.00, and are available from major bicycle shops.

Car rental in New Zealand is hardly cheap. A medium four-seater sedan costs $73.00 per day plus $0.24 per kilometre plus insurance, plus petrol, or $112.00 per day unlimited mileage plus insurance plus petrol. Cheaper rates apply for weekend and long-term rentals. Petrol costs around $0.90 per litre.

Organized cycle tours

Several firms run organized tours through all or part of the country. Guides are provided, bicycles if needed, also a van to carry gear. Accommodation ranges from tents to hotels, depending on the price of the tour. Companies in the field include New Zealand Pedaltours (contact Richard Oddy, P.O. Box 49039, Auckland 4, phone: 3020968 674605) and Paradise Pedallers, 20 Lowry Crescent, Stokes Valley, Wellington. Bikes can also be rented for about $12.00 per day from various bikeshops and tour operators in the main cities and in some tourist centres.

ACCOMMODATION

For the cyclist, camping is the cheapest, most flexible option. Free camping is possible throughout most of the country; organized campgrounds are common, and the solo cyclist rarely if ever needs to book ahead. Youth Hostelling is another budget possibility, possibly combined with camping for extra flexibility. Many New Zealand motorcamps rent out spartan but relatively low-priced cabins. Motels are plentiful. Though too expensive for solo cyclists to consider, they offer reasonable value for groups.

Free camping

Camping is forbidden in water catchment areas, and National Parks, and reserves, except where formal sites have been established. Outside such areas, it is usually legal to camp on public land, unless signposted otherwise. A few heavily touristed areas, however, ban roadside camping. These include the Bay of Islands, Waiheke Island, and the Coromandel Peninsula. To camp on private land, ask permission from the owner.

Roadside picnic areas are common along main roads. Many of these areas have toilets and running water and can be good places for an overnight stop (be discreet). Department of Conservation

Campsite at South Mavora Lake

recreational parks, State Forest Parks and National Parks often have organized campgrounds with basic facilities—toilets, tap water, open fireplaces—for a fee.

Huts

Cyclists who are also hikers will find huts maintained by the Department of Conservation throughout the National Parks. These have bunks and basic cooking facilities, usually open fires. The huts used to be free but, despite considerable opposition from outdoor organizations, the Department has recently introduced a pass system. Charges range from $4.00 to $12.00 per night, according to the standard of the hut. Bivouacs and emergency shelters are still free. Passes are available from Department of Conservation officers and rangers, park visitors centres, and some tramping clubs and outdoor equipment retailers.

In the back-country there are also occasional huts maintained by tramping clubs and privately owned huts. In remote areas, these are traditionally left unlocked, and hikers are welcome to use them as emergency shelters.

Motorcamps

Most New Zealand towns and tourist localities have one or more municipal or privately owned campgrounds, generally known as "motorcamps". Municipal motorcamps are usually slightly cheaper than privately owned ones. Facilities vary in standard, but always include toilets, showers, laundries and kitchens (but not cooking implements). Some motorcamps have small shops and recreation rooms. Charges per adult per night range from $3.00 to $8.00. Solo cyclists with lightweight tents will rarely find it necessary to book ahead, except perhaps during the peak holiday season in Auckland, Rotorua, Queenstown and the Bay of Islands.

Cabins

Many motorcamps provide cabins or on-site caravans sleeping from two to six people. These have bunks and, sometimes, cooking facilities. Users supply their own bed linen, or rent it from the management. Charges start at $8.00 per person per night, but most places charge for a minimum of two people. Solo travellers can often find someone to share. Some motorcamps also have tourist flats, which are better appointed than cabins but also more expensive.

Youth Hostels

New Zealand has 49 Youth Hostels spread around the country. These are open all year round, except for a few "summer" hostels. Members pay $8.00 to $12.00 per night for dormitory beds and use of a communal kitchen and washing facilities. Use of a standard sheet sleeping bag is obligatory. Residents must vacate the hostel between 10.00 A.M. and 5.00 P.M., and there is an 11.00 P.M. curfew.

Overseas visitors who do not hold a valid membership card of their own country's association can take out international membership for $25.00. Join at the Association's offices (36 Customs St., Auckland; 28 Worcester St., Christchurch; 40 Tinakori Rd., Wellington), any Youth Hostel, any University or Technical Institute, student union office, or any branch of the Westpac Bank. The annual *YHANZ Handbook* is free with membership.

Booking is advisable at peak holiday times (Christmas to New Year, Easter, the May and August school holidays), and can be made at individual hostels or via the National Reservations Office, YHANZ, P.O. Box 436, Christchurch.

It is possible to cycle around New Zealand staying at Youth Hostels alone, but the choice of routes in some areas will be limited. Cyclists who want to travel light but still reasonably cheaply could combine Youth Hostelling with occasional nights in cabins or motels.

Some cyclists will find Youth Hostels a little restrictive. In the larger cities there are various "alternative" or "backpackers" hostels offering similar facilities but a less formal environment.

YMCA/YWCA

YMCA hostels in Auckland, Christchurch and Dunedin offer casual accommodation for about $30.00 per night. The YWCA in Auckland (10 Carlton Gore Rd, Grafton) has a backpackers' dormitory open to travellers of both sexes for $7.00 per night. There are also YWCA hostels in Whangarei, Hamilton, Rotorua, New Plymouth, Lower Hutt, Wanganui, Wellington, Christchurch, Dunedin and Gore. Policies on casual accommodation vary from hostel to hostel.

Motels

New Zealand motels can be good value. Even the cheapest motels are clean and well appointed. Motel units are really sleeping apartments which take four to six guests. Each unit has a living room with television and fold-out sofas, one or two bedrooms, a bathroom with shower, and a fully equipped kitchen. All motels have laundry rooms, many have swimming pools, some have shops and restaurants. Units are unserviced. A continental breakfast may be provided, but otherwise guests do their own cooking and cleaning for the duration of their stay.

Prices start at $50.00 per unit per night for two people, with an extra $12.00 per night for each extra person. This is obviously unrealistic for solo travellers, but not unreasonable for groups. Booking ahead is a good idea in the peak holiday season.

Serviced motels are relatively rare. These have bedrooms which double as living rooms. Although they have no cooking facilities, they do offer maid service. For cyclists, they seem to offer less value for money than the usual kind of motel.

Hotels

Hotels range enormously in standard and price, from spartan budget establishments through private hotels and guesthouses, to the local branches of the international luxury chains. Auckland's hotels, for instance, range from the Salvation Army's Railton (upper Queen St.), where bed-and-breakfast is $33.00 per night, to the Sheraton (Symonds St.), where single rooms start at $195.00.

Most country towns, however small, have at least one "pub" (i.e., hotel). The main business of these establishments comes from the bar, but they are obliged by law to offer accommodation and meals as well. Some are very comfortable; others are drab, and staying in them is like going back forty years in decor and service. Of course, that may be an adventure in itself.

Home stays/farmstays

New Zealand has several organizations which will arrange paying stays in private houses and homesteads. Enquire at any tourist office if interested.

Cyclists Accommodation Directory

This is a list of people who are happy to offer free hospitality to travelling cyclists. Anyone on the list can stay with anyone else on the list, but in order to benefit from the hospitality, they must be prepared to offer it themselves. To be included on the directory, cyclists should send name, address and phone number, plus a self-addressed envelope and international reply coupons or cash sufficient for return postage, to Bruce O'Halloran, 40 Amy St., Ellerslie, Auckland 6 (Phone: Auckland 591961).

Directories: accommodation directories are listed in Further Reading.

THE COUNTRYSIDE CODE

New Zealand has a relatively clean and unspoiled natural environment by world standards, and cyclists should do their best to keep it that way. Good behaviour in the countryside is, as elsewhere, largely a matter of common sense and courtesy.

If camping on private land, ask permission from the landowner first. Respect his or her land and property.

Leave farm gates as they are found: open if open, shut if shut. Farmers sometimes leave gates open so that livestock can reach water in the next paddock. If climbing gates, climb them at the hinge end. If climbing fences, climb them near to the strainer post to avoid slackening the wire.

Be careful about fires. Some areas are designated fire-risk areas, and fires are strictly forbidden there. In campsites, light fires only in the official fire-places. Many environmentalists these days disapprove of open campfires in principle, since they use up wood that would otherwise add to the humus content of the soil. This seems less of a consideration if using driftwood at the beach. In any case, light fires with dead wood, never with living wood.

When finished with a fire, dowse it thoroughly. Make sure there are no hot embers left that could rekindle, or hot piles of ash that people could stumble into.

Never leave rubbish behind. Bury human wastes, and bury them deep. But carry everything else out, tins, bottles, empty packets, and all, and dispose of them in the nearest waste bin.

Do not use shampoos, detergents, so-called degradable soaps or other chemicals in streams, rivers or lakes.

Cyclists who do some hiking and use Department of Conservation or private huts in National Parks or the back-country should leave these huts tidy, replace any split wood used, and take all their garbage with them.

In short, leave things as you find them—or tidier.

PUBLIC HOLIDAYS

The following are Public Holidays in New Zealand: New Year's Day, January 2, Waitangi Day (6 February), Good Friday, Easter Monday, Anzac Day (25 April), Queen's Birthday (first Monday in June), Labour Day (fourth Monday in October), Christmas Day, Boxing Day (26 December) and provincial Anniversary Days within each province. Banks, offices, most shops and some museums are closed on those days, and public transport runs to a reduced timetable.

SHOPPING

Throughout this guide, population figures for the 1986 census are given for all towns over 500 people, and for many under. This gives a rough indication of the range of facilities to expect. Towns of more than 5,000 people will have a full range of shops and services including, in almost all cases, at least one bicycle shop. Towns of more than 1,000 people will have several shops, at least one bank, and a Post Office. Towns of more than 500 people, and many even smaller towns, will have at least one general store. Note, though, that New Zealand is a sparsely-populated country. Names on a map in rural localities are sometimes just that, names on a map, with little more than perhaps a rural school or a disused service station to mark their actual location.

Standard opening hours are 9.00 A.M. to 5.30 P.M. weekdays with a late night to 9.00 P.M. either Thursday or Friday. Saturday morning opening from 9.00 A.M. to 1.00 P.M. is becoming more common, with some supermarkets and department stores in the cities, especially in Auckland, staying open to 4.00 P.M. Most shops are closed Sundays and public holidays. Corner dairies, however, selling newspapers, bread, milk, and other basic foodstuffs, are generally open from 8.00 A.M. to 7.00 P.M., sometimes later, every day. Some service stations, open even longer hours, are beginning to stock foodstuffs.

FOOD AND DRINK

Self-catering is the cheapest way to eat. Youth Hostels, motor-camps and motels all provide cooking facilities; motels provide implements as well. Campers can cook on open fires (except in fire-risk areas), or carry portable stoves. Supermarkets are the cheapest place to shop, neighbourhood groceries and corner dairies are more expensive, delicatessens considerably more so.

Fast-food
Fast-food is available from numerous takeaway bars and from outlets of the large franchises such as McDonald's, Georgie Pie and Pizza Hut. Takeaway bars offer fish-and-chips, hamburgers, toasted sandwiches and milkshakes; some also serve allegedly Chinese food. Corner dairies stock hot meat pies, a New Zealand speciality, which make energizing (but less often appetizing) snacks for little more than a dollar.

Eating out
Most towns have lunch bars and coffee bars, which offer self-service snacks of varying value. Tearooms are found along main highways, and can be good places to stop for a rest, a snack and a pot of tea. Small towns usually have at least one "Joe's Diner" type of eatery, which offers plain food of the steak-and-chips, egg-and-chips variety. The cities have a wider range of restaurants, ranging from brasseries and cafés through ethnic restaurants to sophisti-cated imitations of French establishments. Prices are always dis-played outside.

Emergency rations
Rural New Zealand is sparsely populated. In some areas it can be a day's ride or more between towns and villages. It is a good idea to carry 'emergency' rations, perhaps wholemeal bread, cheese, dried fruit, powdered milk, rolled oats, and something to drink. New Zealand cyclists and trampers often carry scroggin, a delicious home-made mixture of nuts, seeds, raisins, dried apricots, sultanas and hunks of dark chocolate.

Alcohol
The official age for public drinking in New Zealand is 20. Al-

cohol is bought by the glass in pubs (bars), by the bottle from hotel off-licenses, and by the crate at wholesalers.

All towns have pubs (bars with hotel accommodation attached) or taverns (bars without accommodation attached). These are open 11.00 A.M. to 10.00 P.M. weekdays and 11.00 A.M. to 11.00 P.M. Saturdays. Most have three bars: house bar, lounge bar and public bar. The first is for hotel guests and their guests, the second for the better-dressed casual customers, the third for the rest. Public bars in many places are very, very rough.

HEALTH, SAFETY AND SECURITY

Emergencies
Dial 111 for police, ambulance and fire-service.

Diet
Tap-water is safe in most places, so is food. There is very little risk of stomach upset anywhere, except for travellers who eat fast-food frequently. Wash fruit and vegetables carefully, however, because of pesticides.

Until quite recently, it was safe to drink clear water from running streams in bush or open country almost anywhere in New Zealand. In 1988, however, *Giardia lamblia,* a water-borne parasite, was discovered in some streams. Ingesting this parasite cause giardiasis, with symptoms including flatulence, stomach pains, nausea and diarrhoea. Giardia will presumably spread throughout the country in the future. It is therefore now advisable to purify stream-water by special filtration or boiling for at least five minutes before drinking it.

Camping out
There are no dangerous animals in New Zealand, few dangerous people (but women travelling on their own should, as everywhere, be careful) and no snakes or poisonous creepy-crawlies. The one exception is the katipo, a red-backed spider which is sometimes found under driftwood on beaches. Encounters with katipos are infrequent and rarely fatal, but anyone who *is* bitten should seek medical attention urgently.

As described in the section on camping, be careful with camp-site fires. Some areas are designated fire-risk areas, and fires are strictly forbidden there. These areas mostly include the large exotic pine-plantations of the central North Island. The tussock country of the South Island also becomes tinder-dry in summer. Signposts along the main roads indicate the degree of fire risk.

Major bush fires in New Zealand, however, unlike Australia, are uncommon.

Health

No vaccinations are required for entering New Zealand, except for travellers coming directly from an area where an epidemic is current. Serious infectious diseases are rare in New Zealand, and AIDS is not yet widespread. Prophylactics are available from chemist shops. Carry a basic medicine kit when on the road: antiseptic, plasters, tweezers, scissors, needle and thread, aspirin. Take sunscreen, insect repellent and sunglasses as well.

The accident-compensation system in New Zealand covers most accident-related medical expenses for everyone, including visitors. Travellers should have medical insurance as well, however, since accident compensation does not include the cost of repatriation, and ceases on the moment of departure from New Zealand.

Citizens of Australia and the United Kingdom are entitled to emergency medical care for sickness on the same terms as New Zealand citizens. Visits to the doctor cost between $15.00 and $25.00, with social security already deducted; hospital care is free; and there is a basic charge for prescriptions. All other visitors must pay for all sickness-related care and for dental care. Costs are substantially lower than in the United States.

Addresses for doctors, hospitals and urgent dispensaries are given in the front of telephone books. Visitor centres, libraries, and the yellow pages will provide the addresses of practitioners of alternative medicine.

Property

Most New Zealanders are honest, especially in small-town and rural New Zealand. But, since there are, as everywhere, exceptions, cyclists should always take care of their property. When leaving a bike and luggage anywhere, lock the bike securely through both frame and wheels to an immovable object, and remove any valuables. Your bike will be safer beside a busy thoroughfare than up a dark alley. Avoid large bike racks: these are where thieves look first. If camping out, lock the bike securely to a handy tree or post.

Railway terminals in the main cities have cheap and secure left-luggage facilities and will take bikes for a fee. Be careful about opening hours. Campground proprietors are usually helpful to cyclists who want to leave their bikes somewhere safe.

If anything does get stolen, report the loss to the police for insurance purposes. Property is rarely recovered, however, unless discarded by the thieves.

Personal safety and the law

New Zealand is a much more violent society than it was a generation ago, but most violence is domestic and/or alcohol-related. Keeping out of trouble, therefore, includes keeping out of the wrong sort of pub. Personal handguns are illegal; as is carrying a knife in a public place without good cause. New Zealand policemen generally do not carry firearms.

Consulates

The United States has consulates in Auckland (Shortland/O'Connell Sts), Wellington (29 Fitzherbert Tce) and a consular representative in Christchurch (Lawrence Anderson Buddle, PO Box 13250). Canada is represented in Auckland (2 Princes St) and Wellington (67 Molesworth St); likewise Australia (32 Quay St, Auckland and 72 Hobson St, Wellington). Japan, the United Kingdom, Belgium, and West Germany are represented in Auckland, Wellington and Christchurch; Denmark, Finland, France, Italy, Norway and Sweden all have consulates in Dunedin as well; and Sweden has one in Invercargill. Ireland and Austria are represented in Auckland and Wellington.

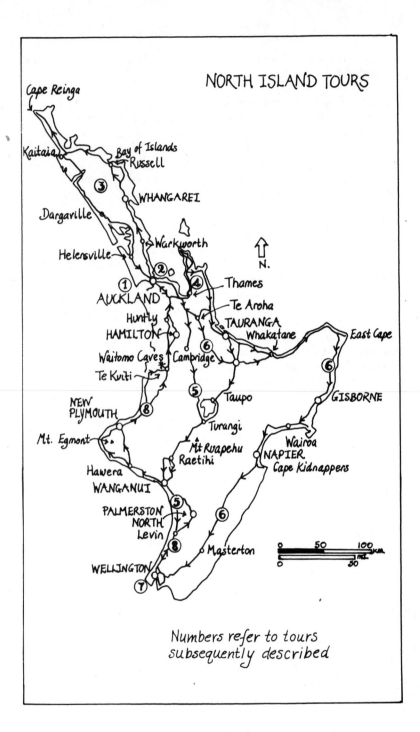

NORTH ISLAND TOURS

Cape Reinga

Kaitaia

Bay of Islands
Russell

③

WHANGAREI

Dargaville

Warkworth

Helensville

N.

②

④ Thames

AUCKLAND

Te Aroha

Huntly

TAURANGA

HAMILTON

Whakatane

East Cape

Waitomo Caves

Cambridge

⑥

Te Kuiti

⑤

⑥

NEW
PLYMOUTH

Taupo

GISBORNE

⑧

Mt. Egmont

Turangi

Wairoa

Mt Ruapehu
Raetihi

NAPIER

Cape Kidnappers

Hawera

WANGANUI

PALMERSTON
NORTH

⑤

Levin

⑥

⑧

WELLINGTON

Masterton

0   50   100
                    KM.
                    mi.
                    50

⑦

Numbers refer to tours
subsequently described

PART II

THE
NORTH
ISLAND

TOUR 1. GETTING AWAY FROM THE AIRPORT

ROUTE 1 AUCKLAND INTERNATIONAL AIRPORT TO DOWNTOWN AUCKLAND

20 km

Coming into Auckland from overseas by day, as the plane comes in to land, you will see a blue harbour and green fields and a vast expanse of brightly coloured houses. You are in a new country; your adrenalin is flowing; you are ready to set up your bike and go.

Like most airports, Auckland International Airport is built on the outskirts of town. From the airport terminal to downtown Auckland is about 20 km. Allow two hours for the ride since you will have to consult maps or this guide along the way. I recommend the ride as a good introduction to New Zealand's largest city. If you would like to do it, skip the next few paragraphs and turn straight to the route descriptions beginning on page 54.

If, however, you arrive tired and jaded after a long flight, or if you arrive late at night, there are alternative ways into town. If you arrive very late, you might like to wait for morning in an unobtrusive corner of the terminal before setting off. Otherwise, there are a number of hotels and motels within a few kilometres of the airport, mostly situated along Massey Road (see Route 3). The Youth Hostels and the budget hotels—and the night life and the bright lights—are nearer to the centre of town.

Airporter buses run between the International Terminal and Customs Street downtown every half-hour between 7.00 A.M. and 10.00 P.M. seven days a week. The fare is $8.00 and bikes are taken as luggage.

If aiming for the Mt. Eden Youth Hostel in Oaklands Road, ask the driver to indicate the nearest stop along Manukau Road, then take Epsom Avenue or Owens Road eastward 1 km to Mt. Eden Road, turn right into Mt. Eden Road, and right again into Oaklands Road. If you want go to the Parnell Youth Hostel in Churton Street, take the bus all the way to the Customs Street terminal. The Youth Hostel is less than 2 km away to the southeast. Head along Customs Street east into Beach Road, up Parnell Rise, left into Garfield Street, and left again into Churton Street.

The New Zealand Tourist and Publicity Department has an office at 99 Queen Street, Auckland's main commercial street,

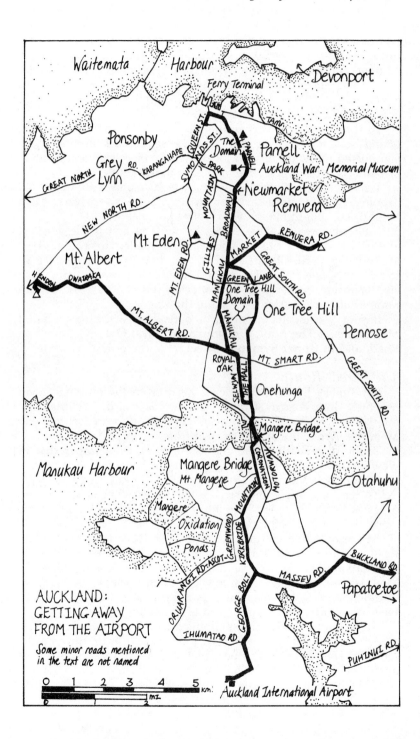

AUCKLAND:
GETTING AWAY
FROM THE AIRPORT
Some minor roads mentioned
in the text are not named

which leads south from Customs Street. Opening hours of the office are 8.30 A.M. to 5.00 P.M. Monday to Friday and 9.30 A.M. to 12 noon Saturday (phone 798-180). The Auckland Visitors Bureau is in Aotea Square, further up Queen Street. Opening hours are 8.30 A.M. to 5.00 P.M. Monday to Friday and 9.00 A.M. to 3.00 P.M. Saturday and Sunday (phone 31-889).

Taxis serve the airport round the clock. There is a taxi rank (stand) outside the terminal, otherwise contact numbers are signposted in the terminal. Most taxis take bicycles but, since few of them have bike racks, the bike goes in the trunk.

The current (1989) fare to downtown Auckland is about $28.00. Tipping is neither necessary nor expected but, if the driver is extra helpful, you might like to show your appreciation.

I describe two possible routes below. The first is the quickest and the most direct, but uses busy arterial roads. This route is best avoided during rush hours (say 7.30 A.M. to 9.00 A.M. and 4.00 P.M. to 6.00 P.M. weekdays). The second route is less direct, using back streets wherever possible, but offering the chance to take in a number of Auckland's sights along the way.

If your bike needs attention or parts, you will find **specialist bike shops at The Mall, Onehunga, in Royal Oak, on Manukau Road, and in Upper Symonds Street,** all more or less en route.

The Direct Route

Ray Emery Drive, which leads away from the terminal, soon becomes Tom Pearce Drive, heading eastward. At the first intersection, turn left (northwest). You are now in George Bolt Memorial Drive, the main exit road from the airport.

Traffic is generally busy and fast-moving. **Remember that in New Zealand You Drive and Cycle on the Left!**

George Bolt Memorial Drive winds for 3.5 km, first past quiet fields then past a new industrial estate to terminate at another set of traffic lights. Turn left here into Kirkbride Road. One kilometre along, Kirkbride Road forks; take the left fork.

At the next intersection, veer right (northeast) onto Mountain Road. Continue for 1.2 km, then turn left (northwest) onto Coronation Road. Carry on up a short rise, passing Mangere Mountain to your left, and freewheel down through the Mangere Bridge shopping centre. **(There is a hardware store which sells basic bike parts at the upper end of the shopping centre.)**

At the bottom end of the shopping centre is an intersection with a roundabout. Take the northern road, which leads towards the harbour. Then take the second street to the right (east) which runs alongside a small park. This street is Waterfront Drive, and it brings you to a signposted cycle track leading to the Mangere

Bridge underpass.

The underpass segregates pedestrians and cyclists from the fast-moving traffic of the motorway above. It is sheltered, and its gradient is gentle, but watch out for broken glass. Solo cyclists should avoid the underpass at night.

At the northern end of the underpass, turn right, beneath the bridge. The cycleway joins Onehunga Harbour Road, from which take the second turn left (west) into Princes Street, then the first turn right (north) into Selwyn Street. Continue along Selwyn Street, climbing for five blocks, then veer left (northwest) along Mt. Smart Road.

Mt. Smart Road leads to Royal Oak roundabout. **There is a specialist bike shop at the southern side of the intersection.** Traffic can be very busy here, and you may want to walk your bike around. Take Manukau Road out of the roundabout; this road is the fourth one around after Mt. Smart Road, and leads northeastwards. Stay on Manukau Road for 2 km until you come to the busy Greenlane intersection, where you turn left.

Get into the right lane here as soon as possible, since you turn right (north) at the first set of lights into The Drive, which shortly veers left, then right, and becomes Gillies Avenue.

If heading for the Mt. Eden Youth Hostel, take the fifth street to the left (west), Epsom Avenue, which passes the Auckland College of Education. Turn left from Epsom Avenue into Stokes Road. Then take the first right turn into Mt. Eden Road and the first right turn again into Oaklands Road.

If continuing downtown, ignore Epsom Avenue, but take the next street left off Gillies Avenue. This is Brightside Road, which turns sharply northward to meet Owens Road. Cross Owens Road into Mountain Road and continue northwards. You will shortly pass the Mater Hospital to your right and the Auckland Boy's Grammar School to your left.

Mountain Road passes above the motorway, then intersects with busy Khyber Pass Road. **(There is a large bike shop less than 1 km along Khyber Pass to the left).** Cross into Park Road. As Park Road veers northwest you will pass the main gates of Auckland Domain and the buildings of Auckland Hospital to your right. At the end of Park Road, continue onto Grafton Bridge. Since this bridge has only two narrow lanes, you might feel safer on the footpath.

At the western end of Grafton Bridge, cross busy Symonds Street straight into Karangahape Road. At the first set of lights along Karangahape Road, turn right into Queen Street. This stretch is very busy; again, it might be safer to walk.

Queen Street is Auckland's main commercial street. At the

bottom of the steep slope running down from Karangahape Road is the Auckland Town Hall. Just beyond this is Aotea Square and the city's Visitors Information Bureau.

The Tourist Route

Follow the instructions for the Direct Route as far as Onehunga Harbour Road. Or, if you have time and would like to see some pleasant countryside, you could try the 7 km detour below.

■ **ALTERNATIVE ROUTE:** One kilometre along George Bolt Memorial Drive, turn left onto Ihumatao Road. A tiny wooden Methodist church dating back to 1856 stands on the northern side of this intersection. Ihumatao Road runs past kiwifruit orchards and the green fields of Mangere's few remaining dairy farms. Some of the old drystone walls, built last century when this area was first cleared of its volcanic rock, survive.

From Ihumatao Road, turn right (northeast) onto Oruarangi Road, which takes you through the small settlement of Ihumatao, then along a harbourside ridge with good views over what at first look like gigantic paddy fields, seen at their best when limpid and lovely against the setting sun. They are in fact the settling ponds for Auckland's main sewerage treatment station.

Oruarangi Road joins Ascot Road, where a new industrial estate has developed. Turn left (north) off Ascot Road into Greenwoods Road. This leads into Creamery Road, which in turn joins Kirkbride Road just below the Kirkbride/Mountain Road intersection. Now follow the instructions for the direct route as given above until Onehunga Harbour Road. ■

Once in Onehunga Harbour Road, instead of turning left into Princes Street, continue straight ahead along Onehunga Mall. This is a small but pleasant shopping precinct. Walk your bike through.

After leaving the pedestrian section of the Mall, continue northward for 1.5 km, then cross busy Campbell Road and enter Cornwall park through its southern gates.

Cornwall Park is one of Auckland's largest parks. It was given to the people of Auckland in 1901 by Sir John Logan Campbell, a Victorian merchant and entrepreneur, sometimes known as the "Father of Auckland" because of his association with the city since its foundation in 1840. It is a pleasant semi-rural area, where sheep graze peacefully in the middle of suburbia. The park surrounds the dormant volcanic cone of One Tree Hill, or Maungakiekie (183 m), which offers excellent views of Auckland. At the summit is an obelisk, erected as a memorial to the Maori people. The massive remains of Maori earth fortifications are visible here, as on

Old Saint Mary's, Parnell

Auckland's other volcanic cones. Alongside the drive to the summit is Acacia Cottage, Auckland's oldest surviving wooden building and John Logan Campbell's first home. It dates back to 1841, but was moved here in the 1920s.

From the gates cycle northeast along Grand Drive. Where the road meets Twin Oak Drive, you will have to detour around a barrier which was erected to stop motorists (but not cyclists) from using Cornwall Park as a throughway. Continue along Twin Oak Drive to Pohutakawa Drive. At this point you can detour left up Olive Grove Drive to the summit of One Tree Hill, or you can continue along Pohutakawa Drive to the northern gates of the park.

Cross busy Greenlane West into Puriri Drive, directly opposite the gates. (At rush hour, Greenlane West is very busy. If you cannot find a safe gap in the traffic, make a 1 km detour west to the first controlled intersection, then turn right, or northward, along Manukau Road.)

Puriri Drive veers northeast past the Alexandra Park trotting course, then joins Campbell Crescent. Turn right here, then take the second turn right (north) onto busy Manukau Road. Take the third street to the left (west), Epsom Avenue, then follow the instructions given above for the direct route above as far as Park

Road. From Park Road, turn right (northeast) through the Domain gates.

Auckland Domain is Auckland's most famous park. Within its boundaries are formal gardens, parklands, playing-fields, native bush, a cricket pavilion, even a scented garden for the blind. Auckland War Memorial Museum, which stands in the southeast corner of the Domain, houses, among other displays, important collections of Maori and Pacific Island artifacts. Opening hours are 10.00 A.M. to 5.00 P.M. seven days a week. Admission is free. There is a fine view of the Waitemata Harbour from the Museum steps. The bush-clad and almost perfectly symmetrical volcanic cone which can be seen from the harbour to the north is called Rangitoto Island.

If you take the narrow drive on the eastern side of the Museum southeastward, you will come out of the Domain into Titoki Street. Turn left (northeast) here, then immediately right onto Domain Drive, then left again onto Parnell Road.

Parnell is an interesting area with a number of well-preserved buildings dating back to the last century. On the corner of Parnell Road and Ayr Street, diagonally opposite Domain Drive, is Kinder House (1857), once the house of the Rev. John Kinder, a 19th-century churchman and distinguished artist and photographer. This is open 10.30 A.M. to 4.30 P.M. daily. A short way down Ayr Street is Ewelme Cottage, a charming little house erected by the Rev. Vicesimus Lush in 1863–1864, and now preserved by the New Zealand Historic Places Trust. It is open what are standard hours for New Zealand Historic Places Trust museums, 10.30 A.M. to 12.00 noon and 1.00 P.M. to 4.00 P.M. daily, except for Christmas Day and Good Friday.

Slightly further north along Parnell Road is the Anglican Cathedral. Beside the new brick-built and partially completed Holy Trinity Cathedral stands its elegant wooden predecessor, St. Mary's, dating back to 1888.

Parnell Road veers to the northwest and continues downhill through Parnell village, a shopping complex with restaurants and craft shops and an architecture intended to be reminiscent of Victorian times.

If heading for the Parnell Youth Hostel, just before Parnell Road becomes Parnell Rise and dips steeply downhill, turn right into Garfield Street. From Garfield Street, turn third left into Churton Street.

If continuing downtown, stay on Parnell Rise. This leads into Beach Road, which passes the main railway station, and in turn leads into Customs Street East.

You are now in the centre of Auckland. The main Youth Hostel office is in Australis House, 36 Customs Street East. The main suburban bus terminal is off Commerce Street to the north of Customs Street East. Passenger ferries to Devonport, Birkenhead and the Hauraki Gulf depart from the quays opposite Queen Elizabeth Square, off Customs Street. Auckland's Central Post Office also fronts onto the Square.

Queen Street leads south off Customs Street. The New Zealand Tourist and Publicity Department has an office at 99 Queen Street. The Auckland Visitors Centre is in Aotea Square, half a kilometre further along Queen Street. The main city library is in Lorne Street nearby.

ROUTE 2 AUCKLAND INTERNATIONAL AIRPORT TO AUCKLAND'S MOTORCAMPS

The two nearest motorcamps to the central city are in Avondale and Remuera, both 8 km from downtown.

The Avondale Motor Park, 46 Bollard Avenue, Avondale (phone 887-228) is about 15 km from the airport and 8 km southwest of downtown. Current charges for a tent site are $6.00 per adult per night. There are also on-site caravans and tourist flats.

To get there, follow the instructions for the direct route downtown as given above as far as the Royal Oak roundabout. **(There is a specialist bike shop on the southern side of the roundabout.)** Take the third road out of the roundabout. This is Mt. Albert Road, which heads in a westerly to northwesterly direction.

Continue along Mt. Albert Road for 5 km, then veer left (southwest) into Owairaka Avenue, which merges with Richardson Road. Turn immediately left (southwest) down Range View Road, then take the second road to the right, Hendon Avenue.

Hendon Avenue intersects with New North Road; turn left here. Bollard Road is a few yards along to the left.

■ **Note:** When you want to cycle into the centre of the city from the motorcamp, simply turn right (northeast) into New North Road and follow this for 6 km. This route leads into Symonds Street. Continue down Symonds Street for 1 km. This stretch is especially busy; watch out in particular for buses pulling in and out of stops without warning. Then veer left down Wakefield Street, descending steeply to Queen Street, opposite Aotea Square and the Auckland Visitors Bureau.

If you prefer to avoid riding in traffic, there are frequent buses along New North Road to downtown. There are also occasional suburban trains from Mt. Albert station, 1.5 km northeast along New North Road from the motorcamp.

The Remuera Motor Lodge, 16a Minto Road, Remuera (phone 545-126) has tent-sites for $7.00 per person per night, along with tourist flats and a bunk-room. To get there, follow the instructions for the direct route from the airport to downtown until the intersection of Greenlane with Manukau Road, or, for the tourist route, until Campbell Crescent. Continue northward along Manukau Road from Greenlane, then take the first turn right into Campbell Crescent, and second right (northeast) into Market Road. Continue along Market Road, passing above the motorway until you reach the Remuera Road intersection. Turn right (east) along Remuera Road. Minto Road is just over 2 km along, to the right.

There are also conveniently placed motorcamps offering tent-sites and cabins in Papatoetoe (see Route 3 below) and Takapuna (see Northland, Day 1).

ROUTE 3 FROM THE AIRPORT GOING SOUTH ———

Some cyclists may prefer to leave sightseeing in Auckland for the end of their trip, and instead head south from the airport straight away.

At the time of writing, George Bolt Memorial Drive, leading northeast from the terminal complex, is the only public road leading away from the airport. An eastern access road, however, has been proposed. If this is built, which is unlikely before 1991, it will cut several kilometres from the route described here by linking the eastern end of the airport with Puhinui Road (see below).

In the meantime, George Bolt Memorial Drive remains the only way out. Follow it for 3.5 km from the airport, to the first controlled intersection. Then turn right (east) onto Kirkbride Road, which shortly leads into Massey Road without changing its general direction.

Continue along Massey Road for 3.5 km to the second intersection with traffic lights after leaving George Bolt Drive (the first lights mark the end of a stretch of motorway forbidden to cyclists; keep away). Turn right (southeast) along Buckland Road. After 1.5 km, this road veers left and becomes Portage Road, then right and becomes Station Road. Follow Station Road for another 1.5 km, finally veering left across a humpback railway bridge.

You are now in Old Papatoetoe shopping centre. Papatoetoe

Railway Station is immediately to the left. On weekdays you could catch a suburban train here to Papakura and avoid 20 km of cycling through the suburbs. Otherwise continue for 1 km along St George Street, past the shops and past the fire station, and veer right (southeast) along Carruth Road. **(If your bike needs attention or parts, there is a bike shop in the mall at Old Papatoetoe.)** Follow Carruth Road for 1 km to a roundabout, taking the first road to the left (northeast) off the roundabout. This is Puhinui Road. At the first set of traffic lights you come to, turn right (southeast) along Great South Road.

A short distance to the right along Great South Road is the Manukau Central Caravan Park (phone 266-8016). This has tent-sites, and sometimes on-site caravans, available. Manukau City shopping centre is 1 kilometre to the south of the Caravan Park. Downtown Auckland is 20 km northward along Great South Road.

On the Puhinui/Great South Road intersection, you are about 13 km from the Airport and about halfway to the southern limits of Auckland's urban sprawl. The rest of this route is described in Tour 4, Day 1.

TOUR 2. AUCKLAND

Auckland is New Zealand's largest urban area. Its almost 900,000 people make up more than one-quarter of New Zealand's total population. It is, in fact, not one city, but several, and is New Zealand's commercial, financial and industrial centre.

Auckland straddles an isthmus between two harbours: to the north, the Waitemata, dotted with white sails in summer, and to the south, the tidal Manukau, teeming with bird-life. The urban area stretches more than 30 km from north to south and almost as far from east to west. Beyond the city to the north and east are uncrowded beaches of golden sand. To the west are the bush-clad Waitakere Ranges and the black-sand beaches of the wild West Coast. To the south are quiet farms and green and rolling countryside.

Visitors can climb one of Auckland's numerous volcanic cones—Mt. Hobson, Mt. Eden, Mt. Albert, One Tree Hill—to orient themselves to the city and its environs.

It is largely a low-rise city. There is a cluster of mirror-glass skyscrapers around the commercial centre downtown and occasional tall apartment buildings elsewhere. Otherwise, the suburbs of brick and wooden bungalows on individual sections (lots) stretch for miles, dotted with parks and shopping centres and pockets of industry.

Auckland is a city of recent origin. When Europeans first settled here in 1840, the isthmus had been virtually deserted by the Maori people as a result of tribal wars. Auckland's population at the turn of the century was only just over 66,000. Nonetheless, a number of historic buildings are preserved today, and there are good art galleries and museum.

Since this is a cycling guide rather than a tourist guide, only the sights that actually lie along routes selected are mentioned in the text. The Auckland Visitor's Bureau in Aotea Square can provide further information, and pamphlets and guidebooks.

Three short trips in the city and environs are described below. These will enable you to tone up your muscles, adjust to the roads and drivers, and get your bike and equipment right before setting off on longer tours. There are, of course, a number of alternative rides. *Auckland Bike Rides*, published by the Auckland Bicycle Association in 1982, is now out-of-print, but can be consulted in the New Zealand room of Auckland Public Library. The ARA (Auckland Regional Authority) has also prepared several bike maps covering the urban area. These are available for $3.50 per map from the Auckland Visitors Bureau and from bike shops.

EXCURSION 1 *THE 50 K RIDE*

The Auckland City Council, together with the ARA and local bicycle organisations, has planned and signposted a fifty kilometre cycle route around Auckland's central isthmus. This takes you past many of the city's most interesting sights and through a wide range of its suburbs. The ride can take as little as three hours, or it can take all day; or it can be split into two days, depending on how often you stop to see the sights or just to relax.

Maps are available from the ARA's offices, 121 Hobson Street, or from the Auckland Visitors Bureau.

Start at the Auckland War Memorial Museum in the Domain. Take Maunsell Street southeast from behind the Museum and turn left onto Parnell Road. The upper part of Parnell Road is described in the Tourist Route in the preceding chapter.

Immediately past the Anglican Cathedral, veer right into St. Stephens Avenue. (Bishopscourt, formerly the official residence of Auckland's Anglican bishops, is the fine wooden building to your left.) Take the third street to the left, Gladstone Road, which passes the Parnell Rose Gardens (which often have a fine display of different varieties of roses), then makes a steep, winding descent to the waterfront. Turn right (east) at the bottom, along Tamaki Drive.

Tamaki Drive winds between cliffs and sea for several kilometres, past the pleasant beaches of Okahu Bay, Mission Bay and St. Heliers. A cycle track is marked along the footpath. This is quite narrow, and is obstructed in places by ill-placed powerpoles. If traffic is quiet, it could be easier to cycle on the road.

There are several interesting sights along Tamaki Drive. These include Kelly Tarlton's Underwater World (open 9.00 A.M. to 9.00 P.M. daily) on the point beyond Okahu Bay; the Joseph Savage Memorial on Bastion Point, which offers excellent views of the waterfront and harbour (this is a detour to the right up the cliff-top road just beyond Marineland); and the stone-built buildings of the former Melanesian Mission (1859), on the beach front at Mission Bay.

At the northeastern end of St. Heliers, continue northeastward by climbing Cliff Road. This leads into Springcombe Road, which turns almost full circle. From Springcombe Road, turn left (east) into Glover Road. At the first crossroads, continue straight ahead into Riddell Road, which turns gradually southward then east.

Turn left (south) from Riddell Road into Roberta Avenue, second right into West Tamaki Road, then first left into Taniwha Street. This gradually curves towards the southeast.

> ■ **Side Trip:** Tahuna Torea is a wetlands reserve and bird sanctuary on a spit of land jutting out into the Tamaki River. A signposted walking track circles the reserve. If you want to visit the reserve turn left, instead of right, into West Tamaki Road. The reserve is less than 1 km along.

At the first roundabout on Taniwha Street, 1.5 km beyond the West Tamaki Drive intersection, turn left (south) into Elstree Avenue. Then take the first left turn into Point England Road, followed by the third right into Riverside Avenue.

From Riverside Avenue, veer left into Dunkirk Road. Then take the fifth turn right (west), into Kings Road, which leads to Queens Road and the Panmure shopping centre. This stretch of road is usually busy with commercial and industrial traffic, so take special care.

Beyond the Panmure shopping centre is a busy roundabout. Take the third fork, the Ellerslie-Panmure Highway, which heads just north of east. This is a dangerous stretch of road, but you will shortly leave it behind on taking the third turn right (northeast) into Lunn Avenue, then the first turn left into Marua Road.

Two kilometres along, Marua Road turns southeast and joins Ladies Mile just above the Ellerslie Racecourse. Turn second right from Ladies Mile into Morrin Street. This veers left, after which you turn right into Mitchelson Street, which squeezes between the motorway to the left and racecourse grounds to the right. An underpass leads under the motorway and the railway line into Wairakei Street.

Turn immediately right into Woodbine Avenue, then right (northwest) again into Great South Road. Turn left immediately into Matai Road, then take the first right into Wheturangi Road. Once more, turn immediately left, this time into Atarangi Road, then take the first right into Maungakiekie Road, which intersects with Greenlane West.

Turn left onto Greenlane West. Half a kilometre to the west are the northern gates of Cornwall Park. Turn left (south) here along Pohutakawa Drive.

■ **ALTERNATIVE ROUTE:** If you feel you have done enough sightseeing for one day, this is a convenient point to split the 50 k ride into two. To return to the central city, instead of turning left into Pohutakawa Drive, turn right into Puriri Drive, and follow the instructions given in the preceding chapter for the Tourist Route. ■

Take the right-hand fork out of the roundabout at the end of Pohutakawa Drive. This road leads along Olive Tree Grove past the Cornwall Park tearooms and Acacia Cottage (1841). A steep road to the left offers a short detour to the summit of One Tree Hill or Maungakieke (183 m).

Continuing along Olive Tree Grove around the mountain takes you past the Auckland Observatory before arriving at the park's western gates. Turn right (north) here along Manukau Road. At the first major intersection, which is called Greenwoods Corner, turn left (west) into Orakau Road.

Then follow a zigzag course essentially westward as follows through the pleasant middle-class suburbs of Epsom, Mt. Eden and Mt. Albert: first right along The Drive, first left along Empire Road, first right into St. Andrews Road, immediately left into St. Leonards Road, left into Mt. Eden Road, immediately right into Shackleton Road, third left into Dominion Road, second right into Lambeth Road, second left into Sandringham Road, third right into Taumata Road, first left into Duncan Road, right into Mt. Albert Road.

Follow Mt. Albert Road northwestward for just over 1 km. To your right you will pass the multi-storey offices and laboratories of the New Zealand Department of Scientific and Industrial Research (DSIR) Plant Research Station, and then, hidden by trees, Alberton House (1862), a well-preserved mansion built by a wealthy 19th century merchant and now maintained by the New Zealand Historic Places Trust. To your left is Mt. Albert itself. Turn right down Alberton Avenue, past Mt. Albert Grammar School.

At the bottom of Alberton Avenue, turn right (northeast) into New North Road. At the first set of traffic lights, turn left into St. Lukes Road, which crosses above the Northwestern Motorway to join Great North Road. Opposite is Auckland's Museum of Transport & Technology (MOTAT), which has displays of historic machinery and vehicles and a replica colonial village. Hours are 9.00 A.M. to 5.00 P.M. weekdays and 10.00 A.M. to 5.00 P.M. weekends.

If you want to visit MOTAT, turn right: the entrance is a hundred yards along Great North Road. Otherwise, turn left, then take the first road to the right (north), Motions Road.

Motions Road passes the Auckland Zoo (open 9.30 A.M. to 5.00 P.M. daily), then shortly afterwards veers northeast. Turn left along the pathway which crosses the Motions Creek reserve and MOTAT's aircraft park. Then turn right into Meola Road.

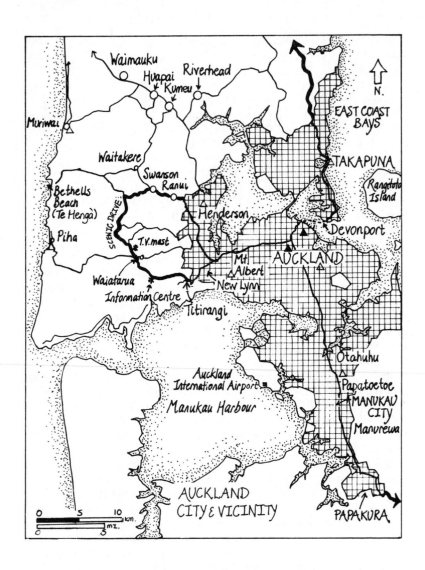

Meola Road climbs to Garnet Road. Turn left here, then take the third street to the right, into West End Road. This dips down to the harbour's edge at Cox's Bay and passes Grey Lynn Domain before climbing to Jervois Road. Turn left (west) along Jervois Road, then immediately right into Masons Avenue. From Masons Avenue, take the first turn right, along Argyle Street, then first left along Cremorne Street, and first right again into Stack Street.

If you feel like a break, you will find a secluded little beach down Wairangi Street to the left. Otherwise continue along Sarsfield Street to Curran Street. Turn left into Curran Street and take the left-hand fork at the bottom which leads to Westhaven Boat Harbour. Do *not* get onto the Harbour Bridge by mistake: this is strictly forbidden to cyclists.

Westhaven is Auckland's premier marina, and is crammed with yachts. Continue past them along Westhaven Drive, which runs between the motorway and the harbour's edge. Turn left off Westhaven Drive into Poore Street, right into Beaumont Street, and left into Fanshawe Street.

Take Fanshawe Street, then Customs Street East, eastward through the city. Customs Street East leads into Beach Road and past the main railway station. From Beach Road, turn right into Stanley Street just before the railway overbridge. Turn left off Stanley Street onto Domain Drive and continue up the bush-clad slopes of the Domain to the Museum. You are back where you started.

EXCURSION 2 *THE WAITAKERES SCENIC ROUTE —*

The Waitakere Ranges are a lovely but precipitous set of hills which separate Auckland from the wild beaches of the West Coast. Suburban sprawl has covered the foothills but, deeper into the ranges, public reserves and water catchment areas preserve large areas of native bush. There are a number of walking-tracks in the ranges, but also enough roads to offer a strenuous but rewarding ride to cyclists who prefer not to get off the saddle.

The route described below covers 68 km. If you cycle all the way, you can regard it as a full day's trip, although stronger riders might add a detour to Bethells Beach (Te Henga). The trip is better done on weekdays than on weekends, when there is a lot of day-tripper traffic on the roads. Weekdays, too, you can save 13 km and a rather dull ride through the suburbs by taking the Waitakeres train from Auckland Central or Newmarket to New Lynn. (Note: As mentioned before, Auckland's suburban train system is under threat of closure. The information given below is valid at the time of writing, but should be confirmed with the Auckland Visitors Bureau or any Railways Corporation office before making plans.)

Trains are infrequent. Morning departures from Auckland Central are at 7.46 A.M. and 10.10 A.M. and from Newmarket are at 6.38 A.M., 6.52 A.M., 7.55 A.M. and 10.15 A.M. Afternoon trains back from Swanson (see later) leave at 1.50 P.M. and 3.30 P.M. and there is a later train from Henderson at 4.43 P.M. Timetables between Christmas and mid-January are further reduced. Phone the Railways Corporation (792500) to check.

If you are cycling the whole way, take Karangahape Road westwards from the top of Queen Street. This leads into Great North Road which continues, mostly in a southwestward direction, all of 12 km to New Lynn.

Continue through New Lynn shopping centre, a little beyond which New North Road veers due west. At the first crossroads past the shopping centre, turn left along Titirangi Road. Titirangi Road climbs gradually for 4.2 km to Titirangi township, a suburban centre perched on a ridge high in the bush-clad hills.

At the western end of Titirangi is a roundabout. Take the third road off this, View Road. One kilometre along, View Road comes to a forked intersection. Take the upper fork. This is Scenic Drive, which can be followed the entire way through the hills.

Four kilometers along Scenic Drive is the Auckland Centennial Memorial Park headquarters, perched on a ridge with magnificent views over the upper reaches of the Manukau Harbour. The information centre here is open 10.30 A.M. to 4.30 P.M. weekdays and 10.00 A.M. to 5.30 P.M. weekends and public holidays.

From Park headquarters to the Piha turnoff is another 4.5 km. Take the right, or upper, fork here, signposted to Swanson.

■ **Side Trip:** If you want to visit one of the West Coast beaches, you can take the left, or lower, fork instead. Piha Beach is 14 km away through the hills. The road, quite a strenuous one and busy in summer, is sealed all the way. Piha is a long black-sand beach famous for its surf. Like all West Coast beaches, it has dangerous currents and rips: surf or swim only in the patrolled areas between the flags. Piha has a shop and a motorcamp (open October to June only).

A further 1.4 km climb along Scenic Drive is the Waiatarua television mast. This marks the highest point along the route: 389 m at the base of the mast. The road is mainly downhill from here on.

Continue another 12 km to Swanson, turning right (east) at the Swanson West Coast Road/Waitakere Road junction. Swanson marks the furthest extent of Auckland's suburban sprawl to the northwest, and is the end of the scenic part of the trip.

■ **Side Trip:** Perhaps a more interesting beach to visit than Piha, and certainly a wilder and more unspoiled one, is Bethells Beach (Te Henga). On leaving the hills 9.6 km after Waiatarua, turn left (west) along Bethells Road. The beach is 10 km down the gentle, gravel road. It is crowded during summer weekends, but undisturbed at other times. There are a few houses at Bethells, but no shops or other facilities.

If you arrive in Swanson by 3.35 P.M., you can catch the last suburban train back to the city (weekdays only). The railway station is on the south side of the road 1 km east of the Waitakere/Swanson Road intersection.

If you decide to cycle, continue through Swanson township along Swanson Road, which gradually turns southeast towards Henderson. Seven kilometres along, in Henderson township, this road becomes Great North Road. The last train back from Henderson leaves at 4.43 P.M. To reach the railway station, turn right (south) down Railside Avenue. Otherwise, continue along Great North Road to the city. From Henderson to downtown Auckland is 19 km.

EXCURSION 3 WAIHEKE ISLAND

Waiheke Island is the largest of the nearer islands of the Hauraki Gulf. Until recently a sleepy and isolated backwater, with the development of rapid boat services, the beachside settlements at its western end (pop. 4,137) are rapidly becoming another commuter suburb of Auckland. Nonetheless, the island retains much of its former charm, and a visit to Waiheke offers the rare chance to combine a harbour cruise and a cycle ride.

The Waiheke hydrofoil departs daily from Ferry Buildings (across Queen Elizabeth Square from Queen Street in downtown Auckland) for Matiata Bay, at the western end of the island. Daily departure times are 8.00 A.M., 10.00 A.M., 2.00 P.M. and 5.30 P.M. On Fridays, there is also an 8.45 P.M. departure. The hydrofoil returns from Waiheke at 8.45 A.M., 12.50 P.M., 4.30 P.M. and 6.15 P.M. There is also a 10.00 P.M. flight on Fridays. The crossing takes 35 minutes. Return fare is $17.00 plus $8.00 for bicycles. There is also a Friday to Sunday service during summer from Panmure wharf (for details of both services, phone Waiheke Shipping at 790-092), and a daily car and passenger ferry from Half Moon Bay, Bucklands Beach (phone Subritzky Shipping at 534-5633).

Most of Waiheke's population is concentrated at the beach settlements of the western end of the island. The beaches on the north side, Oneroa, Palm Beach and Onetangi, respectively 2 km, 4 km and 9 km from the wharf, are good places to swim and relax. Perhaps the best idea for a day's ride, however, is to explore the eastern end of the island. For the energetic cyclist a complete circuit of the island from Matiata back to Matiata is about 75 km. Much of this is over hilly, gravel roads.

Follow the signposts to Onetangi. From Onetangi, continue eastward along Waiheke Road, which shortly turns inland over the hills, before descending into the valley of a small river. Turn left

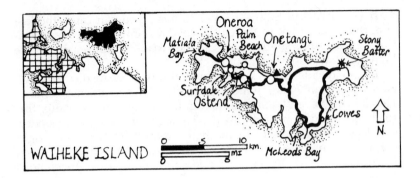

(north) at the first intersection. The gravel road winds through low hills for 7 km, gradually climbing to the islands's eastern ridge.

There is an intersection here. Stony Batter, the site of massive gun emplacements dating back to World War II, is a 2 km detour to the northeast. The road reaches its highest point here at just over 200 m. Otherwise, continue southwards, dropping to the coast, then climbing again past Cowes Bay. After Cowes Bay, the road turns northwest, drops down to skirt the mangrove swamps of McLeods Bay, then climbs inland up a river valley and over a ridge to reach the same Waiheke Road intersection left behind several hours before. Turn left for Onetangi.

If you want to stay overnight on Waiheke Island, there is a Youth Hostel, cabins, hotel and motel in Onetangi, and a motel in Ostend. Booking is advisable in summer. Free camping is forbidden on the island.

TOUR 3. NORTHLAND

12 days: 1010 km–1069 km.

Northland is New Zealand's narrow northern peninsula. It juts into the Pacific for more than 200 km north of Auckland, but is at no stage more than 80 km wide. Northland is hilly, with a coastline deeply indented by harbours and bays and fringed with white sandy beaches. The climate is warm and humid in summer, mild and wet in winter. Cycle touring is possible at any time of year.

Northland's Maori tribes trace their arrival back to the landing of the Mamari, Mahuhu and Te Mamaru canoes from Hawaiki in prehistoric times. Europeans first arrived less than two centuries ago. The first visitors were seamen attracted by the native kauri tree, which they used for ship's spars. Whalers and missionaries were next (New Zealand's first mission was established at Rangihoua in the Bay of Islands in 1814), followed by traders and, finally, government officials. The Treaty of Waitangi, which established the British Crown's claim to New Zealand, was signed at Waitangi, in the Bay of Islands, in 1840.

Russell, situated on Northland's eastern shore, was New Zealand's seat of government for nine months in 1840–1841; the capital then shifted to Auckland. Northland rapidly became a backwater, notable only for its timber and its kauri gum. Poor soils, hilly terrain, and isolation hindered development for decades.

Northland today is largely a farming and a holiday area, with a growing tourist trade centred on the Bay of Islands and the numerous beaches. The only substantial town is Whangarei (pop. 40,179), a port, market town and minor industrial centre.

DAY 1 AUCKLAND TO WARKWORTH
67 km

State Highway One (S.H. 1) north from Auckland is a busy road, in parts too narrow for the volume of traffic it carries. It is not always possible to avoid the busy stretches. I recommend that cyclists take a bus to Whangarei, or at least to Warkworth, and begin their trip there. If you are determined to cycle, however, a description of the route follows.

The Auckland Harbour Bridge is forbidden to cyclists. You may hear of a shuttle service, but this in fact ceased in 1987. To cross the Waitemata Harbour on your way north, take the Devonport ferry, which leaves from the Ferry Buildings, on the seaward side of

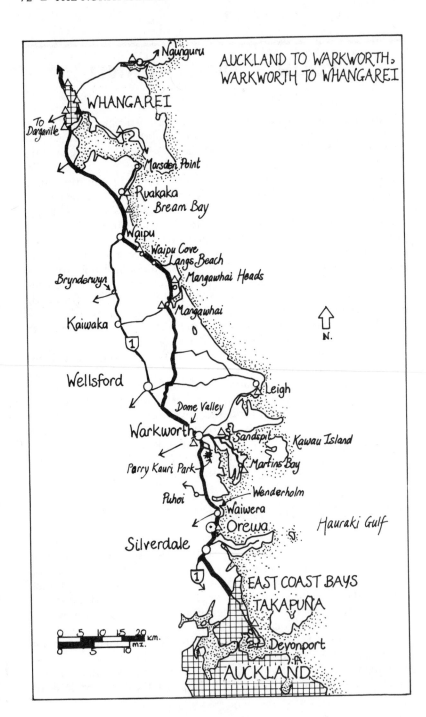

AUCKLAND TO WARKWORTH,
WARKWORTH TO WHANGAREI

Quay Street from Queen Elizabeth Square at the bottom of Queen Street.

Ferries run hourly Monday to Friday between 7.00 A.M. and 11.00 P.M. and half-hourly between 3.00 P.M. and 7.00 P.M.; Saturdays hourly between 7.00 A.M. and 11.00 P.M.; and Sundays hourly between 7.00 A.M. and 10.00 P.M. The crossing takes 15 minutes. A single adult fare is $2.50 plus $1.00 for a bicycle.

Devonport is one of Auckland's oldest suburbs, a quiet seaside community with numbers of well-preserved and restored 19th-century villas. As you approach Devonport's Victoria wharf, New Zealand's largest naval base, Stanley Bay, is to the left; to the right is North Head, a small hill commanding the harbour. This was extensively fortified at the end of the last century against the imagined threat of a Russian invasion, and the former gun-sites and ammunition tunnels are preserved today as an historic monument.

Victoria Wharf leads into Marine Square. Veer right past the small reserve at the Square's eastern end into King Edward Parade. Follow the Parade along the harbour's edge for 1.2 km, then turn left into Cheltenham Road. If you want to inspect North Head, take the second street to the right, Takarunga Road. Otherwise, take the first turn left, Tainui Road. Turn right from Tainui Road into Vauxhall Road.

Vauxhall Road rises slightly as it passes Fort Cautley, a naval establishment, then drops gently to Narrow Neck Beach. From here, at dead-low tide, it is possible to ride or push your bike 3.5 km along the beach to Takapuna. If you feel it is more prudent to stay on dry land, however, turn inland along Old Lake Road, then immediately right onto Hamana Street.

Hamana Street continues into Seacliffe Avenue. Turn left where this joins Winscombe Street, then take the first turn right, into Lake Road. Lake Road is often busy, so take care. Brave the traffic for 2.6 km to the main Takapuna shopping centre, then veer right into Hurstmere Road. Hurstmere Road passes along a narrow stretch of land between Lake Pupuke, a submerged volcanic crater, and the sea. This area contains some of Auckland's most expensive real estate. The Takapuna Motorcamp (cabins) is off The Promenade, the first street to the right off Hurstmere Road.

Hurstmere Road changes its name to Kitchener Road when it veers inland to the north of Lake Pupuke. One kilometre along, this comes to a Y-intersection. Take the right fork, East Coast Bays Road, which undulates along an inland ridge with magnificent views of the northern suburbs and beaches, the Hauraki Gulf and Rangitoto Island.

Twenty kilometres from Queen Street you finally leave the suburbs behind, as East Coast Bays Road turns northeast, passing

Wenderholm (Photo by Mim Ringer)

through green and rolling hills until its junction with State Highway One just south of Silverdale. This stretch of road is well-surfaced, and gradients are usually gentle.

Silverdale (pop. 962), a small market town, is the gateway to the growing coastal resorts of what is known as the Hibiscus Coast. It has a small pioneer village and museum. The road from here to Waiwera is always busy, especially just after Christmas, when queues of traffic several kilometres long can build up.

There is a steep 1 km climb out of Silverdale, then a longer, gentler descent to Orewa, with a narrow and dangerous bridge at the bottom. Orewa (pop. 8,241) is a busy holiday and retirement resort. It has several motorcamps with cabins, numerous motels, a large shopping centre and a long sandy beach.

Between Orewa and the next settlement north, Hatfields Beach, is a short, steep hill, with another steep hill to follow before Waiwera. The 1.4 km descent to Waiwera is narrow and winding, and the seal is broken in parts—keep your speed down.

Waiwera developed last century as a resort around natural hotwater springs near the beach. The mineral pools have been heavily commercialised in recent years and are crowded and noisy during weekends and holidays, but make a pleasant stop midweek. Do not soak too long or you will lose the energy to keep pedalling. Waiwera has a caravan park with on-site caravans for rent.

A very steep 1.5 km climb out of Waiwera is rewarded by a magnificent view over Wenderholm, a regional reserve with a pretty

pohutakawa-fringed beach. (The reserve is open every day 7.00
A.M. to sunset.) A steep descent to the Puhoi River Valley follows.

Puhoi, a village slightly off the main road to the left, is worth a
visit. It was first settled in 1863 by Bohemians from an area which
is now part of Czechoslovakia. Remaining signs of the past are the
little wooden Catholic church of St. Peter and St. Paul (1881) and an
old-style pub with a bar that is as much a museum as a watering-
hole. Midway between Puhoi and Warkworth is one further significant hill, otherwise the remaining 15 km are relatively gentle.

■ **Side Trip:** The Warkworth Museum and the Parry Kauri
Park, with gigantic kauri trees, are a 4.4 km detour along
gravel roads to the southeast of town. Two kilometres be-
fore Warkworth, turn off S.H. 1 to the west, along McKinney
Rd. Take the first turn right (Wilson Rd), then the first left.
To continue to Warkworth from the museum, turn right
rather than left into Wilson Rd, then take the first left along
Pulham Road into town.

Warkworth (pop. 1,889) is a market town set on the tidal
Mahurangi River. It has a hotel and several motels. The Kowhai
Park motorcamp (tentsites only) is situated beside the main road at
the northern edge of town. There are also motorcamps with cabins
at the Sandspit, 6 km east, and at Martins Bay, 15 km southeast.

■ **Side Trip:** From the Sandspit, you can catch a ferry to
Kawau Island, on which is the restored mansion of Sir
George Grey (1812–1898), former Governor and Premier of
New Zealand. Kawau Island ferries leave at 7.45 A.M., 9.30
A.M., 10.00 A.M., 10.30 A.M., 11.30 A.M., 12.30 P.M., 2.00 P.M.
and 4.30 P.M.

DAY 2 WARKWORTH TO WHANGAREI
111km

This is a longish day, but the only really difficult stretch is the
coastal hills between Mangawhai and Langs Beach. However,
cyclists who like travelling at a leisurely pace could split it into two
very easy days: Warkworth to Mangawhai/Mangawhai Heads (42
km) and Mangawhai to Whangarei (69 km).

The day begins gently as S.H. 1 meanders northward along the
Dome Valley, 4 km beyond Warkworth, passing the entrance to
Sheepscene, an agricultural display centre, and beyond that an
earth satellite station. There follows a steepish 1.5 km rise to the
head of Dome Valley (tearooms and an information centre), then a

long descent.

Fifteen kilometres north of Warkworth leave busy S.H. 1 at the first road to the right (northeast) after crossing the Hoteo River. This gravel road climbs gently, joining the sealed Wellsford-Leigh Road 6 km along. Turn right here, then almost immediately left into the Mangawhai Road. Another 8 km of gravel follows, then 13 km of seal to Mangawhai. The terrain is undulating, and most of the last 10 km is a gentle descent to the coast. Once off S.H. 1, traffic is light.

■ **ALTERNATIVE ROUTE:** Cyclists who do not feel prepared for the gravel roads of the Mangawhai route will have to follow S.H. 1 the whole way, a much less interesting route. This involves a long, steep, and winding climb over the Brynderwyn Hills before Waipu. Traffic can be a nuisance on this stretch, especially in midsummer. ■

Mangawhai is a crossroads settlement with a shop, a service station, a school, orchards and two motorcamps nearby, both with cabins. Four kilometres on (turn right at Mangawhai, then take the first left) is Mangawhai Heads, a holiday settlement with a harbourside motorcamp at its northern end, and motels. The main road bypasses the beach, which is a short detour eastward.

From Mangawhai Heads, follow the signposts northwards to Langs Beach and Waipu Cove. The seal ends at Mangawhai Heads, after which there is a winding 5 km ascent and 2 km descent over coastal hills. The ascent is steepish in parts and, because of the gravel, is all low-gear work. You may have to walk stretches. The road is narrow, so keep as far to the left as practicable.

The seal begins again at Langs Beach, and the terrain is virtually flat for the next 30 km. Langs Beach and Waipu Cove are holiday settlements. The latter, well-known as a surfing beach, has a motorcamp and a store.

Nine kilometres from Waipu Cove is Waipu, founded in the 1850s by settlers from Nova Scotia, led by the stern and eccentric Rev. Norman McLeod. There is a small museum crowded with displays, the House of Memories, a short detour down the Auckland road. There are also shops, tearooms, a hotel and a motel. Take the Whangarei road north out of Waipu. You have now rejoined S.H.1.

The next 40 km to Whangarei are rather dull, especially if cycling against a northeasterly wind. A long plain with little shelter is followed by gently rolling country for the last 10 km into Whangarei. Traffic is fast-moving, but the road has a wide shoulder most of the way. Five kilometres north of Waipu, however, there is a Department of Conservation campsite, which gives access to the long lonely sweep of beach along Bream Bay.

■ **Side Trip:** Just off the main road 10 km north of Waipu is Ruakaka, another holiday settlement with a fine beach, a motel and a camping ground. Six kilometres beyond Ruakaka is a thermal power station and, beyond that, the Marsden Point oil-refinery, the flare and smokestack of which can be seen for miles around.

Whangarei (pop. 40,179) has several motels and hotels, a Youth Hostel and several motorcamps along the main road into or out of the city and in the vicinity. The tourist information office is in Forum North, which is off Rust Avenue right in the centre of town. In summer an information cabin is also set up beside the main road at Otaika Park on the way into town.

Perhaps Whangarei's main attraction is its proximity to a number of excellent beaches on the coast to the east of the city. The city itself, however, is not without its own attractions. It can be pleasant to wander around the yacht basin at the bottom of town. The Society of Arts has a gallery in Reyburn House, near the yacht basin. There is a specialist clock museum near the centre of town. The Northland Regional Museum is on the Dargaville road 5 km to the west of the city. Whangarei Falls is 5 km northeast along the Kiripaka/Ngunguru Road; Reed Memorial Kauri Park is also nearby.

Whangarei yacht basin (Photo by Mim Ringer)

DAY 3 WHANGAREI TO RUSSELL VIA KAWAKAWA — 73 km

You should set off from Whangarei quite early, aiming to reach Russell at least by mid-afternoon, leaving time to find accommodation and to see some of the sights.

Take Bank Street northward from Whangarei central. The road forks after 1 km, just before an Anglican church. Take the left fork, signposted for Kamo. Kamo, 3 km further north, marks the end of Whangarei's urban area. There is a steep dip beyond Kamo, then S.H.1 enters an area of low, rolling farmland, interspersed with

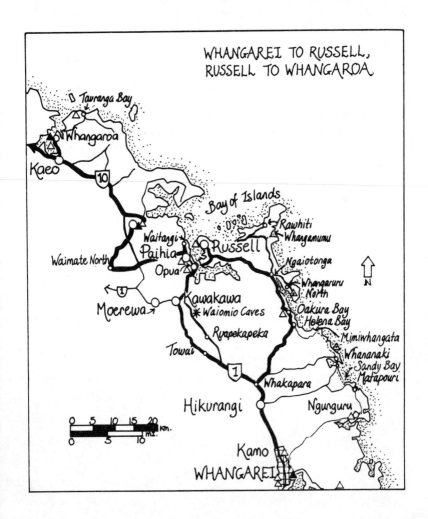

patches of bush.

The first 12 km out of Kamo through Hikurangi (pop. 1,334) is mostly relatively gentle, with some flattish stretches. After Whakapara, the terrain becomes hillier, gradually rising to 221 m beyond Towai. The last 5 km into Kawakawa are mostly downhill.

■ **ALTERNATIVE ROUTE:** 10 km beyond Whakapara, a gravel road turns right, almost due north, climbing high into the hills. Five kilometres along is Ruapekapeka ("bat's nest"), the site of a massive pa (fortification) built by warriors of the Ngapuhi tribe and besieged by British troops in 1846. Defended by 500 or so Maori, it was attacked by 1500 soldiers assisted by cannon. Even so, the soldiers were unable to take the pa until they made a surprise attack on Sunday, when the defenders were at their prayers. A difficult gravel road descends to Kawakawa from here, passing the Waiomio limestone caves en route. ■

Kawakawa (pop. 1,538) is a farming centre, with a hotel and service motel but no campgrounds. Leave S.H. 1 here, turning northeast towards Opua, Russell, Paihia and the Bay of Islands. The road climbs a minor saddle, skirts mangrove swamps along the upper reaches of a tidal inlet, and enters Opua (pop. 339), a small port and growing holiday settlement set on a ridge above the harbour. Turn down to the harbour's edge along Franklin Street and take the car ferry to Okiato across the inlet, from where a good sealed road leads 12 km to Russell.

■ **ALTERNATIVE ROUTE:** You could continue instead to Paihia, 4 km north of Opua, and visit Russell as an excursion via the frequent passenger ferries that cross the bay from Paihia Wharf (these take bikes). Although there are numerous hotels and motels in Paihia, it is an expensive, heavily touristed town. There is a motorcamp with cabins midway between Opua and Paihia, and several other motorcamps in the vicinity of Haruru Falls, 3 km west of Paihia. ■

Russell (pop. 1,052) is one of New Zealand's most historic towns. In the 1840s it was a crowded port, notorious for its grog shops and gambling dens. It served briefly in 1840 as New Zealand's capital, and was sacked by Maori rebels during Heke's war in 1845.

Original buildings include Christ Church (1835), the oldest surviving church in New Zealand, and Pompallier House (1841–2), a pisé-de-terre structure erected by Bishop Jean Baptiste Francois Pompallier, the first Catholic Bishop of New Zealand. Russell also

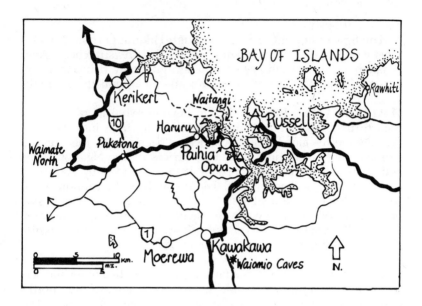

has a small but interesting historical museum.

There are several hotels and motels, which are generally booked heavily in mid-summer. There are also two motorcamps, one 3 km south of Russell on the road from the car ferry, and the other on the northeastern edge of town.

■ *ALTERNATIVE DAY 3A* WHANGAREI TO RUSSELL VIA HELENA BAY
87 km–99 km

Cyclists who do not mind gravel roads might care to approach Russell via the longer and more demanding, but far more beautiful, coastal road via Helena Bay.

Turn off S.H. 1 at Whakapara, northeast toward Helena Bay. Between Whakapara and the coast are 16 km of winding road, involving first some substantial climbing, then a long downhill swoop. The road is sealed for a few kilometres beyond Whakapara; from then on the surface is gravel much of the way to Russell. The surface is usually quite rough, especially in summer, when excessive holiday traffic causes ruts to form, which can have quite a jarring effect on cyclists.

At Helena Bay, the road turns north, climbing up and down over low coastal hills for the next 23 km. The lovely beaches of

Oakura Bay (motorcamp with cabins), Whangaruru South and Whangaruru are short detours to the east.

At the northern end of the Whangaruru Harbour, the direct road turns inland (Russell is now 25 km away) and climbs through the bush-clad hills of the Ngaiotonga Scenic Reserve, reaching 304 m before descending to the Waikare Inlet to follow the harbour's edge to Russell.

■ **ALTERNATIVE ROUTE:** You can avoid the longish climb outlined above by turning coastward rather than inland at Ngaiotonga, taking the indirect road to Russell via Taupiri Bay and Parekura Bay. This adds 12 km to the total. There are a number of interesting excursions off this road, and you may want to put aside an extra day for exploration.

South of Ngaiotonga, the narrow Whangaruru Peninsula juts into the sea. The road down the spine of the peninsula gives access to several golden, pohutakawa-fringed bays and beaches. There is a campground beyond Whangaruru North, an 8 km detour to the south.

Three kilometres north of Ngaiotonga is Whangamumu. An easy 3 km walk from the road brings you to a scenic and historic reserve, the site of a shore whaling station between 1890 and 1931.

Four kilometres further on is Parekura Bay. Another 8 km detour from here takes you to Rawhiti, a tiny Maori settlement in the northeastern corner of the Bay of Islands, and the end of the road. Beyond is only the scrub- and bush-covered promontory which ends in Cape Brett. ■

DAY 4 RUSSELL TO WHANGAROA ────────────
57km–72km

This is an easy day by the direct route, but there should be time for excursions to Kerikeri, and perhaps to Waimate, en route.

Take the passenger ferry from Russell to Paihia. Paihia (pop. 2,533) originated as an Anglican mission station in 1823. New Zealand's first church was erected here—the site is marked by the memorial church of St. Paul (1926). Paihia is today a brash tourist town, crowded with visitors in summer. There is a Public Relations Office in Williams Road, the main waterfront road.

Across Waitangi Bridge at the northern end of Paihia is the Waitangi Historical Reserve. The Treaty House here was built in 1833 by the then British Resident, James Busby, and is restored and furnished as a museum. A flagstaff marks the site of the signing of the Treaty of Waitangi. Nearby is the Maori Centennial

Memorial (1940), a meeting-house with carvings representative of many of New Zealand's Maori tribes; also a Maori war canoe.

It is possible to cross the hills to Kerikeri direct from Waitangi by way of forestry roads—but the route is a difficult one, narrow, winding and gravel all the way, with little of interest to see. I recommend taking the main road as described below.

From Paihia, turn westward past Haruru Falls. There is a short steep climb between Paihia and Haruru, then the road gently ascends the valley of the Waitangi River to join S.H. 10, 14 km from Paihia. Turn north here.

■ **ALTERNATIVE ROUTE:** An excursion to Waimate will add only 8 km to the day's total. Just north of Puketona, turn west. An easy sealed road leads 6 km to Waimate North, a tiny village with an English atmosphere, and the site of the Waimate Mission House (1831–1832), one of the oldest buildings in New Zealand. The old oak tree nearby was planted at the same time the house was erected. The Church of St. John the Baptist stands nearby.

From Waimate North, a gravel road meanders northeast to rejoin S.H. 10 opposite the turnoff to Kerikeri. ■

From Puketona to the Kerikeri turnoff 6 km further north, the road passes through undulating countryside. The choice at the Kerikeri junction is to continue straight ahead due north or to detour to Kerikeri itself, adding 7 km to the day. I recommend the latter course.

Kerikeri (pop. 1,753) is the centre of an area of citrus and kiwifruit orchards. It is also a tourist centre, with a motorcamp, Youth Hostel and several hotels and motels.

One kilometre east of the township is the Kerikeri basin, an area of great historical interest. The Stone Store (1832–1835) which stands above the basin was an early trading post. Next door is Kemp House (1822), New Zealand's oldest building. Nearby is Rewa's Village, an authentic reconstruction of a pre-European Maori village.

Climb the rise beyond the Kerikeri basin and turn west towards Waipapa, rejoining S.H. 10 going north. For the next 23 km the road snakes through partly-forested hills, climbing to 235 m midway to Kaeo, a small market town spread out along the highway.

Three kilometres beyond Kaeo, turn off S.H. 10 northeast towards Whangaroa. The road leads 5 km along the harbour's edge to this pretty harbourside settlement. There is a motorcamp with cabins 2.5 km before Whangaroa, and a motel, hotel and Youth Hostel in the waterfront village itself.

Whangaroa street scene (Photo by Mim Ringer)

DAY 5 *WHANGAROA TO PUKENUI/HOUHORA* ──────
107 km; with detour to Karikari Peninsula: 147 km

Return to S.H. 1 from Whangaroa. Turn west along S.H. 1. For 9 km the road skirts the southern reaches of the harbour, then turns inland through 20 km of low rolling hills to the Mangonui Harbour.

Mangonui is a seaside village with a number of fine old buildings. Just beyond, over a short hill, is Coopers Beach, a popular holiday settlement. There is a hotel and budget lodge at Mangonui, and a motel and motorcamp with cabins at Coopers Beach.

Beyond Coopers Beach, the road passes through Cable Bay and Taipa, both well-known beaches (Taipa has a motorcamp with cabins), then leaves the coast and passes through gently rolling country, as it gradually turns southwest. At Taipa, a memorial to Kupe, the great Polynesian seafarer, who is said to have discovered New Zealand in 950 A.D., stands beside the bridge.

■ **Side Trip:** Cyclists in search of out-of-season isolation could turn north along the Karikari Peninsula 15 km beyond Mangonui. The Karikari Peninsula is an area of swamp, and dry and desolate scrub-covered hills, but it has long, isola-

ted and beautiful beaches. The best of these, perhaps, is
Matai Bay, 20 km along a rough gravel road off S.H. 10.
There is a Department of Conservation campsite here, with
fireplaces and tap-water. There is also a motorcamp with
cabins at the northern end of Karikari Bay.

A major tourist resort is planned for this area. Over the
next few years the roads and facilities may improve, but the
sense of loneliness and isolation will be lost.

About 10 km before Awanui is a steepish hill to cross. At
Awanui (pop. 355), a crossroads settlement, turn north here along
the Aupori Peninsula. A good sealed road leads to Houhora
through flat to undulating country. There is a country store at
Waiharara en route.

■ **ALTERNATIVE ROUTE:** You may prefer to explore the Aupori
Peninsula by bus, in which case turn south to Kaitaia (pop. 5,011)
from Awanui rather than north to Houhora. Tour buses run daily
from Kaitaia to Cape Reinga and back. ■

Whangaroa (Photo by Mim Ringer)

■ **Side Trip:** Four kilometres south of Houhora, and 34 km
north of Awanui, a minor road turns off towards Houhora
Heads, an inlet which offers a good view of Mt. Camel
standing in isolation across the Houhora Harbour. At
Houhora Heads are the old Subritzky Homestead, built in
the 1850s, and the Wagener Historical Museum. There is a
campground here.

At Pukenui, just south of Houhora, is a motorcamp with
limited cabin accommodation, a motel with hostel attached, and a
shop. Check that the store and tearooms at Waitiki Landing are
still open before setting off, or stock up here. Houhora itself is a
tiny settlement with a few houses and a pub.

DAY 6: PUKENUI TO CAPE REINGA
68 km

Check with the local warden of the Department of Conservation
at Te Kao (phone Te Kao 540) about the availability of campsites at
Tapotupotu Bay near Cape Reinga before continuing northwards
from Houhora.

The road is sealed for the first 24 km to Te Kao, a roadside settlement with a tearoom, and for 5 km beyond, but is gravel from there
to Cape Reinga. The last 36 km are quite strenuous. The road initially winds up and down over low hills around the Parengarenga
Harbour, then at Waitiki Landing (store, tearooms and cabins),
turns inland up the Waitiki Valley past Te Paki Station and climbs
through the hills to Cape Reinga. Just before Cape Reinga, it
reaches more than 200 m. Gradients are not particularly steep, but
the surface of the road is often corrugated by traffic and weather,
and the dust and the frequent tour buses can be a nuisance.

The Parengarenga Harbour is the gathering ground for godwits
in February to March, before they make their annual migration to
Siberia. Near the entrance to the harbour, pure white silica sand is
mined for New Zealand's glassworks.

Not long ago virtually the whole of the Aupori Peninsula was a
scrubby wilderness, dug over for kauri gum in past years, and
with vast sandhills pushing in from the east. Now large areas have
been stabilised with marram grass or planted with pine trees, and
the Government has established a large cattle station and recreational farm park at Te Paki in the north.

Cape Reinga, according to Maori mythology, is where the
spirits of the dead depart Aotearoa for Hawaiki, their homeland.
You will sense little of the mystery of the place in high summer

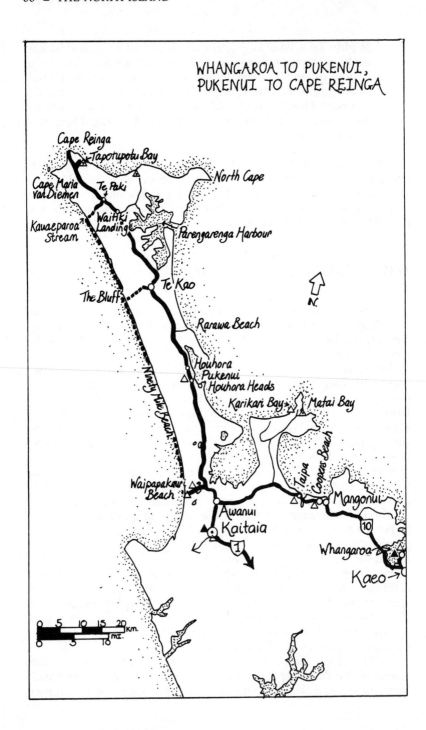

WHANGAROA TO PUKENUI,
PUKENUI TO CAPE REINGA

perhaps, since Cape Reinga is visited by more than 50,000 people a year, but the views over steep cliffs and golden beaches to Cape Maria van Diemen to the southwest are magnificent. There is a light-house at Cape Reinga, and a souvenir shop.

The nearest campground to the Cape is at Tapotupotu Bay, down a steep descent 5 km by road southeast of Cape Reinga. This has only basic facilities: fireplaces and tap-water. The campsite is sheltered in most weathers, but very exposed in a northeasterly.

The nearest accommodation otherwise is cabins at Waitiki Landing, and a guesthouse at Te Kao.

■ *ALTERNATIVE DAY 6A* AWANUI TO CAPE REINGA VIA WAIPAPAKAURI AND NINETY MILE BEACH
79 km

Ninety Mile Beach is a long stretch of sand running along the eastern side of the Aupori Peninsula. Despite its name, the beach is in fact only 64 miles (103 km) from head to foot. It can be travelled by vehicles at low tide, when the hard sand below the tideline is exposed.

Since the beach is very open, plan this stretch around the winds. The prevailing wind in the region is a southwesterly, so the trip is usually best done south to north; but a strong northeasterly can make things very difficult indeed. When the wind is right, however, this is a glorious ride, with the hard-packed sands forming a smooth surface little inferior to a paved road, and pipi and cockle shells crunching under the tires.

Ninety Mile Beach can only be recommended to fit and energetic cyclists who are equipped to camp out. Take food with you, and water, since good freshwater streams are infrequent. The route is an isolated one, but not a lonely one, since tour buses and some private cars use it. If you run into trouble, help will probably not be far away.

Descend to the beach at Waipapakauri (motorcamp with cabins) and turn north. There are 47 km of unbroken sand to the Bluff. Just south of the Bluff, a gravel road leads inland through pine plantations 8 km to Te Kao, where you rejoin the main road.

If the tide is right, you can, however, continue around the Bluff, from where another 19 km of unbroken sand brings you to the mouth of the Kauaeparoa Stream (sometimes called the Te Paki Stream). A four-wheel drive track leads up the stream to Te Paki, from where Cape Reinga is another 19 km away. The Kauaeparoa Stream route is the route that tour buses take. I cannot recommend it to cyclists unfamiliar with the area, however, since there are shifting quicksands along the bed of the stream.

After returning from the Cape, you may have to strip your bike down and regrease it since sand will have worked its way into the hubs. **The nearest bike shop is in Kaitaia.**

DAY 7 *CAPE REINGA TO KAITAIA*
114 km

This long and arduous day will see you retracing your steps to Awanui. Kaitaia (pop. 5,011), 7 km south of Awanui, is the largest town of the Far North. It has several motels and hotels, a Youth Hostel; and a motorcamp with tourist flats just off S.H. 1 at the southern end of town.

The tourist information centre is in the Far North Regional Museum, South Road, Kaitaia.

DAY 8 *KAITAIA TO RAWENE*
67 km

The next three days are relatively short days, although the terrain is difficult in parts. Stronger cyclists might consider covering much of the distance in two days: Kaitaia to Opononi (102 km) and Opononi to Dargaville (89 km). Youth Hostellers will certainly do so, since both Opononi and Dargaville have youth hostels.

The most difficult part of this day comes in the morning. Leave Kaitaia via S.H. 1 to the southeast. For most of the next 20 km this ascends the bush-clad Maungataniwha Range to a peak of 390 m. The last 3 km of the ascent are steepish. Summertime heat can make this an arduous and sticky stretch.

From the top there is a fast 2 km descent, followed by another short rise, then another 3 km descent, levelling off over the last 4 km to Mangamuka. Two kilometres beyond Mangamuka, at the Mangamuka Bridge, turn of S.H. 1 to the right (west), following signposts to Kohukohu and Rawene.

The road follows the Mangamuka River for several kilometres, turns briefly inland, then rejoins the Mangamuka. This enters the upper reaches of the Hokianga Harbour and, for the next 15 km into Kohukohu, winds between the hills and the mangrove-strewn reaches of the upper Hokianga.

Kohukohu (pop. 148) is a small town with an old-world atmosphere. Long ago it was a timber-milling town; now it is a centre for craftspeople and alternative-lifers who joined the drift to the

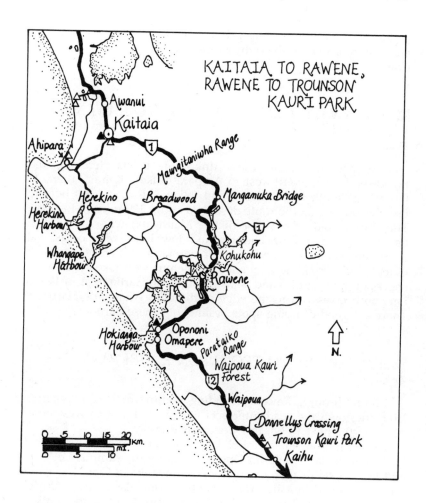

KAITAIA TO RAWENE, RAWENE TO TROUNSON KAURI PARK

countryside in the last two decades. There is a hotel here.

Not far around the harbour's edge from Kohukohu is the ferry to Rawene. This leaves at 7.45 A.M., 8.30 A.M., then hourly on the hour from 9.00 A.M. to 4.00 P.M., then half-hourly to 6.00 P.M. The crossing takes about ten minutes.

The Hokianga Harbour was, in the 19th century, a centre of missionary activity, ship-building and timber-milling. Rawene (pop. 408) is its largest town. Among its older buildings is Clendon House on the waterfront which, during the 1860s, was the home of James Clendon, the first United States consul to New Zealand, 1840–1841. This is preserved by the New Zealand Historic Places Trust.

Rawene has a motorcamp with cabins. To get to the motorcamp, take the third road to the right off the main street as it climbs away from the harbour.

■ *ALTERNATIVE DAY 8A KAITAIA TO RAWENE VIA BROADWOOD*
77 km

A longer but equally interesting route is via Herekino and Broadwood. Turn southwest to Ahipara outside Kaitaia, then, 11 km along, south to Herekino, and follow the road from here to Broadwood, to join the route described above 19 km from Rawene. This road avoids the worst of the Maungataniwha Range, but passes through rolling country and low hills, with occasional short, steep climbs on both sides of Herekino. It is gravel for much of its length. From Herekino, a 5 km detour west takes you to the shores of the beautiful and isolated Herekino Harbour. A further 5 km south takes you to the edge of the tidal Whangape Harbour. There are good camping spots beside both these harbours.

DAY 9 RAWENE TO TROUNSON KAURI PARK
76 km

Climb through Rawene, heading southward. Six kilometres from the town the road intersects with S.H. 12. Turn west here. Much of the next 15 km to Opononi is gravel.

Opononi (pop. 407) is a holiday resort, once famous for the activities of the tame dolphin Opo here during the summers of 1955 and 1956. A statue on the foreshore commemorates Opo. There is a motorcamp with on-site caravans at Opononi; also a Youth Hostel in the old school. There is a hotel and a motel in Omapere 3 km south.

Now comes the difficult part of the day. From Opononi the road skirts the harbour to Omapere, climbs steeply over hills to the south, descends, climbs again, descends, then climbs gradually up the valley to the Waimamaku River.

The seal ends 12 km south of Omapere. There follows a tough 5 km ascent of the Parataiko Range, reaching 390 m. The road then drops briefly to the Wairau River and climbs again to 360 m, entering the Waipoua Kauri Forest. This preserves some of the last of Northland's great kauris, massive trees which in maturity (and some of them are up to two thousand years old) can reach 16 m in girth and 50 m in height. The greatest of them are found along short walks signposted from the road.

The road climbs a ridge to 260 m south of Waipoua. Five kilometres beyond Waipoua, turn west off S.H. 12 towards Donnellys Crossing. The road drops steeply to a minor river and follows its valley for several kilometres. This brings you to the Trounson Kauri park, which has another reserve of fine kauris. There is a Department of Conservation campsite on the outskirts of the forest, and a private motorcamp with cabins 3 km further south.

DAY 10 *TROUNSON KAURI PARK TO PAHI* ———
98 km

The seal begins shortly after leaving Trounson Park. The road gradually climbs a ridge, then descends steeply to the upper reaches of the valley of the Kaihu River, where it rejoins S.H. 12. The next 30 km into Dargaville are through rolling to undulating to flat countryside.

Dargaville (pop. 4,859) is a pleasant riverside town, once a mill

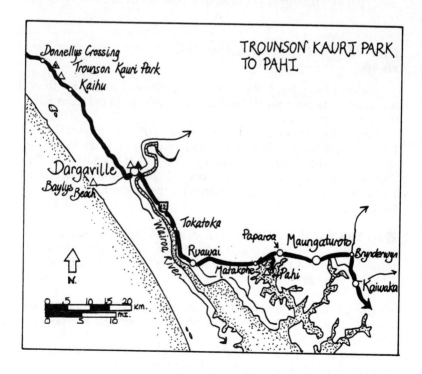

TROUNSON KAURI PARK TO PAHI

town and now a market town. It has a good local museum, the Northern Wairoa Museum, in Hardy Park. There are several hotels and motels in the town, a Youth Hostel and a motorcamp with cabins in Onslow Street. There is another motorcamp at Bayleys Beach, on the west coast, 14 km from Dargaville. Bayleys Beach, like many west coast beaches, is dangerous for swimming.

Leave Dargaville to the west in the direction of Whangarei. Just outside the town, turn south towards Maungaturoto and Wellsford. S.H. 12 leads through rich farmland reclaimed from wetlands along the Wairoa River to Ruawai (pop. 509), 29 km south. Turn east here, skirting the northern reaches of the Kaipara Harbour.

The road enters low hills 5 km from Ruawai before descending again to the harbour's edge. There is an excellent local museum, the Otamatea Kauri and Pioneer Museum, in the tiny settlement of Matakohe, 16 km from Ruawai. This displays the largest collection of kauri gum in New Zealand and relics of the timber-milling days. Five kilometres beyond Matakohe is the turn-off to Pahi.

Pahi is situated at the tip of a promontory which juts 7 km into the Kaipara. There is a motorcamp here and a store. The beach is tidal, but swimming is possible from the wharf at most tides.

DAY 11 PAHI TO HELENSVILLE
116 km

This is a long day, but easier towards the end of the day than at the start. It takes a much quieter road into Auckland than S.H. 1 through Warkworth.

Return to S.H. 12 and turn eastward. The road passes through low hills and through Paparoa and Maungaturoto (pop. 868) before climbing gradually to the junction with S.H. 1 at Brynderwyn. Both Paparoa and Maungaturoto have country hotels and there is a tearoom at Brynderwyn. At Brynderwyn, turn south. You are now back amongst busy traffic.

■ **ALTERNATIVE ROUTE:** You can save a few kilometres and some climbing by turning south 1 km east of Maungaturoto along a minor gravel road, which comes out on S.H. 1, 4 km south of Brynderwyn. ■

The 28 km to Wellsford are through pleasant rolling countryside, though with longish climbs both through Kaiwaka and into Wellsford, which is itself set on a ridge. Wellsford (pop. 1,627) is a town of no great distinction, though it has several tearooms and fast-food outlets; also a hotel and a bed and breakfast.

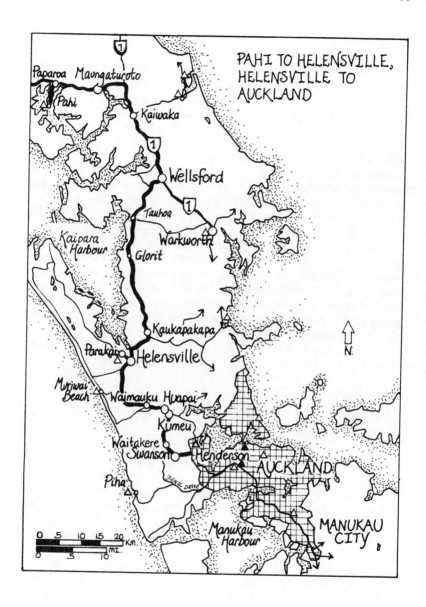

■ **ALTERNATIVE ROUTE:** Instead of continuing to Helensville, you can follow S.H. 1 toward Warkworth, retracing the route described for the second day of this tour. The next day should see you back in Auckland. The distance from Pahi to Warkworth is 75 km. ■

At Wellsford turn southwest along S.H. 16. The intersection is towards the southern end of town.

Wellsford is on a ridge and the road drops gradually for most—though not all—of the next 15 km. The seal ends 5 km south of Wellsford. Do not let your speed get up too much on the downhill stretches. Although this is a quiet road, it is a narrow one, and you never know what you might meet coming the other way.

At Tauhoa, the road almost touches an arm of the Kaipara, then climbs a low ridge before descending to the harbour again. There is another moderate climb past Glorit, 22 km south of Wellsford, where the seal begins again. The next 17 km to Kaukapakapa involve a succession of minor climbs over ridges running down from the hills to the harbour. The last 10 km of the day from Kaukapakapa to Helensville are almost completely flat.

Helensville (pop 1,347) began life as a timber town, and is now a rather shabby but pleasant market town. It has a small pioneer museum. In the town itself is a hotel; 3 km further on, at Parakai Hot Springs, a short detour from the main Auckland road, there are several motels and a motorcamp. There you can soak the aches and pains of the day away in natural hot pools.

The National Roads Board plans to seal the whole of the Helensville to Wellsford road by 1991. It will then become a viable alternative to S.H. 1 for holiday-makers and traffic will increase.

DAY 12 *HELENSVILLE TO AUCKLAND*
48 km

This is a short day. If there is nothing to keep you in Auckland, you could pass through the whole urban area on your way south (see below).

Rejoin S.H. 16 from Parakai and head south. The road passes through flat to gently rolling countryside south of Helensville, becoming marginally hillier as it approaches the urban area.

Instead of continuing along S.H. 16 all the way, I recommend turning south for Waitakere at Kumeu 20 km southeast of Helensville. The road is clearly signposted. From Waitakere continue through Swanson and Henderson towards the city. At Henderson, join Great North Road which continues virtually all the way to the centre of the city.

If Auckland's suburban trains are still running, you will be able to avoid the rather boring ride through the suburbs by catching the train at Waitakere. Departure times (weekdays only) include 9.18 A.M., 11.15 A.M., 1.45 P.M. and 3.30 P.M. There is also a 4.43 P.M. train from Henderson. You can change trains at Newmarket if you wish and continue south as far as Papakura, right through the urban area.

Cyclists who want to get through the city, avoiding the city centre and pedalling all the way, should continue along Great North Road through Henderson and New Lynn as far as Avondale. At the roundabout just before the Avondale shops, take St. Jude Street uphill to the right, then veer right at the first major intersection into New North Road. Take the second turn right (southeast) into Hendon Road, then follow the instructions (in reverse) given for the route from Auckland International Airport to Avondale Motorcamp (see Tour 1, Route 2). From the turnoff to the airport on Massey Road, follow the instructions given for the route from the Airport going south. From Helensville to Papakura by this route is about 86 km.

Hills above Manaia, near Coromandel (Photo by Richard Oddy)

TOUR 4. COROMANDEL PENINSULA

7–9 days: 466km–897km

The Coromandel Peninsula is about 40 kilometres due east of Auckland. Its ranges are visible from parts of the city, the highest mountain being Moehau (891 m). The Coromandel is an area of bush and beaches, with pockets of rough farmland, and holiday settlements sprinkled along its coast.

Captain James Cook, the English navigator, touched at Mercury Bay on the eastern side of the Peninsula in the *Endeavour* in 1769. He hoisted the British flag, claiming the country for George III. Permanent European settlement began much later, with traders and timber millers living here under Maori protection from the 1830s onward.

In the 1850s gold was discovered at Coromandel and later at Thames, and these towns boomed. Their streets became crowded with diggers and lined with pubs, and the hills around were strewn with mine tailings and denuded of trees. In less than twenty years, however, the boom was over and the Peninsula became a backwater of rugged terrain, poor soils and poor roads. There is still gold in the hills, however, a source of conflict between mining companies and environmentalists who want to preserve the area as it is.

Today the Coromandel Peninsula has gained new life as a tourist area, with thousands of holidaymakers passing through at the height of summer. The rest of the year it is a quiet rural haven. And this is when it is seen at its best.

The distances given on this tour are generally short. This region is far too beautiful to hurry through. The main itinerary takes you on a circuit of the Peninsula, returning to Auckland via Te Aroha and Kaiaua. The option is also offered of continuing south to join either of the Auckland to Wellington routes. From Whangamata, you can head southeast to Tauranga instead of southwest to Te Aroha, and from Tauranga continue either to Whakatane or to Rotorua. At either Whakatane or Rotorua, you can join Tour 6; or you can continue southwest from Rotorua to Taupo and Tokaanu to join Tour 5 (see Tour 6A).

Note that free camping on public land is forbidden on the Peninsula. In summer, the parks and beaches are patrolled by wardens. They have the power to move you on if your tent is pitched on an unofficial site.

DAY 1 AUCKLAND TO THAMES ─────────
90–121 km

If Auckland's suburban trains are still running, the quickest and most sensible way out of Auckland to the south is to take the train to Papakura. This saves 31 km of dull and sometimes dangerous suburban streets.

Trains run from Auckland Central Station between 6.10 A.M. and 6.30 P.M., weekdays only. Avoid rush-hour. There are no trains on Saturday or Sunday or on public holidays. The trip takes 43 minutes. Tickets can be bought at any station or on the train itself. Bikes are carried free. Load your bike on and off the luggage compartment yourself. In some luggage compartments space is limited and the bike must be suspended from hooks by its front wheel; this means unloading your gear.

On emerging from Papakura station, turn left (southeast) along Railway Street and left again into Onslow Road. From Onslow Road, take the third turn right onto Hunua Road.

If you leave the city during the weekend you will have to cycle. The most practical route is Great South Road, which was the main road south before the southern motorway was built.

Great South Road is an easy road with gentle gradients; but it can not be called a picturesque road, since it mostly passes through industrial areas and shopping centres. Traffic is busy much of the way on weekdays and on Saturday mornings, but moderate for the rest of the weekend.

(By the way, if your bike needs some last-minute attention before leaving town, **there are bike shops at Greenlane, just south of Newmarket, and in Otahuhu, Hunters Corners, Manurewa and Papakura.**)

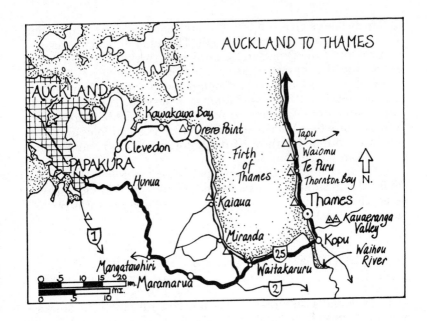

From Newmarket, take Manukau Road southwards. At the first set of traffic lights beyond the motorway underpass, Great South Road forks to the left. Follow this road south all the way to Papakura.

After 3 km you come to the Harp of Erin intersection. Take the right fork here (the left leads across the motorway and into Ellerslie). Two kilometres further on, the road turns sharp left over a humpbacked bridge to cross the railway line. Penrose Station is just beyond.

From here to the Westfield Freezing Works is 3 km. Another 2 km takes you through Otahuhu shopping centre. (Just before Otahuhu is a compulsory left turn into Princes Street, then right into Atkinson Avenue, which rejoins Great South Road 1 km along.) From Monument Corner at the southern end of Otahuhu to Hunters Corner shopping centre is another 2.5 km.

From here to Manukau City centre is 3.5 km. Manukau City (pop. 177,248). Is New Zealand's largest city in area, taking in as it does most of the suburban sprawl that is South Auckland and vast stretches of the countryside beyond.

From Manukau City to Manurewa is 3.9 km. If you feel like a short break for sightseeing, Hill Road, to the left just before reaching the Manurewa shops, leads 2 km uphill to the Auckland Regional Authority Botanical Gardens. From the Hill Road intersection itself to Papakura is 6 km.

Papakura (pop. 23,357) was originally a military settlement. Among its oldest buildings is the Selwyn Chapel (1862) of Christ Church, seen to the right just before entering the Papakura shops. There is a small museum in the old Courthouse 1 km further south.

Continue along Great South Road through Papakura shopping centre. Half a kilometre beyond the main Post Office veer left onto Opaheke Street. Continue in a southeasterly direction for 1 km, turning into Boundary Road, the eighth street to the left. This shortly crosses the railway line, and less than 1 km along joins Hunua Road.

Hunua Road passes through an industrial estate on the outskirts of town, climbs eastward and upward for 8 km through the picturesque Hunua Gorge, turns southeast through the pleasant farmlands of the Wairoa River valley and Happy Valley, then climbs a small saddle and drops briefly and sharply to Mangatawhiri. Turn eastward here along S.H. 2 towards Thames.

From Papakura to Mangatawhiri traffic is usually light; from then on until Thames it can be very busy, particularly at the beginning of the summer holidays.

Twenty-five kilometres of rolling country with a downhill trend follows from Mangatawhiri, where the road forks. Take the left fork (S.H. 25) for Thames. The 30 km from here to Thames across the Hauraki Plains are virtually flat. This is a fast road if you have a good southwesterly wind behind you.

> ■ **Side Trip:** Thirty kilometres from Mangatawhiri is the small roadside settlement of Waitakaruru. Nine kilometres to the north, near the coast of the Firth of Thames, are open-air thermal pools, with an associated campsite.

Seven kilometres before Thames the road crosses the muddy and tidal Waihou River, where the long one-way bridge can be a bottle-neck. There are traffic lights at either end of the bridge and passing bays, which allow slower vehicles to pull over so others can pass, at intervals along it. Across the bridge is the crossroads settlement of Kopu (hotel, motel, tearooms). Turn north here for Thames.

Shortly beyond Kopu you will see the Kauaeranga Valley signposted to your right. This beautiful bush-clad valley, about 15 km in length, gives access to a number of walking-tracks into the ranges. The Department of Conservation runs several campsites along the valley. There is an information centre 5 km along the northern side of the river.

If you would like more formal accommodation, continue into Thames which has several hotels and motels. Thames (pop. 6,461) a century ago was a rip-roaring mining town with 60 taverns in the main street alone. It now has a mere five. A number of old buildings, the Thames museum, and the School of Mines Museum (Cochrane/Brown Street) recall the past. The nearest motorcamp to Thames itself is at Dickson Park, 3 km north of the town. This has cabins. There are other motorcamps at Te Puru, 11 km north, Waiomu, 13 km north, and Tapu, 19 km north. All have cabins.

The Thames Information Office is at 405 Queen Street, the main road through town.

DAY 2 THAMES TO COROMANDEL ───────────
55 km

This may seem like a short day but you will probably want to linger on the attractive coast north of Thames, and there are two steep hills to cross in the latter part of the day.

The road northward from Thames hugs the coast for 30 km, passing through the seaside settlements of Thornton Bay, Te Puru, Waiomu and Tapu. Pohutakawas fringe the road, and there are sandy beaches and a myriad of rocky coves to swim from. The flat to undulating road is sealed.

At Wilsons Bay the road turns inland, winding up a steep hill, going from sea-level to 243 m in just over 4 km. This ascent is followed by an almost equally steep descent to the farming settlement of Manaia.

A short flat stretch through Manaia is followed by another, but less demanding, climb and descent. The last 3 km into Coroomandel are flat.

Coromandel (pop. 940), like Thames, is a former gold-mining town. Many of its older buildings, such as the wooden Courthouse and the School of Mines Museum, are preserved from last century. The hills around are honeycombed with former mines. Coromandel is now a centre for a number of artists and craftspeople. There is a hotel in the township, also motels and a guesthouse. The Coromandel Motorcamp (cabins) is in Rings Road: turn right at the main intersection in town. There is another motorcamp at Longs Bay, 1.5 km to the east.

SIDE TRIP: NORTH OF COROMANDEL CIRCUIT ───
100–110 km

This is a rugged trip recommended only to experienced cyclists who are happy with gravel roads. A mountain bike is the most useful sort of bike for much of the distance. A strong cyclist could possibly do the circuit in one day, starting early and going hard at it all day. But most cyclists should allow at least two days with a loaded bike, and will probably want to linger for several more.

As mentioned, free camping on public land is not allowed on the Coromandel Peninsula, and the northern coast is patrolled in summer to prevent it. Official accommodation north of Coromandel consists of motorcamps (with cabins) at Papa Aroha and Amodeo Bay respectively, 12 km and 18 km north of the

Coromandel township, and motels at Papa Aroha and Colville. There are also campsites on farm parks operated by the Department of Conservation at Fantail Bay, Port Jackson, Fletcher Bay, Stony Bay, Port Charles and Waikawau Bay.

Leave Coromandel by Rings Road, to the northeast. The road climbs into the hills briefly before descending to the coast again, then hugs the coast for much of the next 10 km to Amodeo Bay. Here the road turns inland, and the seal ends.

A 3 km ascent is followed by a 7 km descent down a river valley to Colville, a roadside halt with a pub, a store, a motel (down Wharf Road) and little else. The store is the northernmost one on the Peninsula. The road north from Colville to Port Jackson, 33 km away, is rugged but delightful, winding along a rocky coast fringed with pohutakawas. Port Jackson is an open beach, a port in name only. The road continues over the hills for another 4 km to Fletcher Bay, then peters out in the hills.

This is where you decide whether to turn back or continue, perhaps at some risk to your bike and yourself. The Coromandel Walkway leads around the coastal hills at the eastern end of Fletcher Bay, joining the end of the west-side road 7 km southeast at Stony Bay. The track is steep and narrow in parts. Anticipate about 3 to 4 hours with a bike since you will be pushing it perhaps one-quarter of the way. There are several creeks to cross and, when riding on narrow stretches, you must be careful of your pedals snagging on bushes and rocks beside the track.

A gravel road leads from Stony Bay over the hills to Sandy Bay and Port Charles, then inland, climbing to 198 m before descending to a river valley. The road forks just beyond the river. Either take the right fork for Colville, returning to Coromandel the way you came, or turn left for Waikawau Bay, a beachside farm park maintained by the Department of Conservation. South of Waikawau Bay the road rises to 200 m before descending to Kennedy Bay. From Kennedy Bay to Coromandel is 14 km, involving a gradually steepening 8 km climb to 400 m and a very steep and winding descent. Seal begins again just outside Coromandel.

DAY 3 *COROMANDEL TO WHITIANGA* ————
46 km

This route is demanding and hilly but very scenic. Except for short stretches of seal outside Coromandel and Whitianga and at Te Rerenga and Kuaotunu, the road is gravel all the way. Distances are short, however, and if you leave Coromandel after breakfast you could reach Kuaotunu in time for a leisurely picnic lunch on the beach and a swim. Traffic is light except for peak holiday periods, when both cars and the dust they create can be problems.

Leave Coromandel southwards by the main Thames road. The Kuaotunu road is signposted eastward less than a kilometre outside the township. A short stretch of seal is followed by a 1.5 km climb to 364 m on a winding and sometimes rugged gravel road. The reward is a magnificent panorama of bays, beaches and harbours to both east and west of the summit.

A more gradual 3 km descent follows. The road then skirts the southern side of the Whangapoua Harbour, with one or two short climbs over secondary ridges. Native bush gives way to dairy farms and pine plantations. Continue all the way to Kuaotunu. Alternatively, about 20 km from Coromandel turn left through farmland and swamp toward the developing holiday resort of Matarangi Beach. Then follow the narrow and ill-kept but beautiful stretch of coastal road eastward past Rings Beach to Kuaotunu.

Less than a century ago, Kuaotunu was a bustling gold-mining town. Today it is a quiet farming and holiday settlement, and the centre of resistance by local residents to mining companies once again prospecting in the hills. There is a motorcamp with cabins midway along the beach, and a combination dairy-tearooms and petrol station at the eastern end.

> ■ **Side Trip:** If you decide to stay in Kuaotunu for the afternoon—or for a day or two—possible excursions include Otama and Opito Beaches and Waitaia. Otama is a short, steep climb away over Black Jack Hill at the eastern end of Kuaotunu. Otama has brilliant white sand which squeaks when walked on, but swimming is unsafe except in the lagoon. Opito, five or six kilometres further on, is a safe and pleasant beach, although lined with holiday homes.

> ■ **Side Trip:** Waitaia is a small, secluded and very beautiful beach four kilometres southeast of Kuaotunu. Turn left where the Whitianga Road enters the hills. The Waitaia Road is a clay road, impassible except to four-wheel-drive vehicles and off-road bikes during much of the winter.

There are a number of abandoned gold mines in the hills around Kuaotunu. It is unwise to explore them but, if you must, do not go alone, take a good torch, and watch out for unexpected holes. Otherwise you just might not come back.

From Kuaotunu the road gently climbs and descends through bush-clad hills, comes out into open farmland, then hops over a last brief hill between Wharekaho Beach and Buffalo Beach before entering Whitianga township.

Whitianga is a fishing port and seaside resort with a permanent population of 2,503 that increases to at least 35,000 in summer. The town has a small local historical museum and offers a wide selection of motorcamps with cabins, motels, hotels and guesthouses. If all of these are full, continue to Cooks Beach (see the next day's tour).

DAY 4 WHITIANGA TO WHANGAMATA
71 km

From Whitianga, S.H. 25 leads southward out of town then turns inland to avoid the upper reaches of the Whitianga Harbour. This dog-leg, however, can be avoided by taking the launch across the harbour instead. The launch crosses from Whitianga wharf to Ferry Landing directly opposite the town. It runs all day during summer, and the crossing takes no more than five minutes.

The stone wharf at Ferry Landing dates from the 1830s and is said to be the oldest in the country. From the wharf, take the Cooks Beach road eastward around a low headland. The road skirts a small beach and climbs a low saddle before Cooks Beach. To the left, a side-road leads 1.5 km to the Cook Memorial above Shakespeare Cliffs. Captain Cook landed and observed the transit of the planet Mercury from the far end of Cooks Beach in 1769.

Cooks Beach is a holiday settlement with a motorcamp. The road leads southeast and inland from here to rejoin S.H. 25 at Whenuakite.

> ■ **Side Trips:** 5 km south of Cooks Beach a gravel road leads eastward 5 km to Hahei, a beach renowned for the colour of its sand, which is tinted a delicate pink. Hahei has a motorcamp with cabins. A further 4 km south of Cooks Beach, just before Whenuakite, another side-road to the east leads to Hot Water Beach 6 km. away. This is notable for hotwater springs in the sand at the northern end of the beach, where holidaymakers can dig their own temporary open-air spa pools. Hot Water Beach also has a motorcamp with cabins.

S.H. 25 leads southeast, climbing a river valley and ascending a range of coastal hills (212 m) before descending steeply to Tairua (pop. 1,109). A small market town and holiday settlement, Tairua has a hotel, several motels and three motorcamps (with cabins). Just across the estuary by boat, but a circuitous 25 km trip by road,

Flaxmill Bay, near Cooks Beach (Photo by Joan Oddy)

is Pauanui, one of New Zealand's plushest holiday resorts.

At Tairua the road turns inland along the northern edge of the Tairua Harbour and the Tairua River. Gradients are gentle for the next 16 km to Hikuai. Beyond Hikuai the road forks.

Keep to S.H. 25, which continues southeast towards Whangamata. The first 10 km are gravel, winding, and involve several short, steep climbs and descents. From then on the seal begins, and the terrain is slightly gentler.

> ■ **Side Trip:** Midway to Whangamata a side-road turns east to Opoutere, 5 km away. This is a small harbourside settlement as yet unspoiled by tourist developments. It has a mangrove-lined harbour, a lagoon and a long, uncrowded beach. There is a Youth Hostel here and farm campsites. Opoutere will suit get-away-from-it-all cyclists much better than Whangamata.

Whangamata (pop. 2,475) is a bustling holiday town with a beautiful beach, several motels, and motorcamps with cabins.

DAY 5 WHANGAMATA TO TE AROHA ————
71km

From Whangamata southwards the road is sealed and traffic becomes heavier. The road skirts the Otahu River, gently climbs the valley of a minor stream, and drops to Whiritoa, a holiday settlement with another attractive beach.

Waihi (pop. 3,679) is a farming centre and old mining town. The shell of the former pumphouse of the Martha Mine, closed down in 1952, can be seen on Martha Hill on the way into town. Waihi has hotels, motels, and a motorcamp with cabins.

At Waihi you decide whether to turn west for Te Aroha, and thence back to Auckland (or on to Rotorua via Matamata), or to turn south to Tauranga and join either tour 5 or 6 heading to Wellington. The options via Tauranga and Whakatane (see Tour 4A), or via Tauranga and Rotorua (see Tour 4B) are described at the end of this itinerary. For a description of the route linking Rotorua (Tour 6) and Tokaanu (Tour 5), see Tour 6A.

To continue to Te Aroha, take the Paeroa road westward from Waihi. This winds through the Karangahake Gorge, rising slightly for the first 5 km beyond Waihi, then dipping into the Gorge, then is mostly level until a short steep rise outside Paeroa.

Waikino and Karangahake, small settlements in the Gorge, are former mining towns. There are tearooms and an open-air mining museum at Karangahake, 16 km from Waihi.

As an alternative to cycling, an excursion train runs on the hour every hour 10 km along the Gorge during holiday periods, less frequently at other times. This will take bicycles. By the end of 1989, it is planned to extend the railway line to link with the eastern end of the Karangahake Gorge Historic Walkway. This runs for 5 km along the southern side of the Gorge from Owharoa Falls (across the first bridge to the left after Waikino) to Karangahake, passing through a former railway tunnel on the way. The surface of the track is good and the gradients easy.

Paeroa (pop. 3,661), once a river port, is now a service centre best-known for the production of its namesake soft-drink, Lemon & Paeroa. Paeroa has several hotels and motels. There is an interesting Maritime Park on the Waihou River 3 km northwest of town, where examples of the old river steamers that served the region are preserved.

At Paeroa, turn south along S.H. 26 for Te Aroha. The road runs through gently rolling country between the Waihou River and the Kaimai Ranges.

Te Aroha (pop. 3,510) is a former spa town with some elegant old buildings. In the Tourist Domain are hot baths and mineral

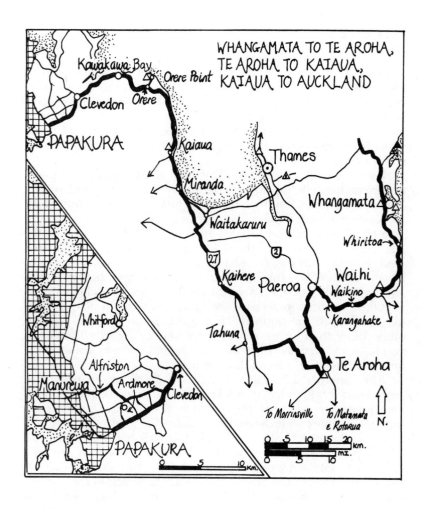

drinking waters. A steep walking-track behind the Domain leads up Mt. Te Aroha (952 m) which offers magnificent views on either side of the Kaimai Ranges. The ascent takes 2 to 3 hours by foot. There are mini-bus tours up the mountain by road.

Te Aroha has a hotel, motel and Youth Hostel. The motorcamp (cabins) is on the Matamata Road, across the river westward from the main part of the town. There is a Public Relations Office at 102 Whitaker Street.

Te Aroha is a convenient point to turn south to Wellington via Wanganui or via Rotorua and around East Cape (see Tours 5 and 6). Otherwise return to Auckland via Kaiaua, as described below.

DAY 6 TE AROHA TO KAIAUA
72 km

Leave Te Aroha via S.H. 26, heading southwest across the river toward Hamilton. Take the first road to the right (northwest) after crossing the bridge and continue through Te Aroha's leafy western suburbs. Take the second road to the left beyond the outskirts of town, which brings you to the tiny crossroads settlement of Elstow. Turn right here, continuing northeast for 5 km, then turn left (southwest).

The road is absolutely flat. This area is reclaimed swampland and immediately to the north is the largest area of peatland in New Zealand. Continue southwestward for just over 7 km, joining S.H. 27 before reaching Tahuna, then turning north.

S.H. 27 is a well-kept sealed road running to the west of the Hapuakohe Range. Until the last year or two it was a quiet rural road, but it is carrying increasing traffic as it is becoming known as an alternative route between Auckland and points south. Around the locality of Kaihere, 20 km north, are several kilometres of rolling country, otherwise the terrain is virtually flat. S.H. 27 joins S.H. 2, 32 km north of Tahuna. Continue northwest for another 3 km, then turn northeast into S.H. 25 towards Thames. If you have followed this itinerary, you passed this way going in the opposite direction, several days earlier.

After another 2.5 km, turn off S.H. 25 along an easy road signposted to Miranda. After 9 km the road joins the Kaiaua road. One kilometre south of this junction is Miranda Hot Pools, a thermal complex with campsites available.

If you do not feel like a hot soak, continue north to Kaiaua. At first sight, Kaiaua is a nondescript settlement straggling along a bare coast, but the area has a certain charm which becomes apparent as you observe the play of light and shade across the shallow waters offshore and note the abundant bird-life. There is a tavern and a takeaway bar at the southern end of the village. 1 km further north is a store and a motorcamp (cabins). Note that free camping is forbidden between Miranda and Matingarahi, 13 km north of Kaiaua.

DAY 7 KAIAUA TO AUCKLAND
61–92 km

The difference in distance depends on whether or not you catch the suburban train (if available) to town from Papakura, or cycle the whole distance. The last afternoon trains from Papakura leave at 4.10, 4.50, 5.10 and 5.35.

Continue north along the flat coastal road from Kaiaua. Seven kilometres along is Waharau Regional Park, from where walking tracks lead into the Hunua Ranges. Waharau Park looks an ideal spot to pitch a tent; unfortunately, camping is forbidden. The campsite above the road to the left is reserved for the sole use of members of the Maori Waikato tribes.

The road turns inland at Matingarahi, 6 km beyond Waharoa, after which there are two substantial hills to climb before reaching Orere.

Orere is little more than an intersection, but there is a pretty beach 3 km away on the coast (motorcamp with cabins). If continuing to Auckland, take the western fork at Orere. A gradually steepening 6 km ascent of the lush, green valley of the Orere River is followed by a steep 3 km descent through bush-clad hills to Kawakawa Bay. This stretch is narrow and winding. On emerging at the coast, turn left (west) for Auckland. Kawakawa Bay has a dairy and a motel.

At the western end of the bay, the road turns inland again. There is a short but stiff climb and descent to a coastal river, then several kilometres of rolling country before Clevedon, a small rural centre and commuter village. There are pleasant tearooms here to the right on the way into the village, a good place to refuel if you are cycling all the way into Auckland.

From Clevedon, continue southwest to Papakura if you intend to catch the train. The terrain is flat. If you prefer to cycle all the way into Auckland, take the second turn to the right 2 km outside the village. Four and a half kilometres along, turn right for Alfriston; and another 3 km on, turn left for Manurewa. You will enter Manurewa at the southern end of the shopping centre. Turn right (northwest) along Great South Road.

Tour 4A Whangamata to Whakatane

DAY 1 *WHANGAMATA TO TAURANGA* ————
91 km; via Waihi Beach: 98 km

For the route from Whangamata to Waihi, see Tour 4, Day 5. From Waihi, take S.H. 2 southeast. This rises gently for the first 5 km beyond Waihi, then dips downhill to the Athenree Gorge. For 5 km along the Gorge, gradients are gentle, then there is a steepish 2 km climb. The following 12 km to Katikati are through undulating to rolling country.

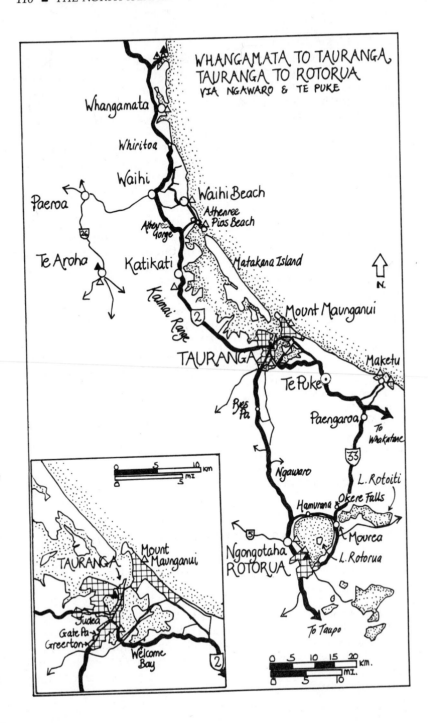

There is a beautiful rest area set amongst trees halfway through the Athenree Gorge. Overnight camping is permitted here, but not longer stays. There are tearooms at the southern end of the Gorge, which also offer accommodation.

■ **ALTERNATIVE ROUTE:** If you like beaches, you could detour south via Waihi Beach instead of via the Athenree Gorge. After descending from the hills between Whiritoa and Waihi, turn left off S.H. 25 onto the Happy Valley road. This winds southward through rolling country, bypassing Waihi and joining the Waihi Beach Rd 15 km south of Whiritoa.

Waihi Beach (pop. 1,500) is a holiday resort set at the northern end of a long beach of golden sand stretching almost 10 km south to Bowentown Heads. It has a motel and several motorcamps (cabins). There is another motorcamp (cabins) beyond Pio's Beach (pop. 347) near the tip of the Bowentown Peninsula.

From Waihi Beach, continue along the coastal road southeastwards. At 3 km along, turn inland along the Athenree road which, after 4 km, joins S.H. 2 just south of the Athenree Gorge. ■

Katikati (pop. 1,921) is a pleasant market town, first settled in the 1870s by immigrants from Northern Ireland. There is a motel in Katikati and a motorcamp (cabins) at Sapphire Springs 3 km south.

For the next 36 km to Tauranga, the road runs through undulating to rolling country. Approaching Tauranga, the rises, although short, become steeper, so this can be quite a demanding stretch of road. Like much of the northern Bay of Plenty, this is a fruit-growing region, with numerous roadside stalls selling local produce.

There is a motorcamp (cabins) at Omokoroa 5 km to the east of the main road roughly halfway between Katikati and Tauranga. Eight kilometres before Tauranga, there is a rest area with toilets and tap-water beside the banks of the Wairoa River.

S.H. 2 enters Tauranga from the west, through the suburbs of Bethlehem and Judea. The centre of the city lies on the Te Papa Peninsula jutting northwards into the harbour. S.H. 2 becomes Waihi Rd as it snakes through the suburbs. Turn left off this into Cameron Rd., which runs along the spine of peninsula.

Tauranga (pop. 41,611) is a prosperous city, the centre of a rich fruit-growing area, and a major port. Because of its sunny, warm climate it has also attracted large numbers of retired folk.

Before the pakeha came, the Bay of Plenty was densely populated by the Maori, although ravaged by tribal wars in the early 19th century. The first pakeha to settle in the Tauranga district were missionaries, who established a mission station in 1835, on the Te Papa Peninsula. "The Elms," the house built by one of the first missionaries, Archdeacon A.N. Brown, still stands on the northern end of the city centre, and is preserved as a museum.

A major battle was fought here in 1864, during the Land Wars. Government forces besieged a Maori fortification, known as Gate Pa, near the foot of the Peninsula. After the wars were over, substantial areas of land were confiscated from the local Ngaterangi tribes, and military settlers moved in.

Relics of the early days in Tauranga include, besides the Elms, the Monmouth Redoubt (the remains of a fort built by British troops in 1864), the Otemataha Pa Military Cemetery, and the site of Gate Pa. There is also a regional museum and replica pioneer village.

Tauranga has numerous hotels and motels, also a Youth Hostel. There are two motorcamps (cabins) in the city itself. These are both off Fifteenth Avenue. Turn right instead of left where Waihi Rd. meets Cameron Rd. Fifteenth Avenue is the fourth road to the right off Cameron Rd. Continue to the end, where the Avenue becomes Turret Rd. and turns south to cross the Hairini Bridge.

This is also the main road out of town to the east, towards Te Puke and Whakatane.

Mount Maunganui (pop. 12,375) lies across the harbour to the northeast of Tauranga. This is Tauranga's port, and one of New Zealand's major export ports. It is also a major holiday town, noisy and crowded in mid-summer. Houses line its long, golden beach, from Mount Maunganui (252 m) at the northeastern end most of the way to Papamoa, 20 km away.

Tauranga and Mount Maunganui are linked by a recently completed bridge which crosses the harbour from the northern end of the city centre to Hewletts Rd. on the southwestern edge of Mount Maunganui. Some older maps may not show this bridge.

DAY 2 TAURANGA TO WHAKATANE
90 km–98 km; with detour to Maketu: 110 km–112 km

Cross the Hairini Bridge to the south of Tauranga. Once across the bridge, you have the choice of following S.H. 2 all the way to Te Puke, or of taking the Welcome Bay road for about two thirds of the distance.

S.H. 2 turns northeast almost to Mount Maunganui, then southeast around the upper reaches of Rangataua Bay. It is a fairly busy road, but flat to undulating the whole way.

For the Welcome Bay road, turn southeast once across the Hairini Bridge. This road passes through rolling to hilly country to

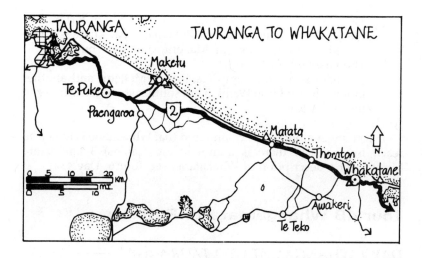

the south of Rangataua Bay, rejoining S.H. 2, 9 km north of Te Puke. It is a quieter road than S.H. 2, but narrower, much more strenuous, and 2 km longer.

Te Puke (pop. 5,106) is a farming and orchard centre set on the edge of a fertile coastal plain. This is kiwifruit country, in local opinion the kiwifruit capital of the world. Virtually the whole region is divided into squares and rectangles by the rows of tall trees which shelter the orchards. Besides kiwifruit, tamarillos, passionfruit, oranges, and other, more exotic, fruits grow abundantly. Te Puke has a hotel, a motel and a motorcamp (cabins).

From Te Puke to Whakatane is flat to gently undulating the whole way, easy riding indeed. S.H. 2 touches the coast 25 km from Te Puke, running between sandhills and the sea for the next 17 km to Matata (pop. 567), then turning slightly inland for the last 22 km to Whakatane.

■ **Side Trip:** Maketu (pop. 802), a farming and holiday village at the mouth of the Kaituna River, 14 km east of Te Puke, is worth a visit. Turn off S.H. 2 towards the coast 8 km beyond Te Puke. Maketu was, according to Maori traditions, the landing-place of the Arawa canoe, the canoe which brought the ancestors of the local Arawa people to this land, in the mid-14th century. Te Arawa fought on the side of British and colonial troops during the Land Wars, and there was a fierce battle here against supporters of the

Maori King in 1864. The remains of a redoubt or fort built at the time stand on the site of Pukemaire pa. There is a fine carved meeting house in Maketu, and the church of St. Thomas, built in 1868.

There is a motorcamp (cabins) in Maketu, and another motorcamp at Little Waihi, 3 km southeast, on the estuary of the Waihi River.

If you linger along the way, and find that Whakatane is too far to reach in one day, there is a motorcamp (cabins) 3 km before Matata. For a description of Whakatane, see Tour 6, Day 4.

Tour 4B Whangamata to Rotorua

DAY 1 WHANGAMATA TO TAURANGA ————————
(see Tour 4A)

DAY 2 TAURANGA TO ROTORUA VIA NGAWERO ——
65 km

This is the "direct road," little-used and very strenuous, but also very beautiful.

Take Cameron Rd. southeast from Tauranga, passing through Gate Pa and Greerton. On the outskirts of the city, this intersects with S.H. 29. Cross this into the Pyes Pa road, continuing first southeast, then south. For the next 10 km the road gradually climbs the lower slopes of the Kaimai Range to the tiny village of Pyes Pa. Here, the seal ends. The next 42 km are gravel, sometimes rough gravel.

Just beyond Pyes Pa, the road forks. Take the right fork. The road drops briefly into a gully, then begins to climb again, ascending most (but not all) of the next 15 km and finally reaching 509 m.

Ngawero, not far beyond the highest point, is just a name on the map in the middle of pine forests. In the coaching days, when this was the main route between Tauranga and Rotorua, it was the site of a hotel. The hotel's foundations and an old horse trough can still be seen beside the first bridge over the Mangorewa River. If carrying provisions, you could decide to stay here for the night. Beware of lighting fires, however; this is a fire risk area.

Beyond Ngawero, the road drops steeply into the Mangorewa Gorge and climbs equally steeply out. You now pass through rolling country before dropping down to the edge of Lake Rotorua north of Ngongotaha. The last 5 km to the lake, and the last 6 km into Ngongotaha, are sealed.

Ngongotaha is a lakeside suburb of Rotorua. The city centre is another 8 km south. For a description of Rotorua, see Tour 6, Day 3

■ *ALTERNATIVE DAY 2A TAURANGA TO ROTORUA VIA TE PUKE*
86 to 96 km

This is, I think, a much less interesting route. It is also much busier, carrying most of the road traffic between Tauranga and the Volcanic Plateau, including logging trucks.

Take S.H. 2 or the Welcome Bay road to Te Puke (see above). At 8 km beyond Te Puke, turn south along S.H. 33 to Rotorua. The road gradually climbs from the coastal plains to the plateau, reaching just less than 300 m at the highest point just before it reaches the lakes.

It then drops slightly to Okere Falls at the western end of Lake Rotoiti, skirts the lake for several kilometres, and crosses a narrow spit of land to Mourea, on the eastern shores of Lake Rotorua.

Just before Mourea, you have the choice of turning south along the eastern shore or west along the northern shore of the lake. By the former route, Rotorua is 16 km away, the latter half of this distance largely through the suburban sprawl of Owhata and Ngapuna.

The latter route is 8 km longer, but circles the lake to north and west, offering some excellent views, and good informal camping spots. The terrain is undulating and the road is sealed.

There is a shop at Hamurana en route.

Mount Ruapehu (Photo by Richard Oddy)

TOUR 5. AUCKLAND TO WELLINGTON VIA WANGANUI

6–9 days: 604 km–761 km

The record by bicycle between Auckland and Wellington is 20 hours 9 minutes, set by 43-year-old Brian Fleck in 1984—fighting sub-zero temperatures and driving rain much of the way. Few cycle tourists will want to emulate him, but some will certainly want to reach Wellington without too much delay. The route described below is for them.

It is not quite, in fact, the most direct route, which would be via State Highway One all the way through Hamilton, Taupo, Waiouru and Bulls, a distance of 660 km, taking the average cyclist five or six days. S.H. 1 however, carries a lot of traffic and is therefore not recommended.

The route described here goes via Wanganui, a longer distance but a far more interesting trip. This itinerary takes you as much as possible along quiet back roads and through unfrequented countryside that, in parts, few New Zealanders know well.

I have split the trip into six to nine daily stages, some quite long. Cyclists who like a more leisurely pace could shorten these stages; cyclists in more of a hurry could perhaps take a train part of the way. This route is most suitable for cyclists who are free campers; cyclists who require formal accommodation may have to accept longer stages.

Stronger cyclists may choose to cover the distance between Auckland and Lake Waipapa in two days instead of three. Logical stages would be: (1) Auckland to Morrinsville (162 km) and (2) Morrinsville to Lake Waipapa (109 km).

The first day, of course, can be reduced to a more manageable 131 km by taking the suburban train (if available) to Papakura, and reduced further to 111 km by taking the Hunua Gorge route from Papakura rather than the Kaiaua route. See Tour 4, for instructions as far as Maramarua. From Maramarua, take S.H. 2 eastward for 15 km, then turn south along S.H. 27. From here, follow the instructions given for Day 2 below.

DAY 1 AUCKLAND TO KAIAUA
61 km–92 km

This can be quite an easy day's cycle, just right to loosen up those muscles and get into the rhythm of the trip, particularly if you avoid 31 km of busy suburban roads by taking the train to Papakura. For directions from Auckland to Papakura, by train or by bike, see Tour 4, Day 1.

If arriving in Papakura by train, head northwest from the station along Railway Street, which runs parallel to the tracks. Take the first turn right (east) then, at the first roundabout, take the northeast fork. This is the Clevedon road, which leaves the suburbs for open country within two kilometres.

If arriving in Papakura by bike along Great South Road, midway through the shopping centre you will come to an intersection with a clock-tower. Turn left here. (The street is called Broadway, but you will quickly see that it has nothing in common with its namesake in New York, USA.) Continue along Broadway over a railway bridge into Willis Road and, at the first roundabout you come to, take the northeast fork towards Clevedon.

The 12 km to Clevedon is a gentle ride through green fields. Clevedon is a small rural centre and commuter village. At the intersection in the middle of the village, veer right onto the Kawakawa Bay road.

Kawakawa Bay is 16 km away through rolling country, with one longish climb in the last stretch before the road drops to the coast. It is a sleepy seaside and retirement village, busy only during the holiday season and on summer weekends. Towards the eastern end of the bay is a small general store. Turn right (south) here to-

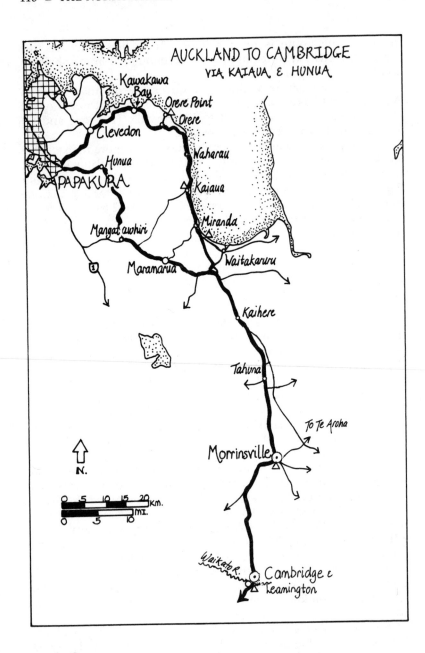

AUCKLAND TO CAMBRIDGE
VIA KAIAUA & HUNUA

wards Orere.

The road climbs through the hills for 3 km, then descends the valley of the Orere River. Orere itself is little more than an intersection, but there is a pretty beach at Orere Point, a 3 km detour to the north. Orere Point has a motorcamp with cabins.

Take the right fork at Orere, heading southeast towards Kaiaua. The 7 km stretch to the coast involves a little climbing and a long descent to the coast at Matingarahi. The last 13 km to Kaiaua are mostly flat.

There is a regional park at Waharau midway to Kaiaua. Walking tracks lead from the park into the Hunua Ranges. Although the park at Waharau may look an ideal place to camp, camping is forbidden here, as is free camping on the entire coastal stretch from Matingarahi to Miranda, 25 km south. The campground to the right of the road at Waharau is reserved for the use of members of the Maori Waikato tribes. Kaiaua is a seaside settlement which straggles along the coast, but has good views across the Firth of Thames to the Coromandel Peninsula opposite.

There is a store and motorcamp (cabins) at the northern end of the village, and a hotel and takeaway shop about 1 km further south. There are also tent sites available at Miranda Hot Pools, 12 km south of Kaiaua.

DAY 2 KAIAUA TO CAMBRIDGE
102 km

Head southward along the coast from Kaiaua. Eleven kilometres south, 2 km beyond the tiny crossroad settlement of Miranda, is an intersection. Take the right fork here to join S.H. 25 9 km further on. Then turn right (west) on S.H. 25. Take the first road to the left which shortly brings you to S.H. 2. Continue south for less than a mile before turning onto S.H. 27.

■ **ALTERNATIVE ROUTE:** You can continue along the coast instead of turning right beyond Miranda. This takes you past the Miranda hot pools and, further south, a bird sanctuary. The shallow waters and mudflats of the Firth of Thames are a feeding and breeding ground for a number of wading birds—godwits, knots and the like. At S.H. 2 turn west, then southeast 6 km along onto S.H. 2. At 3 km along S.H. 2, turn onto S.H. 27. This detour adds a total of 6 km to the day. ■

S.H. 27 passes through pleasant and flat to gently rolling country between the Hapuahoke Range and the Hauraki Plains with some climbing to do just before Kaihere, 12 km south of S.H. 2. At 26 km south the road forks. Take the right fork to Tahuna. Until recently S.H. 27 was a quiet rural road, but it is carrying increasingly heavy traffic as an alternative route from Auckland to points south.

Tahuna is a cross-roads settlement with a tavern. Continue

south from here to Morrinsville, an easy 18 km away. Morrinsville (pop. 5,281) is a market town, centre of a rich farming area. It has a hotel, motel and municipal motorcamp.

Take the Hamilton road (S.H. 26) westward from Morrinsville. The road is flat to undulating. At 12 km from Morrinsville turn south. Twenty kilometres of easy cycling through flat to undulating countryside will bring you to Cambridge.

Cambridge (pop. 10,145) is a notably attractive town with old churches and a village green surrounded by mature oak trees. On Sundays, you might be lucky enough to see a cricket match in progress here.

Cambridge offers a choice of hotels and motels. There is a motorcamp (cabins) in Leamington, across the Waikato River. Continue through town in a southeasterly direction, past the village green, through the main shopping centre to the end of Victoria Street, and across Victoria Bridge.

If continuing further, take the first road to the right beyond Victoria Bridge. This is Pope Terrace, which climbs the river terraces and takes you out of Leamington to the west. If heading for the motorcamp, continue straight along Cook Street from the bridge, take the second turn right into Shakespeare Street, first left into Wordsworth Street, and first right again into Scott Street. (In case you haven't already guessed, most of the streets in Leamington are named after famous English poets and writers.)

DAY 3 *CAMBRIDGE TO LAKE WAIPAPA* ──────────
77 km

From the motorcamp, the most direct route out of Leamington is to continue southward to the end of Scott Street, then turn right into Lamb Street. This brings you out onto the main road heading southwest towards Te Awamutu, which is 23 km away across the plains.

Te Awamutu (pop. 8,096) is a pretty and prosperous town with a small museum, pleasant rose-gardens and an old church, St. Johns, built in 1854. It has hotels, motels and a municipal campground.

Turn south in the centre of Te Awamutu along the Kihikihi road (S.H. 3). Kihikihi is 4 km away. Turn southeast here onto the Arapuni/Putaruru road.

■ **ALTERNATIVE ROUTE:** You can save 4 km by bypassing Te Awamutu and heading direct to Kihikihi. At 17 km from Cambridge, turn left onto the Rangiaohia Road, a minor but sealed

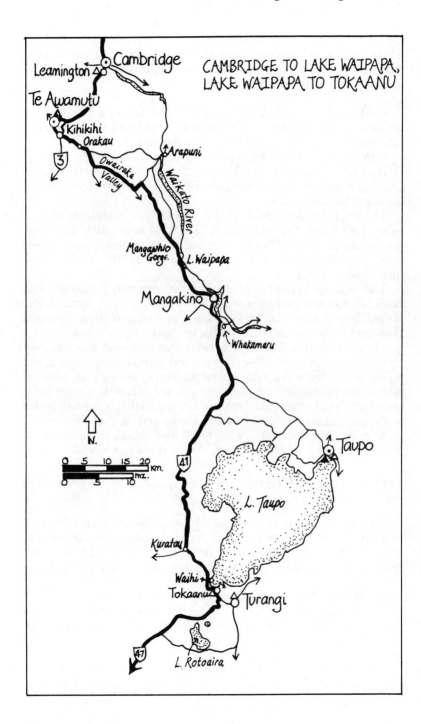

CAMBRIDGE TO LAKE WAIPAPA,
LAKE WAIPAPA TO TOKAANU

road. At the first intersection, 2 km along, turn right. Another 3 km will bring you to the eastern outskirts of Kihikihi. Take the first left turn here to join the Arapuni Road three blocks south, where you turn left again. ■

Orakau, 4 km outside Kihikihi, was the site of a famous and heroic siege during the Land Wars in 1864. A small monument beside the road marks the spot and tells the tale.

Continue through the gently rolling countryside beyond Orakau for 5 km, then turn southeast down the Owairaka Valley. There is a store at the intersection. From here onwards you follow the signs to Mangakino.

The road immediately drops for about 1 km, undulates along a valley for 9.5 km, then rises for 3.5 km, past interesting limestone formations to another intersection with a store beside it. Turn left here. Two kilometres on, turn left again, then, after a hilly 3 km, turn right (south).

The next 15 km are a gradual ascent through farmlands and bush. This is followed by a steep 5 km descent to a spectacularly-placed bridge over the Mangawhio Gorge. From here, Waipapa Dam and Waipapa Lake are almost in sight.

There is little at Waipapa besides the dam and the lake, set amongst bushcovered hills. There is no formal campground and no shop, but there is a wide, pleasant grassy area on the western side of the lake where tents can be pitched. There is a toilet here, and open fireplaces, and a stream. Waipapa Village, a small hydro settlement, is set in the hills above the eastern end of the dam.

Cyclists who do not carry tents will have to continue to Mangakino, 12 km further south, where there is a hotel.

DAY 4 *LAKE WAIPAPA TO TOKAANU* —————
101 km

This a long and strenuous day. The road climbs steeply for 3 km away from the lake, then passes through rolling country for another 8 km. This brings you to the turn-off to Mangakino. Continue straight ahead to visit Mangakino; otherwise veer right.

■ **Side Trip:** Mangakino (pop. 1,572) is a lakeside forestry and hydro town. It has a hotel. The loop through town adds 1 km to your distance. Rejoin the main road just south of the town.

Three kilometres further on is a junction with a shop and a service station where you join S.H. 30, heading southeast. Four kilo-

metres along, just before the hydro village of Whakamaru, turn
south on S.H. 32 towards Turangi.

The next 67 km run through hill-country lying to the north and
west of Lake Taupo. There are only distant glimpses of the lake itself, but the countryside is attractive. The terrain is undulating to
rolling, quite strenuous, with one stiff 3 km ascent which begins
32 km from Whakamaru.

There are no towns or villages or even shops on this stretch,
and drinkable water from streams is hard to find. Carry your own
water.

Turn east at Kuratau Junction (a service station), where S.H. 32
intersects with S.H. 41. There is a moderate 2.6 km climb outside
Kuratau, a 3 km drop, then another 5 km climb. At the end of this
you should catch your first good view of Lake Taupo. The last few
kilometres of the day descend to the lakeside and Tokaanu.

There is a motorcamp (cabins) on the main road at Tokaanu,
also several motels and a hotel, and a general store. Some of the
motels have private hot pools; there is also a public hot pool and a
small thermal area.

The lakeside village of Waihi, just north of Tokaanu, has an interesting old Catholic Church (1889), a carved meeting-house, and
the tomb of Te Heuheu Tukino II, a great chief of the last century.
This area is geologically unstable. In 1846, a mudslide swept away
an entire village near the site of the present Waihi, and there have
been other, though less tragic, mudslides since.

Six kilometres southeast of Tokaanu is the town of Turangi
(pop. 3,913), which was planned and developed in the 1960s as
the centre of the massive Tongariro Power Scheme. This scheme
has been designed to drain more than 2500 square kilometres
of upland, taking water from tributaries of south-flowing rivers
such as the Wanganui, and diverting it to Lake Rotoaira, Lake
Taupo and, finally, the Waikato River, with its string of dams and
generators.

If you cannot find accommodation in Tokaanu, there are motorcamps (cabins) and motels in Turangi. The information centre of
the Tongariro Scheme is on the eastern edge of town.

DAY 5 TOKAANU TO RAETIHI/PIPIRIKI ───────────
Raetihi: 83 km; Pipiriki: 111 km

Leave Tokaanu by the Turangi road to the southeast. At 3 km
from Tokaanu, the massive pipes of the Tokaanu tail-race, part of
the Tongariro scheme, descend the hill. Turn right just beyond,
along S.H. 47 towards National Park and The Chateau.

A demanding 6 km climb follows, taking you from 490 m at the lakeside to 745 m at the top of the bush-clad Te Ponanga Saddle. From the summit, you can see the deep blue expanse of Lake Rotoaira below and, to the southwest, the snowclad peak of Mt. Tongariro (1968 m). Later, Mt. Ngauruhoe (2,291 m) and Mt. Ruapehu (2,797 m) will come into view.

These are active volcanoes: Mt. Ruapehu last erupted in 1970. They were preserved within Tongariro National Park, New Zealand's first national park, by gift of Te Heu Heu Tukino and other chiefs of the Tuwharetoa tribe, in 1887. The park has since been vastly increased by gift and purchase.

There is a steepish 3 km descent to Lake Rotoaira, after which the road passes across a scrubby plain of tussock and gorse, with occasionally pockets of mountain beech and plantations of pine trees. Shortly after leaving the lake, the road crosses over the Wairehu canal, part of the Tongariro scheme.

At 26 km from Tokaanu you pass the signpost to Te Porere Redoubt, an earth fortification dating back to 1869 and the last years of the Land Wars. The redoubt itself is a 1 km walk from the road.

Fourteen kilometres further on, S.H. 47 intersects with the road to The Chateau.

> ■ **Side Trip:** The Chateau, a grand tourist hotel, is a 6 km detour up the lower slopes of Mt. Ruapehu. Just beyond is the headquarters of Tongariro National Park, and a motor-camp (cabins). An unsealed road ascends the mountain further to the ski village of Iwikau. There are skifields on three sides of the mountain, but the area is also popular in summer, when trampers use the walking tracks which criss-cross the mountains.

There is a good campsite beside a stream south of the main road 3 km beyond the turn-off to The Chateau. Another 6 km of S.H. 47 brings you to National Park, a small farming- and ski-town with a number of motels. Turn south here along S.H. 4.

S.H. 4 is a major route south, but it is generally quiet. The terrain is flat to undulating for most of the next 34 km to Raetihi, although there is a short dip to cross the Makatote Stream 11 km south of National Park. Here you get a good view of Makatote railway viaduct (1907) further along the gorge.

Raetihi (pop. 1,323) is a service town for the surrounding farms and timber mills. It was originally laid out in 1892 and was planned to become much bigger. Today it bears some resemblance to a Wild West town, with shops with wide verandahs straggling down its empty streets. Raetihi has served as the locale for several

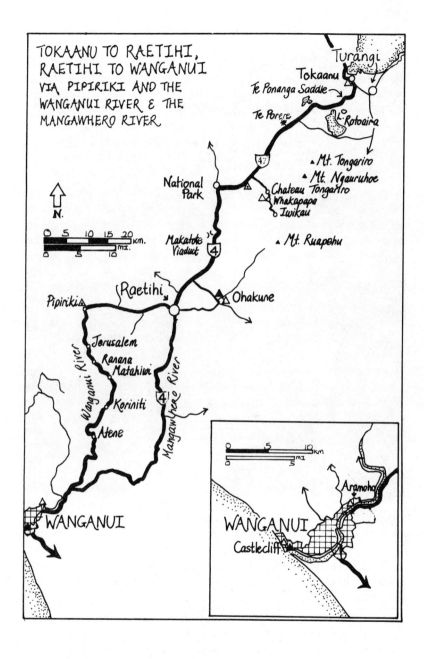

TOKAANU TO RAETIHI,
RAETIHI TO WANGANUI
VIA PIPIRIKI AND THE
WANGANUI RIVER & THE
MANGAWHERO RIVER

New Zealand films, among them *Skin Deep* and *Smash Palace*.

Raetihi is where you must decide whether to take the Wanganui River or Mangawhero River route to Wanganui.

Waterfall beside the Tokaanu–National Park road

The Mangawhero River road is the easier one. It is the main road south and is sealed all the way: the road to take if you dislike cycling on gravel.

If you need formal accommodation, stop in Raetihi and continue downriver the next day. Raetihi has a hotel and a motel, and a motorcamp just south of town. There are no other hotels, motels or even shops between here and Wanganui. If free camping, however, you will easily find riverside sites further south.

To continue on the Matawhero River route, see Day 6A.

The Wanganui River route is a longer and more difficult route, involving more than 50 km of narrow and rough gravel road. It is also a very scenic road, winding for most of its length along the banks of the famous Wanganui River.

If taking this route, you could stop in Raetihi but, if you have a tent, you would be better advised to continue to Pipiriki, 28 km west, thus shortening the next day's more difficult ride. Stock up on provisions in Raetihi, for there are no permanent shops between here and Wanganui (although in summer there is sometimes a mobile food-bar in Pipiriki).

To continue to Pipiriki, take Seddon Street through Raetihi, the third street to the right after entering town. At the west of town, the Pipiriki road drops through mudstone hills covered in rough farmland and pockets of bush.

The first 11 km of this road are sealed; from then on the surface is gravel. The road is very narrow and although traffic is usually light, dust can be a nuisance when cars do pass. The trend is downhill most of the way, the road dropping from 474 m at Raetihi to about 60 m at Pipiriki. At 18 km from Raetihi, you enter the Whanganui National Park.

Pipiriki (pop. 60) was a renowned tourist centre when tourist paddle-steamers used to ascend the river. These ceased to run in 1939, and the settlement consequently declined. The guesthouse and hotel burned to the ground in 1959 and was never replaced, and the village has slept through the decades since.

Now Pipiriki is regaining life as the centre for the new Whanganui National Park. It is the base for bush-walks and tramping, and for jet-boat trips upriver. One of the old river steamers, the *Ongarue*, has been pulled up on dry land as a memorial to the riverboat era. A modern riverboat now runs downriver to Wanganui.

There is a campground in the centre of Pipiriki, and an open shelter opposite. There is a museum and information centre in a restored colonial-style house (ca. 1885) nearby.

DAY 6 *PIPIRIKI TO WANGANUI VIA THE WANGANUI RIVER*
78 km

For most of its length, this is a narrow winding road with a rough gravel surface, though there are brief stretches of seal through the settlements en route. It follows the Wanganui River southwards and offers glorious views. Traffic is light, except perhaps in midsummer, but cyclists need to take care when approaching and crossing any of the numerous one-lane bridges.

Although the Wanganui River drops 60 m or so between Pipiriki and Wanganui, there is some considerable climbing to do along the road at places where it climbs away from the river. As mentioned, there are no shops along the way, nor formal accommodation, but spots for free camping are easy to find, particularly along the middle reaches of the river.

Outside Pipiriki is a flat stretch just over 3 km long, then a gradual 6 km climb as the river passes through a gorge, followed by a 3 km descent to Jerusalem (Hiruharama). Here, the valley opens out, and there are sandy beaches along the river's edge.

Jerusalem, like all villages along the Wanganui, is largely a Maori settlement. A Catholic mission station was founded here last century and was the centre of activity of Mother Mary Aubert, founder of the Order of Daughters of Our Lady of Compassion. During the 1960s the poet James K. Baxter established a famous but short-lived commune and spiritual centre here.

From Jerusalem, a gradual 5 km climb to Ranana (London) follows. The road then passes through 5 km of rolling country to Matahiwi, with a short steep rise just before the village. There is a restored 19th century water-driven flour-mill at Matahiwi. Seven kilometres beyond is Koriniti (Corinth), worthy of note for its carved meeting-house and its old church and mission-house.

At Koriniti, the valley opens out further. The fields are lined with willows and poplars, a beautiful sight in autumn. Also at Koriniti the seal begins, although the road is still narrow until it joins S.H. 4 more than 30 km further south.

Eleven kilometres south of Koriniti is Atene (Athens), and 17 km south of Atene comes the last challenge of the day, where the road briefly leaves the river and makes a steep 3.5 km ascent to 228 m. There is an even steeper drop on the other side, then the road joins S.H. 4. Continue south to Wanganui, which is now an easy 14 km away.

Wanganui (pop. 38,084), founded by the New Zealand Company in 1840, is an attractive city with a good museum, an art gallery (the Sarjeant Gallery) and a number of pleasant gardens and parks. There are beaches to the southwest of town at Castlecliff. On the southern side of the river is Durie Hill, which offers excellent views of the town. An elevator has been tunnelled through the hill to take sightseers to the top.

Wanganui has a number of hotels and motels; also a Youth Hostel. There are two motorcamps, both with cabins or on-site caravans. The Aramoho Motorcamp is 6 km to the north of the city centre on the western side of the river. To reach it, cross the first bridge you come to entering the city from the north, and turn north once across the bridge, along the western bank. The Castlecliff Camp is adjacent to the bank 8 km southwest of the city centre. The easiest way to get there is probably to continue along S.H. 4 on the eastern bank until the Dublin Street bridge, then follow the road along the western bank right through town to Castlecliffe. The motorcamp is beside the beach, 1 km north of the river-mouth.

■ *ALTERNATIVE DAY 6A RAETIHI TO WANGANUI VIA THE MANGAWHERO RIVER*
89 km

This route, as mentioned above, is for cyclists who wish to avoid the gravel and dust of the Wanganui River route. It is perhaps a less challenging route, but it is almost as appealing scenically, particularly in autumn.

Take S.H. 4 south of Raetihi and simply follow this all the way to Wanganui. The road is sealed all the way. Traffic is generally quiet though fast moving.

State Highway 4 basically follows the course of the Mangawhero River, but with numerous short ups-and-downs as it climbs away from and drops back to the river, which has cut deep

Hill country on the Mangawhero road (Photo by Richard Oddy)

into the mudstone hills. The most strenuous climb is the last: a 3.5 km climb from 79 m to 269 m, 55 km out of Raetihi.

The road then descends to the valley of the Wanganui and joins the river 12 km north of the city. From there, see the instructions given in Day 6, above.

Wanganui to Wellington

The stretch from Wanganui to Wellington is the least interesting part of this itinerary. The terrain is flat much of the way and, in parts, rather dull. If you want to cycle all the way, then the quickest and most practical route is via Bulls and Levin, although this does involve some distance on busy S.H. 1. Some cyclists may prefer heading for Palmerston North and catching the train from there, in which case see Alternative Day 7A.

DAY 7 WANGANUI TO LEVIN ─────────────
100 km

This could be a fast day. After the Wanganui River road, the scenery will seem dull, and there is little reason to stop along the way. The terrain is mostly flat, and the road is sealed.

The determining factor really is the wind: the prevailing wind in this area is southwesterly and, if it is strong, there is very little shelter against it en route. If the weather is favourable, however, a strong rider in a hurry could possibly reach Paraparaumu (142 km) in one day, and perhaps take the suburban train into Wellington.

Leave Wanganui by the Victoria Avenue Bridge (the City Bridge) leading southwest from the central business district. Across the bridge, turn right into Anzac Parade, which joins S.H. 3 1 km south. (Note that the signs pointing south from the city centre are intended for vehicular traffic and lead to the Cobham Bridge below City Bridge. This is designated a motorway, and forbidden to cyclists.)

From Wanganui to Turakina, 22 km southeast, is undulating to gently rolling country; the road is bordered by well-kept farms. Traffic is moderate.

> ■ **Side Trip:** At 15 km outside Wanganui, a 4 km detour south will take you to Ratana (pop. 434). This is a village founded in the 1920s by F.W. Ratana, a Maori prophet and healer, and founder of an indigenous Christian sect. There is a fine Ratana temple here with distinctive twin towers.

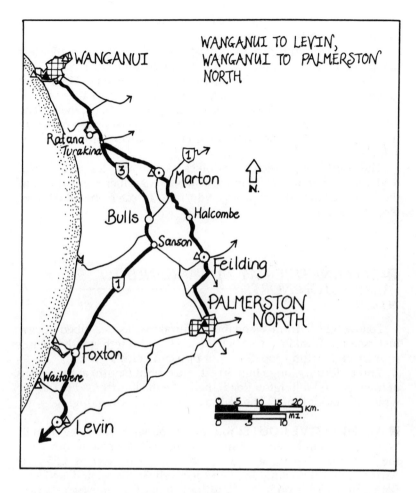

From Turakina onward, the road is virtually flat.

Bulls (pop. 1,799), 22 km beyond Turakina, has a hotel and motel. There is a caravan park (cabins) just south of the town.

Join S.H. 1 at Bulls, turning south to Sanson (pop. 478) and Foxton (pop. 1,448). Traffic becomes busier here. Foxton has several hotels and motels; there is also a motorcamp (cabins) at Foxton Beach, 6 km due west.

Levin (pop. 15,368), 19 km beyond Foxton, is a sizeable town with a number of hotels and motels. There is a motorcamp (cabins) at Waitarere Beach (turn west off S.H. 1, 8 km north of Levin); another in Parker Ave. For the latter, turn off Oxford St., the main road through town, then left into Bath St. Parker Ave. is the third street to the right after the railway line. There is yet another motor-camp 10 km south of town, just off S.H. 1.

If you have found this an easy day, you could shorten the next day's ride by continuing to Otaki, 20 km beyond Levin.

Alternatively, you could catch the train between Levin and Wellington. The *Silver Fern* leaves Levin station at 5.10 P.M. and reaches Wellington at 6.40 P.M. It is a good idea to book ahead. The *Silver Fern* does not take bikes. These have to be sent separately as freight, so arrive at the station before the parcels office closes at 4.30 P.M.

The *Northerner*, which takes bikes as luggage, leaves Levin at 6.50 A.M. and arrives at Wellington at 8.30 A.M. If crossing direct to the South Island, this will give you time to catch the 10.00 A.M. ferry to Picton.

■ *ALTERNATIVE DAY 7A WANGANUI TO PALMERSTON NORTH*
79 km

Follow S.H. 3 from Wanganui to Turakina, as described above. Just beyond Turakina, veer left off S.H. 3 through gently rolling country to Marton (pop. 5,099), a pleasant country town.

Enter Marton along High Street. Turn right (south) at the centre of town down Wellington Road, then take the fourth road to the left which is Station Road. The railway station is 1 km along.

■ **ALTERNATIVE ROUTE:** You can, if you wish, catch the train to Wellington from here. The times may not be convenient, however: the *Northerner* departs at 5.23 A.M. and the *Silver Fern* at 3.55 P.M. Arrival times in Wellington are respectively 8.30 A.M. and 6.40 P.M. Both times also stop at Feilding, but departure times are hardly more convenient: 5.49 A.M. and 4.20 P.M. Palmerston North is a more likely possibility. You could reach it in time to catch the *Silver Fern* at 4.35 P.M., or get up early to catch the *Northerner* at 6.09 A.M.

Bicycles can be taken as luggage on the *Northerner*, but must be sent separately as freight if catching the *Silver Fern*, and may arrive a day later or more. It is a good idea to book ahead, through any travel agent, or any office of New Zealand Railways or New Zealand Roadservices. ■

Just before the railway station, Wings Line Road runs southeast across the tracks. This will bring you out onto S.H. 1. Turn south and follow S.H. 1 for 2 km before turning southeast again through low rolling country to Halcombe. Continue through Halcombe to Feilding. Feilding (pop. 12,116) is a market town founded in 1874 and laid out on a pattern similar to that of a much grander town, Manchester, United Kingdom.

Enter Feilding from the west. Continue down West Street, veering left from this into Manchester Street to the main town square. Take South Street out of the Square; this joins S.H. 54 and continues to Palmerston North.

■ **ALTERNATIVE ROUTE:** For the railway station, turn left across Manchester Square and follow Kimbolton Road for two blocks before turning right down Aorangi Street. ■

Between Feilding and Palmerston North the countryside is mostly flat. S.H. 54 enters the city on its northeastern edge. You cross a railway bridge on the outskirts. Turn right at the first major intersection after this, and head southeastward for 3.5 km to the junction with Rangitikei Road. (The railway station is just beyond this intersection.) To reach the city centre, turn left along Rangitikei Street and continue to the Square.

Palmerston North (pop. 60,503) is a regional centre and University town. Founded in the middle of a plain, it is laid out in a grid pattern around its central square. It is not generally regarded as a tourist town, but the Square, with its flower-beds and trees, clock-tower and fountains, is a pleasant place to spend an hour or two. There is a good regional museum and art gallery nearby; also a rugby museum. The Public Relations Office is in the Civic Complex, the bulky grey modern building which protrudes ominously into the Square.

There are a number of hotels and motels in the city, but only one motorcamp (cabins). This is situated beside the Rangitikei River in the opposite side of town to the station. Take Fitzherbert Avenue, southeast from the square. Four blocks along, turn right along Park Road, then left into Ruha Street.

DAY 8 LEVIN TO WELLINGTON VIA THE AKATARAWA VALLEY AND HUTT VALLEY ————
67 km–100 km

S.H. 1 continues through Levin across the plains. Twenty kilometres away is Otaki (pop. 4,407). This is notable for the magnificent Rangiatea Maori church, built in 1850. There is a monument to the important Maori chief, Te Rauparaha (ca. 1768–1849), near the church. To get to Rangiatea Maori church, turn right from

S.H. 1 into Mill Road, then the fifth right into Te Rauparaha Street. Further north along Convent Road is Pukekaraka, site of a Catholic Mission first established in 1846, where several historic buildings are preserved, particularly St. Marys Church (1859).

Otaki has several hotels and motels. There is a motorcamp at Otaki Beach, a short distance west of the main highway. Offshore is Kapiti Island, a bird sanctuary and reserve.

Fifteen kilometres south of Otaki is Waikanae (pop. 6,117). Turn left (east) here across the railway line, along Elizabeth Street, and up the Akatarawa Valley Road. (If you need any information before approaching Wellington, however, you could first visit the tourist information centre in the Town Centre to the right.)

■ **ALTERNATIVE ROUTE:** You could in fact stay on S.H. 1 and continue direct to Wellington. This is a shorter route (88 km in all), but not really recommended for cyclists since it involves taking increasingly busy suburban roads on approaching the city. Besides, if camping, you will end up in Hutt Valley in any case.

If you do decide to head to Wellington direct, the most sensible option is to cycle to Paraparaumu, 7 km from Waikanae, and catch the suburban train from there. Avoid rush-hour in the morning, when space is limited. There is a vintage car museum in Paraparaumu. ■

The road winds gently up the valley of the Waikanae River for the first 4 km, then climbs steeply to 443 m over 5 km. From the top of the Akatarawa Saddle is a good view of the coast.

For the next 25 km the road descends the Akatarawa Valley to Birchville. The first 5 km are steep, winding and narrow, then the road widens out and the gradient becomes more gentle. Traffic is generally very light until approaching Birchville.

Birchville is the first of the Hutt Valley suburbs (combined pop. 130,923). Follow the signs southward along busy Ferguson Drive from here for the 3 km to Upper Hutt, where you join S.H. 2, which continues through Lower Hutt and Petone to Wellington.

You could catch a suburban train to Wellington from Upper Hutt. Alternatively, you could cycle the whole 33 km along S.H. 2. For the first 10 km, this is a busy and dangerous arterial suburban road, then it widens out virtually to motorway standard. Cyclists are quite safe on the wide shoulders alongside the vehicle lanes. The stretch through the Hutt Valley is flat and rather dull.

■ **ALTERNATIVE ROUTE:** If camping, you will find the nearest motorcamp (cabins) to Wellington in Moera, Lower Hutt. This is the Hutt Park Holiday Village (phone 685 913), 4 km from S.H. 2, 13

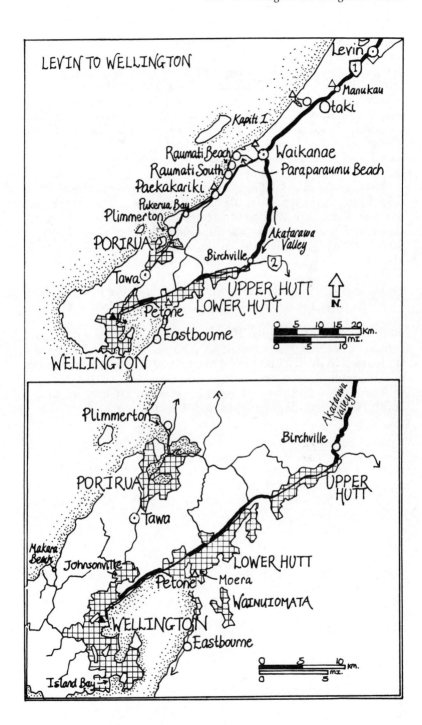

km from the ferry terminal and 17 km from the city centre. To get there, at 18 km along S.H. 2 from Upper Hutt, take the Melling Bridge (Lower Hutt) exit to the southeast. Take the first right turn into Rutherford Street and then the first left into Queens Drive. Follow Queens Drive through Lower Hutt City Centre, veering left (southeast) into Woburn Road, which shortly becomes Ludlam Crescent, heading south. Turn left off Ludlam Crescent into Whites Line West, right into Bell Road past the railway workshops, and right again into Parkside Road. The motorcamp is near the entrance to the trotting course.

To continue into Wellington from the motorcamp, follow Parkside Road westward from the camp entrance, veer right into Seaview Road, take Waione Street northwest from the first roundabout and continue along the Esplanade on Petone foreshore to S.H. 2. Along the Esplanade, on the seaward side, is the Provincial Memorial, erected in 1940 as a centennial tribute to the first pakeha settlers in the region.

There is a public relations and information office in Lower Hutt City Centre, at the corner of High and Margaret Streets. ■

At 22 km south of Upper Hutt, S.H. 2 joins the harbour's edge at Petone. Continue southwestward. The ferry terminal is clearly signposted to the left another 7 km cityward. From here, the centre of Wellington itself is only 4 km away.

There are numerous hotels and motels in Wellington, also a Youth Hostel. For directions through the city, see Tour 7.

TOUR 6. AUCKLAND TO WELLINGTON VIA ROTORUA AND THE EAST CAPE

Auckland to Gisborne: 6–10 days; 670 km–818 km
Gisborne to Wellington: 5–6 days; 521 km–610 km

This is an indirect route south, but takes in some of the most interesting regions of the North Island on the way. It passes through the thermal regions of Rotorua and the Volcanic Plateau on its way to the rugged grandeur of the isolated East Cape region, then heads south through the rich farmlands of Hawkes Bay and the Wairarapa.

If you have time, you could combine this itinerary with the Coromandel tour, turning off at Waihi for Tauranga, or at Te Aroha for Rotorua. Alternatively, if time is limited, you could substantially shorten the trip by cycling as far as Gisborne or Napier, and taking the train to Wellington from there.

DAY 1 AUCKLAND TO KAIAUA
61 km–92 km

See Tour 5, Day 1.

DAY 2 KAIAUA TO TE AROHA
74 km

This is a relatively east day spent cycling through mostly flat to undulating country. You should arrive in Te Aroha early enough for a swim in the hot pools, or to climb Mt. Te Aroha (952 m) behind the town.

Stronger cyclists, however, may choose to combine Days 1 and 2. These total 135 km if you take the suburban train to Papakura. The distance can be further reduced to 115 km by taking the Hunua Gorge road from Papakura rather than the Clevedon road (see Tour 4, Day 1).

For directions from Kaiaua to S.H. 27, see Tour 5, Day 2.

State Highway 27 passes through pleasant and flat to gently rolling country between the Hapuahoke Range and the Hauraki Plains, with some climbing to do just before Kaihere, 12 km south of S.H. 2. At 26 km south of S.H. 2, the road forks. Take the left fork. Four kilometres further on, turn left (east): the road will be signposted to Te Aroha. Just over 7 km further on, take the second road to the right, also signposted to Te Aroha. Continue southeast for 5 km to Elstow, a tiny crossroads settlement, and turn left here (east). Four kilometres further on, the road veers southeast again and, not long afterwards, enters Te Aroha's leafy western suburbs. Just after crossing the railway line, you come to an intersection. The motorcamp (cabins) is straight ahead, then to the left; the centre of town is immediately to the left across the Waihou River.

Te Aroha (pop. 3,510) is a former spa town with some elegant old buildings, and hot pools in the Tourist Domain. There is a hotel, motel and a Youth Hostel. The Public Relations Office is at 102 Whitaker Street.

Mt. Te Aroha (952 m) looms behind the town and offers striking views to the east and west of the Kaimai Ranges. The climb via track from the Domain takes 2 to 3 hours by foot. There is also a steep gravel alternative access road north of the town.

DAY 3 TE AROHA TO ROTORUA
103 km

This could be a longish day. The first 50 km are flat, but are followed by a long 20 km ascent of the Mamaku Range. The climb can be exhausting, especially on a hot day.

Leave Te Aroha via S.H. 26 southwest across the river. One kilometre beyond the bridge, turn south towards Matamata. At 5 km further on, turn left onto the Manawaru road. From Manawaru follow the Turangaomoana road south to southeast.

■ **Side Trip:** At 3 km out of Matamata is a turnoff to Okauia Springs. A 3 km detour eastward brings you to a pleasant hamlet with hot pools. There is a motorcamp (cabins) here.

Approaching Matamata, you will pass the Firth Tower, a blockhouse built in the 1880s by a local landowner, Josiah Clifton Firth, as security against feared Maori attacks. (These never eventuated.) There is an historical museum next to the blockhouse. Nearby is a monument to Wiremu Tamihana, one of the greatest of the 19th century Maori chiefs and a prime mover in the early days of the King Movement, an assertion by Waikato tribes of political independence from the pakeha.

Matamata (pop. 5,701) is a market town. It has a hotel, motels and a motorcamp. Like Te Aroha, it has public hot pools.

From Matamata, take S.H. 27 south across the plains, then

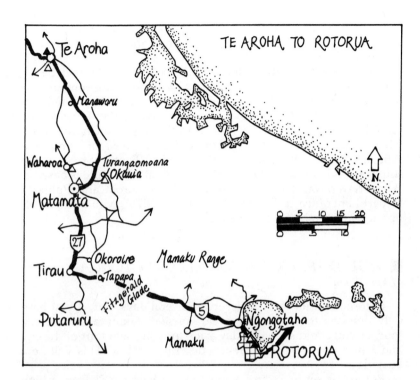

through gently undulating countryside to Tirau. At Tirau (pop. 693), turn east along S.H. 1 for a short, busy stretch, then turn onto S.H. 5 to Rotorua at the first intersection beyond the town.

S.H. 5 from here to Rotorua is usually quite a busy stretch of road, but there is no practical alternative route across the Mamaku Range in the vicinity.

At Tapapa, 9 km from Tirau, the climbing starts. You rise over 11 km from 150 m to 461 m. Fitzgerald Glade, in the early part of the climb, is a noted bush reserve, with trees overhanging the road on either side. The last refreshment stop before the outskirts of Rotorua are tearooms at the upper end of the Glade.

Once on the top of the Mamaku Range, the road undulates along a bleak plateau for another 10 km, gradually rising to a peak of 563 m. The next 13 km to the lakeside are a glorious swoop downhill. Near the end of the descent, you pass the Agridome on the left, an agricultural display area with daily shows of sheep-shearing and such rural activities.

From the lakeside, there are 8 km of urban sprawl into Rotorua. Rotorua (pop. 40,597) is a tourist town, with a wide selection of hotels, motels and guesthouses. There is also a Youth Hostel. You will have no trouble finding a motorcamp: there are as many as twenty in the vicinity.

Scenic attractions in Rotorua City include its thermal baths, Government Gardens (where the Art Gallery and Museum, and an old mock-Tudor bath-house building are located); Ohinemutu Maori Village on the lakeside (have a look at the Tanatekapua carved meeting-house, 1878, and St. Faiths Anglican Church, 1910, which incorporates Maori motifs in its design); and the Whakarewarewa thermal area at the end of Fenton Street at the southern end of town. The Maori Arts & Crafts Institute is based at Whakarewarewa. There is a New Zealand Tourist and Publicity Department office at 67 Fenton St. (phone 85179), with a branch office at 84 Hinemoa St. (phone 80285).

■ SIDE TRIP: EXCURSION FROM ROTORUA
41 km–79 km

Rotorua and its vicinity deserves several days. But, if you have only one day to spare, you could consider taking a commercial tour, or you could set half a day aside for your own tour of the city and half a day for the excursion described below. This will be a busy day.

Rotorua is set in an area known as the Volcanic Plateau, a high triangle of land bordered by the Rotorua Lakes to the north, the Urewera Mountains to the east, and Lake Taupo to the south. The Volcanic Plateau, as its name suggests, is an area of some geological instability, with numerous volcanic peaks and mounds, some extinct, some dormant, some active. The geysers and mud-pools of Rotorua are one example of subterranean activity; the geothermal power produced by the Wairakei power-station near Taupo (see Tour 6A) is another.

Many of the lakes of the Volcanic Plateau were formed by volcanic explosions. The area's soils are mostly pumice soils, formed from the ash of such explosions. Some of these have been recent: in 1886 Mt. Tarawera, near Rotorua, exploded, burying a Maori village nearby, and darkening the skies throughout the North Island.

This region is home to the Te Arawa tribes. It is rich in Maori history and mythology but, until a few decades ago, was also a sparsely populated region covered mostly by scrub and fern. The discovery and treatment of a deficiency of cobalt in the soil opened the area up for farming. Today the Volcanic Plateau is a rich farming area. It is also the centre of New Zealand's timber industry, with vast expanses of pine forest.

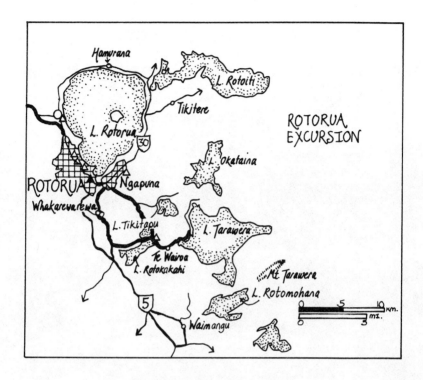

The excursion described here gives a very hasty introduction to the area.

Aim to finish your morning's tour of Rotorua at Whakarewarewa on the southern outskirts of the city. From the entrance, head north along Fenton Street towards the lake, but take the third turn right into Sala Street. Follow Sala Street for 1.5 km (past the Forest Research Institute) until it joins the Te Ngae Road. Turn right (east) here.

Te Ngae Road veers northeast around the lake, becoming S.H. 33. At Ngapuna, 2 km on, turn southeast along the Tarawera Road. This rises gradually from 316 m to 440 m through a forest reserve and past the contrasting Blue Lake (Tikitapu) and Green Lake (Rotokahi). There is a motorcamp (cabins) on the shores of Blue Lake.

The road then drops a further 6 km to the shores of Lake Tarawera, past the ruins of Te Wairoa, a village buried under ash and mud during the Tarawera eruption of 1886. The village has been partly excavated and restored.

Across the lake, to the southeast, rises Mt. Tarawera itself (1,111 m), a volcano cleft by several craters. This summit can be

Government Gardens, Rotorua (Photo by Richard Oddy)

reached by plane or by boat and walking-track.

Retrace your route to the Green Lake. On the narrow isthmus between the Green and Blue Lakes a gravel forestry road leads west. Note that this is open only during daylight hours, and is sometimes closed during times of high fire-risk (in which case you will have to return to Rotorua the way you came).

Continue west for 5 km from the Green Lake until you come to a sealed road. You can turn right (north) here and return to Rotorua, now 11 km away, via Whakarewarewa village.

Alternatively, you can turn left (south) and join S.H. 5. Continuing south another 7 km will bring you to the Waimangu intersection. Seven kilometres down the Waimangu Road is another interesting thermal area. This was the site of the famous Pink and White Terraces, which were obliterated by the Tarawera eruption. The area still retains some magnificent sights, with a boiling lake and a number of craters.

From Waimangu back to Rotorua is 26 km. Rejoin S.H. 5 and follow it the whole way back to the city.

■ **Note:** Cyclists who do not wish to continue to Whatakane have two main alternatives:

1. Follow Tour 6A south to Tokaanu, where they can either continue south to Wellington (Tour 5, Days 5 through 8) or return to Auckland (Tour 5, Days 1 through 4).

2. Return to Auckland via Tauranga (Tour 4B) and the Coromandel Peninsula (reversing Tours 4 and 4A).

DAY 4 ROTORUA TO WHAKATANE
96 km

Take Fenton Street south from the city centre. Opposite the railway shunting yards, veer southeast onto Te Ngae Road, which becomes S.H. 30 leading around the eastern shore of Lake Rotorua.

The first 12 km of the day to Te Ngae are mostly flat, taking you past Rotorua airport and through an uninviting sprawl of motels and holiday houses. At Te Ngae, turn right (northeast) to Whakatane.

A steep 3 km climb follows to the Tikitere thermal area (Hell's Gate)—worth a visit if you still appreciate mud pools. The road then drops to Lake Rotoiti and follows its shoreline for 7 km.

There is a gentle saddle to cross between Lakes Rotoiti and Rotoehu. The road then dips inland for 5 km before running along the southern shore of Lake Rotoma.

Leaving Lake Rotoma, there is a short steep climb through native bush to reach 371 m, the highest point of the day, followed by a long winding descent to the beginning of the coastal plains about 65 km from Rotorua.

From here the road is almost completely flat to Whakatane. After the beautiful Rotorua Lakes, this stretch will seem rather dull. En route are Te Teko (pop. 572), an undistinguished market town, and Awakeri, which has hot springs and a motorcamp (cabins).

Before entering Whakatane (pop. 12,800) you pass to the right a large board mill and pulp-and-paper plant, the mainstay of the town's economy.

Whakatane has a number of hotels and motels. There is also a motorcamp (cabins) in McGarvey Road. You enter the town via a

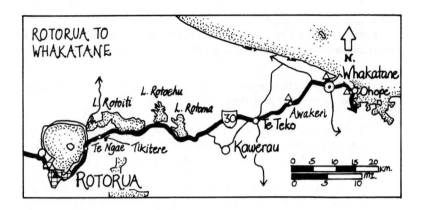

bridge across the Whakatane River. This leads into Landing Road which runs due east, and becomes Domain Road. The third street to the left is McGarvey Road. The motorcamp is at the far end, near the river. The town centre is 1 km further east.

Whakatane was the landing-place of the Mataatua canoe in traditional times. There is a model of the canoe by Pohaturoa Rock in the centre of town. Pakeha settlers first arrived in 1867, and the town developed as a port on the southern shores of the Whakatane estuary.

The most interesting part of town is along the waterfront. Cycle northeastward along the strand towards Kohi Pt. There is also a good regional historical museum in Boon Street. The Public Relations Office is at 10 Commerce Street.

DAY 5 WHAKATANE TO OPAPE
62 km

This is a short stage, as is the next stage, Opape to Te Kaha. Some cyclists may care to combine the two days as one, a more strenuous but very scenic total of 111 km.

There are two routes out of Whakatane. I suggest taking the Ohope Road east from the town over the hills rather than the Taneatua Road south through the Waimana Gorge. The Ohope Road is much steeper, but it cuts 13 km from the total distance.

From Whakatane you climb for 2.5 km steeply into the hills. Then there is an equally steep descent with some sharpish curves to Ohope. Ohope (pop. 1,825) is a beach 12 km long, fringed for much of its length with baches. It is crowded in midsummer and at Easter, but somnolent the rest of the year. It has several motels and motorcamps (cabins).

Two kilometres along the beach, turn right (southeast) onto the Cheddar Valley Road. This winds around the southern reaches of the Ohiwa Harbour and through the green and rural scenery of the Cheddar Valley to join S.H. 2, 16 km before Ohope. Turn left (northeast) here.

Ten kilometres further on, the road touches the coast at Waiotahi Beach and turns due east before turning slightly inland to Opotiki. Opotiki (pop. 3,719) is a market centre, a sleepy and relaxed town. It has a hotels, motels and a guesthouse. There is a motorcamp (cabins) 4 km before reaching Opotiki, another in Opotiki itself, and another at Tirohanga, 6 km further east.

In the town is the Church of St. Stephen the Martyr, built by the Lutheran missionary, the Rev. Carl Sylvius Volkner, who was later killed in 1865 on the orders of the Maori Hauhau prophet, Kereopa. (Volkner had been suspected of spying for the Government forces.) The church was for a time used as a redoubt (fort).

From Opotiki, S.H. 35 leads northeast out of town. It reaches the coast within 3 km, and follows it more-or-less for the next 114 km. Opape motorcamp is on the beachfront 12 km from Opotiki.

DAY 6 OPAPE TO TE KAHA
49 km

This is a short day in distance, though it does involve some climbing. You will want to take it easy, since this stretch of coast is one of the most beautiful parts of New Zealand. Inland are great bush-covered mountains; along the shore are rocky coves and

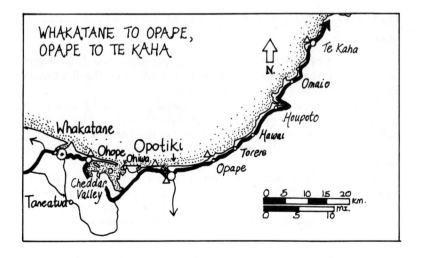

sandy beaches. The area is sparsely populated; you will pass only farms and a few tiny settlements on the way to Te Kaha.

The road is sealed all the way, as it is the whole way to Gisborne. Traffic is light except over the midsummer vacation. However, watch out for trucks carrying stock.

There is a short climb out of Opape, a descent to a small bay, another short climb, then a descent to Torere, 6 km beyond Opape. East of Torere, the road turns briefly inland, climbing slightly, before dropping back to the coast at Hawai.

Beyond Hawai is a demanding stretch: a 5 km climb up Maraenui Hill to the Parunui Lookout (218 m). The road then descends to Houpoto and turns inland for 5 km, crossing the broad lower reaches of the Motu River.

Returning to the coast, it climbs back past Tokata Point and passes two small bays before dropping to Omaio (there is a general store here). From Omaio it hugs the shore closely for the last 13 km to Te Kaha.

Te Kaha, once a whaling settlement, is a tiny village consisting of little more than a store, a garage, a school, a hotel, a motel and a motorcamp. It is nonetheless the largest settlement between Opotiki and Te Araroa, a distance of more than 200 km. Te Kaha, like most settlements on the East Cape, is largely a Maori settlement. The carved meeting-house, Tukaki, is of interest.

The motorcamp (cabins) is 1 km east of Te Kaha village. There are numerous sites suitable for free camping along this coast, but these are under pressure during summer, so take care to respect the environment. In particular, do not take wood from living trees to make fires, and take all your rubbish with you.

DAY 7 TE KAHA TO TE ARAROA
93 km

Northeast of Te Kaha is another exceptionally beautiful stretch of coast. The road turns inland only once (to cross the Raukokere River) in the next 37 km to Waihau Bay.

At Whanarua Bay, 18 km from Te Kaha, you could take a break from cycling and follow the creek inland to a series of bush waterfalls. At Raukokere, 11 km further along the road, is a charming wooden church which stands in isolation between the road and the sea.

At Waihau Bay, there is a general store a short detour from the main road; also a fishing lodge with restaurant. There is a motorcamp (cabins) at Oruaiti Beach 3.5 km further along the coast.

At 11 km beyond Waihau Bay, at Whangaparaoa, the road

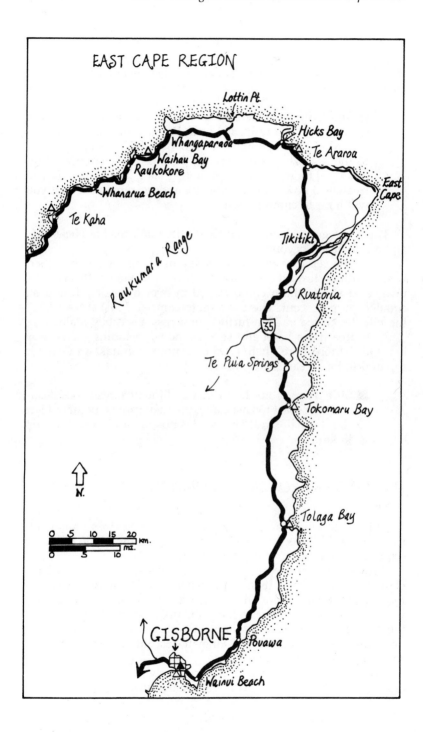

EAST CAPE REGION

Lottin Pt.

Hicks Bay

Whangaparaoa

Te Araroa

Waihau Bay

Raukokore

East
Cape

Whanarua Beach

Te Kaha

Raukumaia Range

Tikitiki

Ruatoria

35

Te Puia Springs

N.

Tokomaru Bay

0 5 10 15 20 km.

0   5   10 mi.

Tolaga Bay

GISBORNE

Povawa

Wainvi Beach

finally turns inland. The next 33 km to Hicks Bay are through gently rolling farmland, with occasional minor hills and flat stretches, crossing the low watershed between east and west midway.

> ■ **Side Trip:** At Potaka, 24 km from Whangaparaoa, a gravel road leads north towards Lottin Point. A stiff 2 km climb is rewarded by a magnificent view over hills sweeping down to the sea. The road drops to the coast and continues another 6 km westward, but note that it is no exit. If you freewheel down the hill in exhilaration, remember that you will have to climb back up.

There is a general store slightly off the main road at Hicks Bay, and a fine beach beyond.

You could set up your tent in the lupins along the beach. Otherwise, continue towards Te Araroa, which is 12 km southeast. This involves a short, sharp climb to 130 m over a headland, and an equally sharp descent. There is a motorcamp (cabins) at the foot of the hill. Te Araroa is 7 km further on across a scrubby plain.

Te Araroa has a hotel and several shops, including a takeaway bar. On the foreshore, there is an enormous pohutakawa which is reputed to be at least six centuries old.

> ■ **Side Trip:** From Te Araroa a difficult gravel road leads around the coast to East Cape, the easternmost point of New Zealand's mainland. This road is no-exit, and the round trip is 46 km.

DAY 8 TE ARAROA TO TOKOMARU BAY ──────────
81 km

This stage involves some strenuous climbing. In summer, try to set out as early as possible in order to get some of the hills over with before the worst of the day's heat.

Turn south at the western end of Te Araroa. A very steep 2 km climb to 113 m follows, then an even steeper descent to the valley of the Awatere River. There are five gentle kilometres along the river valley, then another steep 3.5 km climb up Letterbox Hill (200 m). A breakneck descent follows, then yet another steep climb over 5 km up Gudgeons Hill (220 m). A longish descent to Tikitiki, a small roadside settlement, follows.

The next 19 km stretch is flat to gently rolling. Shortly after crossing the Waiapu River, you will see the turnoff to Ruatoria, the only town for miles, and a detour 2.5 km northeast of the main road. It has a hotel and several shops.

Continuing south, the road winds gradually for 16 km up the Makatote Valley before climbing a saddle to 290 m, descending briefly, and climbing gradually again for another 6 km to Te Puia Springs.

Te Puia Springs is a pretty little country town set around a small lake high in the hills. It has a hotel, a motel and a general store. The hotel was once a spa resort with hot pools, but these have recently been covered over.

There is another short climb out of Te Puia, then—thankfully—an 8 km descent to Tokomaru Bay. There are good free camping sites beside the shallow Mangahauini River along the way.

Tokomaru Bay is a settlement which has seen better times. There is a disused wharf at the northern end of the town. This once

Pakiriki marae, Tokomaru Bay (Photo by Bronwyn Sheppard)

served a freezing works, now derelict. There is a tearoom and a general store on the beachfront. The Mayfair Cabins offers accommodation and tent sites.

DAY 9 *TOKOMARU BAY TO GISBORNE*
89 km

A 4 km climb out of Tokomaru Bay up Purau Hill (205 m) is followed by a short, steep descent and a long, gentle 11 km glide down the valley of the Hikuwai River to Tolaga Bay.

Tolaga Bay, like Tokomaru Bay, was once a thriving port. Its wharf, claimed to be the longest in the southern hemisphere, is now virtually disused. Tolaga Bay, however, survives as a farming and a tourist and crafts centre. It has an excellent beach—the motorcamp (cabins) is near the wharf. There are several shops, a tearoom, a bank, a hotel, a motel.

After Tolaga Bay the road runs inland through rolling coastal hills before it touches the coast again at Pouawa. This is quite a strenuous stretch, a constant series of ups and downs, though without any exceptionally demanding individual climbs.

The road virtually hugs the coast for the next 15 km from Pouawa, running between the hills and golden dunes and beaches. At Wainui (motel), it turns inland for the last 5 km to Gisborne.

Gisborne (pop. 38,269) is a quiet, sunny city intersected by three rivers, and is the administrative and commercial centre of the East Cape region. It has a number of hotels and motels, also a Youth Hostel. There are three motorcamps, all with cabins. To reach the nearest one to the city centre, almost immediately after passing Gisborne's port and crossing the Turanganui River on your way into the city, turn left along Customhouse Street. Then turn right along Awapuni Road at the end of Customhouse Street and continue to Grey Street. There is a motorcamp off Grey Street, and another on Salisbury Road which leads off Grey Street, parallel to the beach, and yet another at the town racetrack, further west.

Gisborne's Tourist Information Centre is at 209 Grey Street, northeast towards the city centre. The railway station is also handy.

Captain Cook landed near Gisborne at Kaiti Beach in 1769, the first European, as far as is known, to actually set foot on New Zealand soil. A series of unfortunate skirmishes with the Maoris of the region left six dead. Difficulties in obtaining supplies led Cook to name the area, quite inaptly, Poverty Bay, a name still found on maps, but otherwise little used.

The first European traders arrived here in the 1820s; whaling began in the 1830s; and missionaries were active in the 1840s. A few pakeha settlers followed. The local Maori, however, initially sold little of their land, but farmed and traded successfully themselves.

In 1865–1866 and 1868–1870 there was war in the region, the latter time between Government and loyal native forces on one side, and followers of the Maori prophet and warrior Te Kooti (ca. 1830–1893) on the other. Among the bloodiest episodes were the Matawhero massacre, where Te Kooti's forces killed 33 pakeha settlers and 37 Maori. Eventually Te Kooti was driven from the region (he ended his days, having been pardoned, as a Government pensioner at Ohiwa near Opotiki).

Pakeha settlement began in earnest with peace in the 1870s. Farmers moved into the hills, felling and burning the bush to make way for pasture for sheep. Such uncontrolled clearance later caused widespread erosion and even today, despite subsequent attempts at conservation, much of the East Cape region and Poverty Bay suffers from landslips and flooding.

Maori influence in the region is strong. Pakeha run many of the sheep-stations inland but much of the land remains in Maori ownership. Most rural villages and settlements are largely Maori; even Gisborne is one-third Maori. In every town and village are marae with carved meeting-houses; and the Maori language is still widely spoken.

Gisborne's past is recalled in its excellent regional museum and art gallery, across the river from the centre of town. A good view of the city is obtained from Kaiti Hill lookout. This is reached via the Esplanade leading off Wainui Road beside the port. On the way up you pass the noted Poho-o-Rawiri meeting-house, built in 1925. There is a memorial to Captain Cook on Kaiti Beach at the foot of Kaiti Hill.

Gisborne to Wellington

The stretch from Gisborne to Wellington takes you through "real" rural New Zealand, through Hawkes Bay, an area of great sheep-stations and fertile vineyards and orchards, and the Wairarapa, a wealthy farming region. Scenically, however, it is perhaps less interesting than the East Cape region. Cyclists with limited time to spare might well choose to take the train to Wellington.

The daily railcar leaves Gisborne at 9.35 A.M. and reaches Wellington at 7.35 P.M. Stops en route include Wairoa, Napier, Hastings, Dannevirke, Palmerston North and Levin.

For those who are determined to cycle the whole way (and why not?) the best route is described below. The stages given are in some cases relatively long.

DAY 10 GISBORNE TO WAIROA ————————
96 km

If leaving Gisborne from the city centre, head northwest along Gladstone Road, the main road through town. This forks in the western outskirts of the city—take the southern fork.

If leaving from the motorcamps on Waikanae Beach, simply continue westward via Centennial Marine Drive along the waterfront. Take the first turn right after the sports stadium, then turn immediately left onto Awapuni Road, which joins S.H. 2 near Matawhero, 4.5 km away.

Turn west along S.H. 2. Three kilometres from Matawhero (site of the massacre), on the far bank of the Waiapaoa River, is a major intersection. Turn south here, keeping to S.H. 2. Five kilometres south of Matawhero is the village of Manutuke. There are two important carved meeting-houses here, Te Mana o Turanga (1883) on Whakato marae and Te Poho o Rukupo (1887) on Manutuke marae. These were largely the work of the master carver, Raharuhi Rukupo (1800–1873) and his pupils, and have recently been restored under the supervision of the New Zealand Historic Places Trust. There is also a fine church, Holy Trinity (1913), nearby, with a carved interior.

The hills begin 20 km onwards, at the southern end of Poverty Bay. The first significant climb is the 2 km Kopua Hill (121 m). You descent to the coast again at Bartletts, then begin a long, hard 8 km climb through pine forest to the Wharerata Saddle. At 510 m, this is the highest point of the day.

The next 15 km to Morere are downhill in trend, but also include several minor climbs over saddles between river valleys. Morere is a roadside settlement with a store and a motorcamp (cabins). There are hot pools here.

From Morere the road winds down the Tunanui Valley to Nuhaka, a coastal farming settlement 70 km from Gisborne.

■ **Side Trip:** Ten kilometres east of Nuhaka is Opoutama, at the eastern end of a long, lovely sweep of beach. There is a motorcamp (cabins) here; and another at Mahia Beach at the

further end of the bay. From Mahia Beach, rough gravel roads wind southward over the bare hills of the isolated Mahia Peninsula.

Continue westward from Nuhaka. Wairoa is 32 km away, mostly through flat to gently rolling terrain, but the last 5 km involve some minor climbing.

Wairoa (pop. 5,094) is a farming town and market centre set on either side of the broad Wairoa River. It is notable largely for the fact it has a lighthouse in its main street. Takitimu, a carved meeting-house near the river, was erected in 1938, as a memorial to Sir James Carroll (1853–1926), the first Maori politician to achieve Cabinet rank in a New Zealand Government. Wairoa also has a local museum.

S.H. 2 enters town from the northeast. At the centre of town turn left (south) down Bridge Street. This leads to the banks of the Wairoa; the main part of town is across the river, including the motorcamp (cabins). Wairoa also has several hotels and motels.

Note: the only road bridge across the lower Wairoa was swept away by floods in early 1988. At the time of writing, the river is crossed by barge. A permanent replacement is planned and should be completed by 1991.

DAY 11 WAIROA TO NAPIER
105 km

This is a difficult day, with the road passing through demanding but beautiful countryside.

Continue along S.H. 2 westward from Wairoa. For 5 km this follows the banks of the Wairoa River, then turns up the valley of a minor tributary, crosses a short steep saddle, and drops to the coast at Waihua 20 km from Wairoa.

From Waihua, the road climbs the valley of Te Kiwi Stream for 6 km and crosses another steep saddle to Raupunga. Upstream from Raupunga, 17 km beyond Waihua, it passes under the railway line at the spectacular Mohaka Viaduct.

The next 37 km to Lake Tutira are particularly hilly, the longest climb being to 259 m, just beyond Kotemaori, 10 km from Raupunga.

Lake Tutira is a well-known bird sanctuary. There are good spots for free camping here. Beyond the lake, the road drops sharply from 197 m to 64 m, but immediately climbs even more

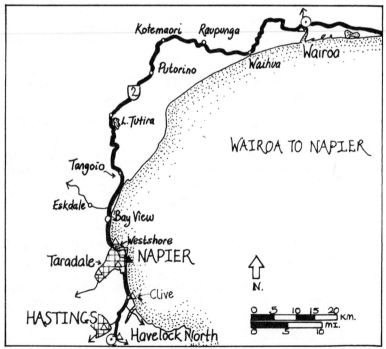

WAIROA TO NAPIER

N.

2,8

sharply over 4 km to 352 m. From here to Tangoio, beyond which the road touches the coast again, is downhill in trend.

The last 18 km to Napier are virtually flat. Most of this stretch was formerly a lagoon, but was lifted by a major earthquake in 1931. The earthquake also toppled most major buildings in Napier and Hastings, and killed 256 people.

You can continue right into Napier via S.H. 2, but the waterfront approach is probably more interesting. At Westshore (there is a motorcamp with cabins here), just past the airport, veer left from S.H. 2 onto Meeanee Quay. Cross the harbour by the Pandora Road bridge and turn immediately left along West Quay. This leads into Customs Quay then Bridge Street. Turn right along Hardinge Road, which leads into Breakwater Road past the port, and turns south past Bluff Hill into Marine Parade.

Napier (pop. 49,428) is a port, seaside resort, and regional business centre. Rebuilt completely after the 1931 earthquake, it is also a treasure-house of 1930s Art Deco architecture, with fine examples of the genre in almost every street of the central business district and the older suburbs.

Marine Parade, which stretches along the foreshore, includes a Marineland and an Aquarium, swimming pools, gardens, amusement centres, etc. The Hawkes Bay Art Centre and Museum is situated at the northern end of the Parade; the Tourist Information Centre is a little further south.

Napier has a wide selection of hotels, motels and guesthouses; also a Youth Hostel. If you have decided not to stay in Westshore, the nearest motorcamp (cabins) to the city centre is near the Rose Gardens, 2 km southeast.

To get there, turn right into Sale Street from Marine Parade just south of Marineland, continue across the railway tracks into Latham Road, then turn right into Douglas Street and left into Kennedy Road. There are other motorcamps at Taradale, 6 km southwest of the city centre, and at Clive, 10 km south. The Taradale motorcamp has cabins; the Clive motorcamp does not.

■ SIDE TRIPS: *HAWKES BAY EXCURSIONS* ────────

Napier is a pleasant place to relax for a day or two, with a number of interesting spots to visit in the vicinity. Potential excursions include a vineyards tour, and a day-trip to Cape Kidnapers. If you decide to visit Cape Kidnappers, I suggest planning the day to end up in Havelock North, 22 km south. This will save you backtracking to Napier and will reduce the distance of the next day's longish ride to Dannevirke.

Napier is noted for its grapes, and Hastings, just to the south, for its stone-fruit. The Information Centre will provide information on local wineries. The best-known include Glenvale (at Eskdale 17 km north of Napier), Mission (the vineyard of a local monastery, at Greenmeadows, 5 km southwest of central Napier), and Te Mata (near Havelock North).

Free samples are given out—it may be more prudent to book a tour.

A far more strenuous option is to ride out towards Cape Kidnappers, the gaunt eroded promontory 30 km southeast of the city that is a famous breeding-ground and sanctuary for gannets. This is best visited between early November and late February, and is closed between July and October. The trip from Napier to the Cape and on to Havelock North is a total of 61 km, including a 16 km walk or tractor ride.

Take the coast road from Napier southwards to Clive. At Clive, turn off S.H. 2 southeast towards Haumoana, across the Tukituki River. From Haumoana continue along the coast to Te Awanga and

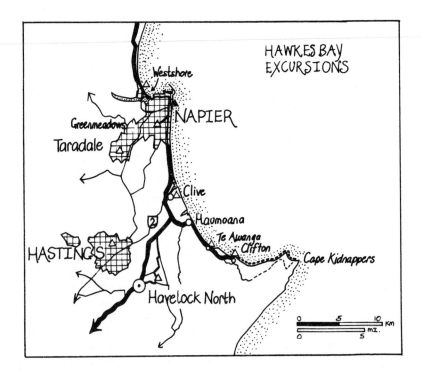

towards Clifton. There are motorcamps (cabins) at both Te Awanga and Clifton.

The gannet colony is about 8 km from Clifton, a 1½ to 2 hour walk along the beach and up the cliffs. Access is only possible at low tide. As a general rule, leave Clifton no sooner than 3 hours after high tide, and Cape Kidnappers no later than 1½ hour after low tide.

There is a rest area with shelter, water and toilets about 1 km before reaching the colony itself.

As an alternative to walking, tours of the colony operate from Te Awanga. One tour takes tractors along the beach; the other takes four-wheel-drive vehicles along a private road through the hills.

To get to Havelock North, you must return to Haumoana and cross the Tukituki River again. Take Lawn Road, the first road to the left (southwest) after the bridge. Within 7 km, this brings you to the main road into Havelock North.

Havelock North (pop. 9,036) is a pretty town with tree-lined streets, the most select and prosperous part of Hawke Bay, and home to some well-known private schools. It has several hotels and motels, also a motorcamp (cabins).

The motorcamp is situated to the northeast of the town. To get there, approaching from Haumoana, turn left from Lawn Road into Te Mata Road, right into Thompson Road, left into Brookvale Road, and left again into Arataki Road.

DAY 12 NAPIER TO DANNEVIRKE ─────────────
108 km–137 km

If starting from Napier, this will seem a long day, but it is not necessarily a strenuous one, since there are no difficult hills en route.

Leave Napier by Marine Parade and continue southward along the coast to Clive. From Clive S.H. 2 continues southwest to Hastings. 4.5 km from Clive, turn off S.H. 2 due south to Havelock North.

The road leads straight through town. In the centre of Havelock North is an intersection with six streets radiating from it. Take the south-west arm ("Middle Road").

The Middle Road is a minor but quiet and well-kept highway that runs southeastward virtually parallel to but at 10 km distance from S.H. 2, the main road through Hawke Bay. The Middle Road is less-known and is therefore less-used; much the preferable route for cyclists.

South of Havelock North, the road winds up a gentle valley be-

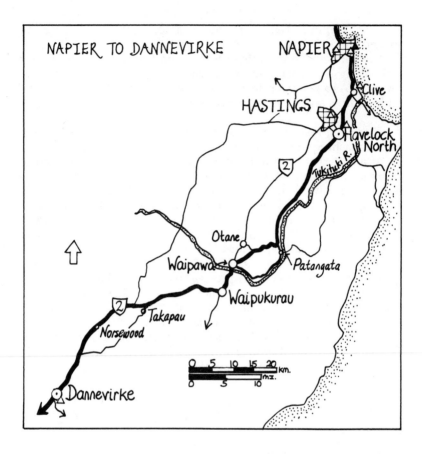

low the Kaokaoroa Range. At 12 km south of Havelock North, it rises over a low saddle and drops to the pleasant valley of the Tukituki River. This is a braided shingle river which, like most major rivers in the region, has over the years carried countless tons of shingle down from the eroded hills of the interior to the sea.

There are some undulating to gently rolling stretches in the upper valley, but the terrain is mostly gentle. Good spots for free camping are easy to find.

At 27 km south of Havelock North, just past the bridge over the Papanui Stream, you have the choice of turning inland direct to Waipawa, or of following the longer and prettier road along the river valley.

If you decide on the direct route, veer right along Te Kura Road after crossing the Papanui Stream. Five kilometres on, veer right onto Racecourse Road; then, another 7 km on, turn left along S.H. 2. Otherwise, simply continue south along the river road, which gradually turns west as it approaches Waipawa. (This route adds 7 km to the day's total.)

Waipawa (pop. 1,849) and Waipukurau (pop. 3,862), 7 km further south across the river, are twin towns and rivals. Both have hotels, motels and motorcamps. The Waipukurau camp has cabins.

S.H. 2 leads out of Waipukurau to the west. There is a brief hilly stretch 5 km beyond the town; otherwise the road is flat to undulating most of the 51 km to Dannevirke.

Dannevirke's name is a reminder of the first European settlers in this area, immigrants from Denmark, who arrived in the 1870s and under conditions of great hardship, with fire and axe, cleared the dense, primeval bush for farms.

Dannevirke (pop. 5,873) has a hotel and a motel. There is a pleasant municipal motorcamp (cabins) in the Domain, which also has a boating lake, a deer-park and a swimming pool. To get to the motorcamp, follow High Street north through the town. One kilometre from the outskirts you come to a Y-intersection. Take the right fork here, then turn immediately right into Christian Street and drop down to the motorcamp, which is set in a bend of the Mangatera Stream.

DAY 13 DANNEVIRKE TO MASTERTON ───────
109 km

This is a longish distance to cover, but again, thanks to the gentle terrain, the day should be a relatively easy one.

Continue southeast from Dannevirke to Woodville (pop. 1,582), 27 km away along S.H. 2. Turn south here for Pahiatua and Masterton. For 50 km the road gently and almost imperceptibly ascends the valleys of the Mangatainoka and Makakahi Rivers, through prosperous green farmland with views of the Tararua Range to the west.

■ **ALTERNATIVE ROUTE:** If you want to save time you could catch a train between Woodville, Pahiatua or Masterton and Wellington. The railcar departs from Woodville Mondays to Fridays at 7.19 A.M. and arrives in Wellington 10.35 A.M. Fridays only there is a 5.00 P.M. service which arrives at 8.23 P.M., and Sundays only a 5.40 P.M. service which arrives at 9.25 P.M.

Respective departure times from Pahiatua, 15 km south of Woodville, are 7.37 A.M., 5.20 P.M. and 6.25 P.M.; and from

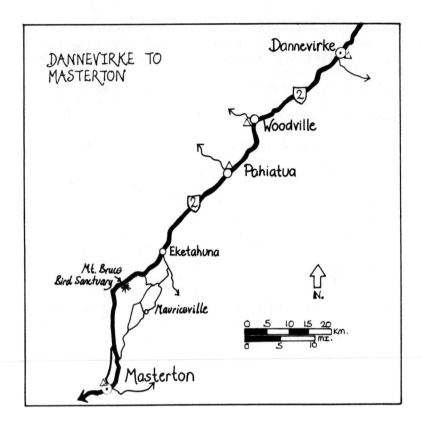

Eketahuna, a further 26 km on, 8.06 A.M., 5.50 P.M. and 6.50 P.M.

Masterton has several extra services. Departure times Monday to Friday are 5.55 A.M., 6.45 A.M. and 8.55 A.M., Fridays only at 6.35 P.M., Saturdays only at 9.10 A.M., and Sundays only at 7.40 P.M. The trip to Wellington from Masterton takes about 1¾ hours. You can also catch the railcar at Carterton and Featherston, which are respectively 15 km and 38 km south of Masterton. ■

The towns of Pahiatua (pop. 2,681) and Eketahuna (pop. 635) lie en route. Pahiatua is notable chiefly for its exceptionally wide main street, originally laid out to allow the railway through (it eventually took another route). Eketahuna is a byword in New Zealand for the back-of-beyond ("nothing ever happens in Eketahuna"). It is in fact a pretty, leafy little town. Pahiatua has a motel and a motorcamp; Eketahuna has a motel and a municipal motorcamp (cabins) set on the edge of the Makakahi River.

Ten kilometres south of Eketahuna is Mt. Bruce Bird Sanctuary, where rare species of native bird such as the takahe and the kakapo are bred and protected. The road ascends a low saddle here, then crosses the Upper Opaki Plain to Masterton.

Masterton (pop. 18,511), the chief town of the Wairarapa, is a conservative farming centre with several well-known schools. It has some fine parks and a museum and arts centre. There is a choice of hotels and motels. The motorcamp (cabins) is beside the bridge across the Waipoua River where S.H. 2 enters town, and the tourist information centre is on the corner of London Road and Chapel Street.

DAY 14 MASTERTON TO WELLINGTON ———
102 km

Chappell Street and High Street lead southeast through Masterton to S.H. 2. For the next 38 km the road is dead flat as it crosses the Taratahi Plain. There are three towns en route, Carterton (pop. 3,902), Greytown (pop. 1,882) and Featherston (pop. 2,516). Carterton has a hotel, a motel and a caravan park, Greytown a motel and a municipal motorcamp (closed in winter), and Featherston a hotel and a motel.

There is a museum at the southern end of Greytown. To the southwest of town is the Papawai Marae, billed in the 1890s as the

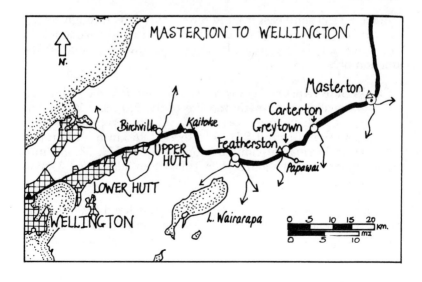

"Maori capital" of New Zealand, being the centre of the Kotahitanga or Maori Parliament movement, a political organization advocating complete self-government for the Maori.

Just beyond Featherston, a long climb up the Rimutaka Ranges begins, the road rising by 520 m in just over 9.5 km. You may find the wind a problem: according to rumour, cars and caravans have been blown over the edge on occasion.

There is a tearoom at the summit. A 3 km descent follows, a hilly stretch for 5 km (there is a Youth Hostel at Kaitoke en route), then a 4 km drop to the Hutt Valley.

To cyclists, the Hutt Valley means 25 km of flat, urban sprawl. The road continues another 11 km beyond, around the harbour's edge to Wellington City itself. The best way into Wellington by far is to take the suburban train from Upper Hutt (avoid the morning rush-hour). Otherwise, keep to S.H. 2 all the way. This may look like a motorway for much of its length, but there is a wide shoulder for cyclists, at least from Silverstream onwards.

The route into Wellington is further described on page 167, along with directions to the nearest motorcamp to Wellington which is situated in Lower Hutt.

Tour 6A Rotorua to Tokaanu

DAY 1 ROTORUA TO TAUPO
82km–96km

Take S.H. 5 southeast from Rotorua. This runs through rolling country for 26 km, past Whakarewarewa Forest and Lake Rotokahi (the "Green Lake") before turning south towards Taupo at the junction of S.H. 38.

> ■ **Side Trip:** On the way, you could detour to the Waimangu thermal area, formerly the site of the Pink and White Terraces, which were destroyed in the eruption of Mt. Tarawera. Turn off S.H. 5 to the left 16 km from Rorotua. From Waimangu continue south to join S.H. 38 and turn right (west) to rejoin S.H. 5. This detour adds about 7 km in distance.

After the junction with S.H. 38, you pass Rainbow Mountain scenic reserve and thermal area to your left and Waiotapu thermal area to your right. If you spent a day or two in Rotorua, however,

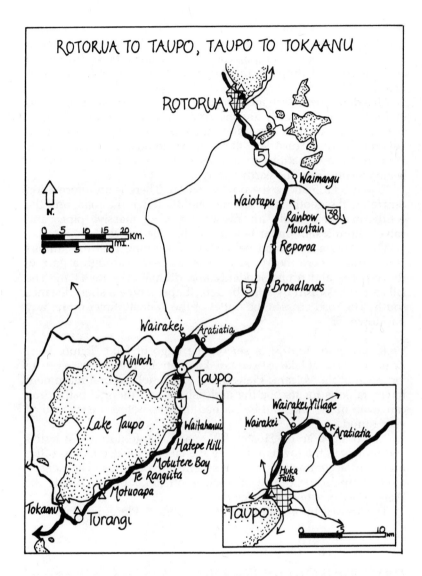

you may well have seen enough thermal areas by now.

At 8 km from the junction, turn off S.H. 5 to Reporoa and Broad-lands. This is a sealed road, which allows you to escape the traffic of S.H. 5. It continues the whole way to Taupo, mostly flat to un-dulating, but rising slightly a few kilometres before the end, then dipping down to the town and lakeside.

■ **ALTERNATIVE ROUTE:** You can make an interesting alternative trip, adding perhaps 7 km to the day, by turning north to
Aratiatia 8 km before Taupo. The road bypasses the hydro village
of Aratiatia, and drops to the Aratiatia dam to cross the Waikato
River.

This dam, the first in a chain along the Waikato, was completed
in 1964. Below the dam are the Aratiatia Rapids, once a famous
beauty spot, but now dry unless the dam's sluice-gates are open.
Beyond the dam, turn left along the riverbank. The road passes
Wairakei power station, reliant on geothermal power or super-
heated steam from the earth's core.

Rejoin S.H. 5 above the power station. There is an information
centre for the geothermal scheme slightly down the road, and the
geothermal field itself, an awesome area of massive pipes and
valves set in a semi-lunar landscape shrouded in steam.

Then take a loop road below S.H. 5 running past the famous
Huka Falls, where the Waikato River squeezes through a narrow
rocky gorge and drops suddenly and dramatically for 11 m. The
falls are overlooked by a footbridge. Taupo is now a short distance
south. The road crosses the outlet of the Waikato River on its way
into town. ■

Taupo (pop. 15,873) is set on the edge of Lake Taupo, New
Zealand's largest lake (619 square kilometres). It is a service centre
for much of the Volcanic Plateau, but also a holiday and retirement
town, famous for its boating and fishing and thermal baths. You
can swim in the lake, but be warned that the waters are icy cold all
year round.

Taupo has a Youth Hostel. There are a large number of hotels
and motels in the town and along the lakeshore; also lodges offering cabin accommodation, and several motorcamps. The nearest
motorcamp to the centre of town is off Redoubt St., beside the
Waikato River where it leaves the lake.

The Tourist Information Centre is in Story Place, nearby.

DAY 2 TAUPO TO TOKAANU
57 km

This road is a beautiful one, passing along the eastern shore of
Lake Taupo. It cannot be unreservedly recommended to cyclists as
it carries a high volume of traffic. However, the alternative route,
around the north of the lake via the Kinloch road and south via
S.H. 32, is almost twice as long (106 km) and much more difficult.

Rapids above Huka Falls (Photo by Richard Oddy)

Pause for refreshment, Lake Taupo (Photo by Richard Oddy)

Take S.H. 1 south from Taupo. The first 12 km to Waitahanui are flat to undulating and a little dull, much of the way passing a long string of motels and holiday homes. But the road then turns inland and climbs into the hills, rising from 369 m at the lakeside over 5 km to a peak of 465 m. This is Hatepe Hill, once a notoriously narrow and winding stretch of road, now a broad smooth highway.

The road then descends again to the lakeside and keeps close to the water much of the way to Turangi. There are several pleasant little settlements en route: Motutere, Waitetoko, Te Rangiita, Motuoapa. There is a motorcamp at Motutere Bay 32 km south of Taupo, and a motel and a motorcamp at Motuoapa 11 km further on.

Turangi (pop. 3,913), once little more than a fisherman's camp, was expanded in the 1960s as the service town for the Tongariro Power scheme. It is famous for the excellent trout-fishing in the vicinity.

Turangi has several hotels and motels and a motorcamp (cabins), but you may prefer to continue to Tokaanu, 6 km northwest. S.H. 1 bypasses most of Turangi. Turn right onto S.H. 41 just south of town. For Tokaanu, see Tour 5, Day 4.

TOUR 7. WELLINGTON

Wellington has been New Zealand's capital city since 1865. It was founded in 1840 by immigrants of the New Zealand Company, who first settled in Petone in the Hutt Valley but, because of flooding, soon moved to Thorndon, where the central business district now stands.

The centre of Wellington is a narrow strip of land squeezed between the hills and the sea. The foreshore has been extended over the years, both by earthquakes and by reclamation, but the city still lacks space for expansion. Its suburbs have spread over the hills and along the valleys for many miles north and south. The population of Wellington City itself is only 136,911; that of the whole urban area including the Hutt Valley is 325,697.

Wellington, being extremely hilly, is not an ideal place for cyclists. It is also very windy, being subject to strong winds funnelled through Cook Strait.

Nonetheless, it is an interesting place to spend a day or two, or more. Among the sights to see are Parliament Buildings, and the old Government Buildings, said to be one of the world's largest wooden buildings. Old St. Pauls (1866) is one of New Zealand's most beautiful churches. The National Art Gallery and Museum are also situated in Wellington. There is also a good Maritime Museum, and botanical gardens.

A cable-car runs up the hill to Kelston from Lambton Quay in the centre of town. Other good places to view the city include Mt. Victoria (170 m) and Tinakori Hill (300 m) The bleak coastal areas to the south and west of the city can also make an interesting excursion, as described later.

Getting Through Wellington

These directions assume you are approaching the city from the northeast, that is, from Petone and the Hutt Valley along the harbour's edge.

THE COOK STRAIT FERRY TERMINAL ───────

This is clearly signposted to the left from the Hutt Rd. (S.H. 2), 8 km southeast of Petone and 3 km before the city centre. For the ferry timetable and other details, see p. 175.

WELLINGTON YOUTH HOSTEL

S.H. 2 leads into Thorndon Quay. Tinakori Road branches southeastward from the northern end of Thorndon Quay. The Youth Hostel is on the right side of Tinakori Rd. Be warned: Thorndon Quay and most of the other roads described here and below are busy and crowded. Strong winds are frequently an additional hazard.

PARLIAMENT BUILDINGS

Thorndon Quay passes to the west of Wellington's central railway station. Turn right along Molesworth St. just after passing the station. Old Government Buildings (1876) are now to your left. One block further on are Parliament Buildings.

The central edifice of Parliament Buildings, with its massive portico and pillars, was completed in 1922. This houses the debat-

Wellington Harbour from Mount Victoria (Photo by Richard Oddy)

ing chambers. The "Beehive", the circular building to the left, completed in 1977, houses most of the ministerial offices. The Victorian Gothic General Assembly Library to the right dates from 1897.

Further along Molesworth St. are old St. Pauls (1866), the new Anglican cathedral, and the National Library building (1986).

Continuing along Molesworth St. brings you to Tinakori Rd. Turn right for the Youth Hostel, which is about 100 m down. Alternatively, if continuing into the city after this sight-seeing excursion, turn down Pipitea St. beside the National Library, then right into Mulgrave St. This brings you back to Thorndon Quay and the central railway station.

THE PUBLIC RELATIONS OFFICE

This is in Mercer St., (phone 735063) conveniently placed next to the main city library. Continue along Molesworth St. into Featherston St.

> ■ **Side Trip:** Turning right into any street which leads off Featherston St. will bring you out into Lambton Quay, one of Wellington's main shopping streets. The Kelburn cable car ascends the heights to the Botanic Gardens, above the central business district, from a small lane off the southern end of Lambton Quay.

Six blocks from the railway station, turn left into Panama St., then first right into busy Customhouse Quay.

> ■ **Side Trips:** The Maritime Museum, which you may wish to visit in passing, is across Customhouse Quay opposite Panama St. Two blocks further south, in the triangle formed by Customhouse Quay, Lambton Quay and Hunter St., is a remarkable historical precinct which preserves some of New Zealand's finest Victorian and Edwardian commercial buildings. Elsewhere in Wellington, because of commercial pressures and earthquake regulations, the older commercial buildings have been razed to the ground, and replaced by anonymous tower blocks. In this small corner, a few elegant examples from the past survive, their styles ranging from classical revival through Edwardian baroque to Art Deco.

Customhouse Quay continues into Willis St. Turn left into Mercer St. two blocks along.

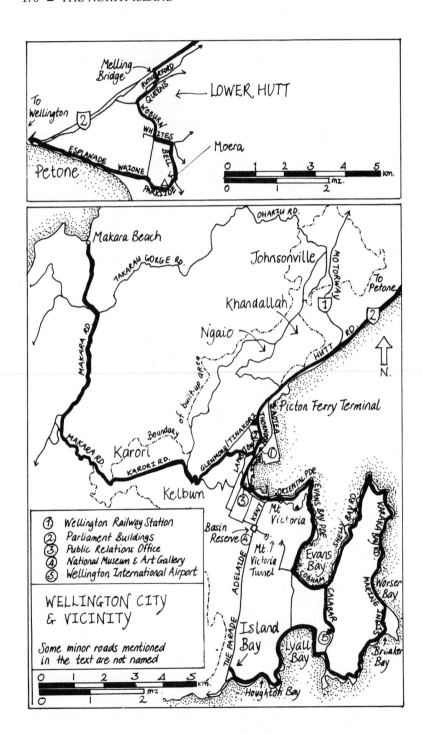

WELLINGTON CITY & VICINITY

① Wellington Railway Station
② Parliament Buildings
③ Public Relations Office
④ National Museum & Art Gallery
⑤ Wellington International Airport

Some minor roads mentioned in the text are not named

WELLINGTON AIRPORT ─────────────

The Airport is 6 km from the city centre, by the direct route via the Mt. Victoria tunnel; an extra 2 km by the more scenic route, via Oriental Bay.

Continue down Mercer St. from the Public Relations Office. Turn right into Cuba St., which runs between the old Town Hall and the modernistic Michael Fowler Centre, then take the first turn left. This brings you into Wakefield St. Five blocks along Wakefield Street, turn left into Oriental Parade.

■ **ALTERNATIVE ROUTE:** If you would like to visit the National Art Gallery and Museum—or to take the direct route to the airport—turn right instead along Kent Terrace. This leads to the Basin Reserve (a sports ground), just under 1 km away. Turn left along Buckle St. and circle the Basin Reserve clockwise until you rejoin Buckle St., then turn left for the Museum.

The road to Mt. Victoria Tunnel is at the southeast end of Basin Reserve. The tunnel itself is a short, nasty, noisy and dangerous stretch of road—best wheel your bike through on the footpath. Once beyond the tunnel, simply follow signs to the airport, turning right into Ruahine St., then taking the third left into Wellington St., continuing from this direct into Cobham Drive. ■

Oriental Parade becomes Evans Bay Parade as it rounds the first headland from the city. The airport is at the southern end of Evans Bay. Turn left off Evans Bay Parade into Cobham Drive, which passes along the northern end of the airport. Turn right at the second roundabout, 1.5 km along Cobham Drive. The airport entrance is another 1.5 km south, down Calabar Rd. and Stewart Duff Drive.

Wellington Excursions

Because of its hilly terrain, Wellington's road patterns are very complex. If you want to spend some time in the city, you really should buy a map. Some interesting excursions around and outside the city are also described below.

EXCURSION 1 ISLAND BAY ─────────────
30 km+

The coastal road from the city to Island Bay offers good views both of the harbour and of Cook Strait. If the day is sunny, this is a delightful ride, with numerous places to stop for a swim en route.

If the day is stormy, however, go elsewhere, since the road is very exposed. Most of the roads described below are main roads and relatively busy; unfortunately, Wellington's topography allows few alternatives.

Follow the directions to the airport via Oriental Parade as far as Cobham Drive. At the eastern end of Cobham Drive, turn north along Shelley Beach Rd.; then follow the coastal road as it rounds a headland and turns south through Scorching Bay, Karaka Bay and Worser Bay.

At the southern end of Worser Bay, turn inland briefly along Inglis St. This leads to the Breaker Bay road on the southern end of the Mirimar Peninsula. Keep to the coast again from here, passing through a succession of rocky coves, and continue past Lyall Bay (at the southern end of the airport) and Houghton Bay into Island Bay.

Island Bay is a maritime suburb and fishing port 6 km south of the city centre. You can return to the city from here by heading northwards along the Parade. Alternatively, you can follow the road to its end several kilometres further along the coast, leaving the suburbs behind, and passing between bare hills and the wild sea.

EXCURSION 2 MAKARA
30 km +

This is a shingle beach on the eastern coast, 15 km from the city. It is unpopulated and lonely (except on summer and holiday weekends).

Climb the hills behind the city through Karori, following successively Bowen St. (off Lambton Quay beside Parliament Buildings), Glenmore St., Chaytor St. and Karori Rd. At the northeastern end of Karori, turn right along the Makara Rd. This climbs briefly but steeply to a high ridge, then makes the long descent of the Makara River Valley to the sea. The road is sealed, but narrow.

The climb back up the valley is strenuous. If you prefer not to retrace your route then, 3 km back from the beach, turn left up the rough gravel Ohariu Valley Rd. This climbs through the hills to Johnsonville, 10 km away. The city is 9 km south of Johnsonville. Take the suburban train back, or follow the old main road southward, winding through Khandallah, Ngaio and Wadestown.

EXCURSION 3 RIMUTAKA CIRCUIT
130 km–179 km

This is a very demanding trip designed for off-road enthusiasts. It is best done on a mountain bike, but a sturdy and lightly loaded touring bike would be adequate.

If cycling the whole way, anticipate taking at least two days. You can however, save 49 km of distance by taking the train in and out of Wellington. Stock up with whatever provisions you need before leaving Eastbourne; there are no shops, indeed very few habitations of any sort, between there and Featherston. Take rainwear and warm clothes.

Head for Petone via S.H. 2 (or take the suburban train). Follow the Esplanade southeast along the Petone waterfront. This leads into Seaview Rd which turns southward past Lowry Bay, York Bay, Mahina Bay and Days Bay, running along the eastern edge of Wellington Harbour to Eastbourne, 11 km from Petone central.

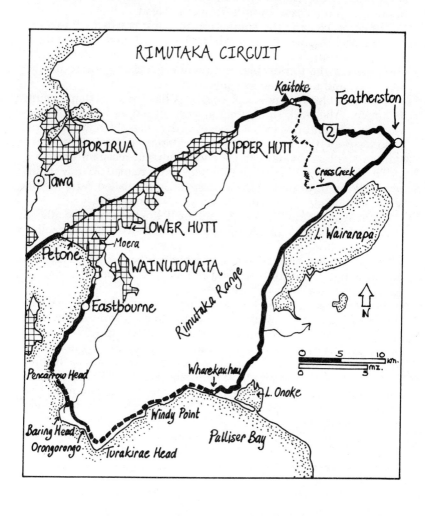

Eastbourne (pop. 4,494) is a pleasant seaside, commuter and retirement town. Just south of Eastbourne, the seal ends, but a flat, well-formed gravel road leads for another 10 km to Pencarrow Head lighthouse.

From here, a four-wheel drive track continues along Fitzroy Bay towards Baring Head. There are one or two fords to cross. At the southern end of Fitzroy Bay, the track climbs a low ridge to join the road which services the Baring Head lighthouse. Turn left, and descend to the Wainuiomata road 1 km away. Turn right here.

The gravel road continues downriver then along the coast to Orongorongo Station (this is a sheep-station not a railway-station). Traffic is light, except during holiday weekends. The road ends at the Orongorongo Stream, but a four-wheel drive track continues along the coast towards Turakirae Head.

Turakirae Head is the southernmost point reached on this excursion, and the road turns northeast here. Although the terrain is mostly flat to undulating, the surface now becomes rough. A few stretches may be unrideable, and there are locked gates to lift the bike over, and unbridged streams to cross.

This is a bleak, windswept coast, its bleakness perhaps being its appeal. The track runs along a series of ledges lifted from the sea over the centuries by successive earthquakes. Strong southerly winds sweep the area, and the vegetation consists mostly of stunted scrub and karaka trees, and tough salt-resistant grasses.

There is little shelter until after aptly named Windy Point where, 9 km from the roadhead, a sparsely furnished A-frame hut is situated. A stream nearby serves as a water supply.

From Windy Point, there are another 10 km to the next roadhead at Wharekauhau, an untidy row of fishermen's cottages straggling along the bare coast. From here, a gravel road climbs up the Wharepapa River and crosses a stretch of wetlands and gently rolling farmland at the southern end of Lake Wairarapa. The seal begins again 10 km from Wharekauhau.

Featherston is now 30 km away, an easy ridge along the eastern shores of the lake. You can return to Wellington from Featherston via S.H. 2 across the Rimutakas, or by train (see pp. 159).

Alternatively, you can take a much more demanding and exciting route through the mountains over the old Rimutaka Incline. This was the route trains took between 1878 and 1955, pulled by Fell locomotives especially designed to cope with the extreme gradients of the track. Most of the now disused track is still negotiable by foot or bicycle.

Thirty kilometres north of Wharekauhau, turn west along Cross Creek Rd. This peters out 3 km into the hills. Fifteen kilometres of off-road slog now follows before you emerge onto S.H. 2 at

Kaitoke. There is a Youth Hostel at Kaitoke.

Continue up the foot track leading along Cross Creek. This soon rises steeply up a ridge to the first of the four tunnels you will have to negotiate. These are damp and dark and unrideable. A torch will help. Some of the rest of the track is rideable, much is not, and most of it is steep.

For directions to Wellington, see Tour 6, Day 14.

WELLINGTON TO PICTON VIA THE COOK STRAIT FERRY

The wild waters of Cook Strait separate the North Island of New Zealand from the larger but less-populated South Island (sometimes known, particularly to people who live there, as the "mainland"). Cook Strait is crossed by roll-on/roll-off ferries sailing between Wellington and Picton.

Ferries leave Wellington at 8.00 A.M. (not Mondays and Tuesdays), 10.00 A.M., 4.00 P.M. and 6.40 P.M. (not Sundays). Timetables may change during holiday weekends. Cyclists will almost always find space. If you have not booked, however, you should arrive at the ferry terminal an hour or so before departure in case you need to queue for tickets.

The ferry terminal is 3 km northeast of the city. Follow Customhouse Quay, Waterloo Quay and Aotea Quay northwards. The terminal is signposted to the left off Aotea Quay. Note that these roads are all busy roads with fast-moving traffic.

Ride or wheel your bike on board up the vehicle ramp. Once on the vehicle deck, attach your bike to stanchions along the sides with the ropes provided. Take your valuables with you above deck.

The ferry sails southward through Wellington Harbour, turns eastward once in Cook Strait proper, then turns southward again along the sheltered waters of Queen Charlotte Sound. The crossing takes just over three hours. Each ferry has several lounges and observation decks, a small shop, and a cafeteria.

On arrival in Picton, cyclists can disembark almost immediately.

Most cyclists will want to catch one of the morning crossings. This means arriving in Picton at 11.00 A.M. or 1.00 P.M. In summer, this allows several hours cycling before the end of the day.

Cyclists arriving later, at 4.00 P.M. or 9.40 P.M., may wish to stay in Picton overnight. There is a wide choice of hotels, motels and guesthouses in the town, also a summer Youth Hostel.

Picton (pop. 3,536) is a port and holiday centre. The tourist information centre is near the disembarkation point. There is a pleasant park on the waterfront at the head of the sound, and a whaling museum in adjacent London Quay.

There are also several motorcamps (cabins). The nearest to the ferry terminal is in Canterbury St. To get there, continue down Auckland St. due south from the port—the main route south—veer right into Wairau Rd., take the second turn left into Devon St., and the second left again into Canterbury St. There are other motorcamps along the Waikawau Bay Rd. to the northeast of town.

Even if you do not intend to overnight in Picton, I suggest spending an hour or so there, to allow traffic from the ferry to pass. The road will then be much quieter when you do leave.

The ride from Picton to Christchurch can be a rewarding one. The road runs along the beautiful Kaikoura Coast for nearly a third of the total distance.

If you have limited time, however, take the train, since the railway-line also runs along the most scenic parts of the coast. The 10.00 A.M. ferry from Wellington connects with a daily train which leaves Picton at 2.10 P.M. and arrives in Christchurch at 7.55 P.M. Stops en route are made in Blenheim, Seddon, Kaikoura, Scargill and Waipara.

TOUR 8. WELLINGTON TO AUCK-LAND VIA TARANAKI AND THE KING COUNTRY

8–10 days: 731 km–819 km

This tour takes you back to Auckland through the western side of the North Island. It is not a direct route, though it can be shortened by taking the train at either end, and it passes few major tourist attractions. Nonetheless, it is on the whole as rewarding as any other tour in the book.

First, head north across the Horowhenua Plain to Palmerston North, the market centre and University town, then turn northeast through the Wanganui to Taranaki regions. (If you came south this way some days or weeks before, you may care to take the train to Palmerston North instead.)

Visible from all parts of the Taranaki region, and standing almost exactly in its centre, is the tall volcanic cone of Mt. Egmont (2,518 m). Most of the province consists of land gently sloping away from the mountain, bordered by rugged hill-country to the west and by the sea to north, south and east.

The Maori name for Mt. Egmont is Mt. Taranaki. Taranaki is recognized as an official name, but most maps and guidebooks still refer to the mountain as Mt. Egmont. According to tribal mythology, Taranaki once stood in the central North Island alongside Tongariro and Ruapehu, but was banished here after quarrelling with Tongariro over the latter's wife. The quarrel has never died; even today when Tongariro catches sight of Taranaki he erupts in fury.

New Plymouth (pop. 36,865) is the region's largest city. It was first settled by pakeha in 1841, by immigrants of the Plymouth Company. As the settlement expanded, the new settlers eyed with envy land owned and cultivated by the local Ngati-Awa people. Some Maori wanted to sell; many did not. This naturally led to a series of disputes, which escalated into full-scale war in 1860, the immediate cause being a fraudulent sale of land at Waitara near New Plymouth.

The British and colonial troops, superior in numbers and weaponry, gradually defeated the Maori forces, but guerilla warfare continued spasmodically in the region for some years. As an aftermath of the fighting, considerable areas of land passed from

Maori to pakeha hands.

Relics of the war are common in the area: pa-sites where battles were fought, blockhouses and redoubts erected by the Army.

For more than a century, however, there has been peace. Taranaki is today one of New Zealand's richest farming areas, densely settled, and famous for its lush pastures, its dairy farms, and its cheeses. It is also the site of recent and massive energy projects. There are natural gas fields both offshore from New Plymouth and at Kapuni, south of the mountain.

From Taranaki, you head up the coast then inland through the King Country. It was into the King Country that supporters of the Maori King retreated after defeat in the Land Wars. For some years this region was closed to pakehas; any unwary enough to cross its boundaries risked their lives.

The King Country was opened up for settlement when peace was made in 1881, but in some ways it still seems a pioneer country. Some of its rugged hillcountry has been developed for sheep-farms, but much still remains covered in native bush. King Country towns mostly developed around the railway when the Main Trunk Line between Auckland and Wellington was pushed through in the latter part of the 19th century.

Beyond the King Country, you pass into the fertile plains of the Waikato, once largely peatland and forest and swamp, now another rich farming and dairying region. You have a choice of detouring into Hamilton (pop. 94,511), New Zealand's fourth largest city, sited pleasantly beside the Waikato River, or of heading direct to Auckland.

From Hamilton itself, Auckland is as little as one day's ride away—though you can take the train if you prefer.

DAY 1 *WELLINGTON TO PALMERSTON NORTH* ———
92 km–115 km

As mentioned above, if you have done this stretch before, you may prefer to take the train. The *Northerner*, which takes bikes as accompanied luggage, leaves Wellington daily at 8.45 P.M. and arrives in Palmerston North at 10.57 P.M.; the *Silver Fern*, which does not take bikes, leaves Wellington at 8.20 A.M. Monday to Friday and arrives in Palmerston North at 10.23 A.M.

I do not in any case recommend cycling out of Wellington northwards along the former main road through Johnsonville, Tawa, Porirua and Plimmerton. This stretch is hilly, busy, and dull, no sooner passing out of one suburb or commuter town than entering the next.

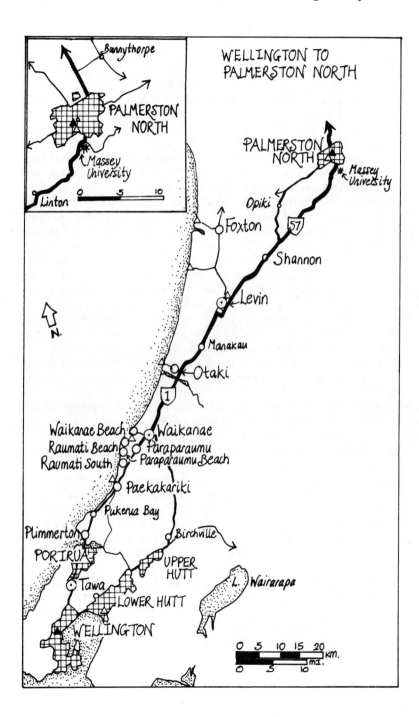

WELLINGTON TO
PALMERSTON NORTH

Take the suburban train instead, at least as far as Plimmerton, a pleasant beachside settlement to the north of Porirua Harbour, or perhaps as far as Paraparaumu, the end of the suburban line. This will save 28 km (to Plimmerton) or 51 km (to Paraparaumu), and puts Palmerston North within one day's easy reach. Avoid rush-hour trains from mid-afternoon onwards.

From Paraparaumu, continue north along S.H. 1, following this for almost 40 km, most of the way to Levin. It is a busy road but fortunately has wide shoulders much of the way. Watch out for a squeeze point at the narrow, hump-backed railway bridge just north of Waikanae. The terrain is virtually flat.

Fifteen kilometres north of Waikanae is Otaki (pop. 4,407), quite a historic town. Levin (pop. 15,368) is 20 km further on. It is a prosperous market town, with hotels, motels and a motorcamp (cabins). However, since the main road through the town is usually busy and crowded, I suggest bypassing it. Turn to the right (east) just beyond Ohau, a small village 3 km south of Levin, then take the first turn left. This bypass brings you to S.H. 57, which you can follow for the remaining 50 km to Palmerston North.

Twelve kilometres north of Levin the road climbs moderately for 2 km, then descends for 3 km to Shannon (pop. 1,584), a small farming centre that was in former times a flax-milling centre.

Much of the rest of the distance to Palmerston North is flat, though there are a few kilometres of mildly rolling country before the city.

There are in fact two alternative routes into Palmerston North. At 5 km north of Shannon there is an intersection where a road veers left towards Opiki. This continues on to join S.H. 56 and enters Palmerston North from the south. The Opiki route is dead flat all the way, but I recommend staying on S.H. 57, which is more scenic, running as it does closer to the Tararua Range to the east.

S.H. 57 passes Massey University campus just outside Palmerston North. (A short detour to the right will take you around the campus.) The bridge across the Manawatu River between the campus and the city is quite narrow, and very busy in the afternoons during term-time, when lectures are out.

The bridge leads into Fitzherbert Avenue, which continues northeast direct to the Square, the centre of the city. If heading for the only motorcamp (cabins) in town, take Park Rd., the fourth road to the left after crossing the bridge, then turn left into Ruha St. less than 1 km along. The motorcamp is set beside the river.

For a description of Palmerston North, see Tour 5, Alternative Day 7A.

DAY 2 PALMERSTON NORTH TO WANGANUI ────
Via Feilding: 79 km

Take Rangitikei St. northeast from the Square. This is the main road out of town and almost always busy. At 1.5km from the Square, turn right (northeast) along Tremaine Ave. East. (The railway station, by the way, is a short distance down Tremaine St. West.)

At 2.5km along Tremaine St. East, turn left into Railway Rd., shortly crossing a railway bridge and leaving the city behind. S.H. 54 is clearly signposted to Feilding and runs through flat countryside most of the way.

Feilding (pop. 12,116) is a market town. It was founded in 1874 and laid out in a pattern similar to that of Manchester, United Kingdom. Note the spelling of the name—Feilding *not* Fielding. The town was named not after its bucolic setting but after a Lieutenant Colonel W.H.A. Feilding, agent of the Emigrants' and Colonists' Aid Corporation, who selected the land on which Feild-

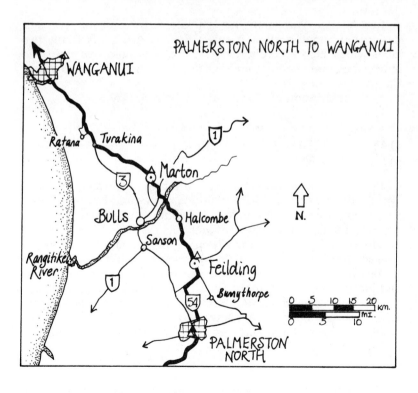

ing stands.

Feilding has a hotel, several motels, and a motorcamp.

From Feilding you continue northeastwards out of town on the Halcombe road, through a stretch of gently rolling country. Beyond Halcombe, the road crosses the Rangitikei River and joins S.H. 1. Turn north here but, within 1 km, turn east again for Marton.

Marton (pop. 5,099) is a pleasant country town. It has a hotel, motels, and a motorcamp (cabins). From Marton, the road leads just north of east to Turakina, from where you follow S.H. 3 for Wanganui, now 22 km away across low, rolling country. The road now becomes busier, but is rarely crowded.

> ■ **Side Trip:** At 2.5km beyond Turakina you can, if you wish, make an interesting detour south to Ratana Pa (pop. 434). This is a village founded in the 1920s by F.W. Ratana, a Maori prophet and healer, and founder of an indigenous Christian sect. There is a fine and distinctive Ratana temple here.

Just outside Wanganui the last kilometre or so of S.H. 3 is designated a motorway as it enters the city (it is in fact only two lanes wide). Bicycles are forbidden here: you must veer right and enter Wanganui slightly to the north across the Victoria Avenue or City Bridge.

For a description of Wanganui, see Tour 5, Day 6.

DAY 3 WANGANUI TO HAWERA
90 km

Leave Wanganui on S.H. 3 running northwest. Between Wanganui and Waverley (45 km) and Waverley and Patea (62 km) is low rolling country, with no long hills but with a number of minor but occasionally strenuous rises and falls.

There is a hotel at Waverley (pop. 1,112), a market town largely set back from the main road. There is also a motorcamp at Waverley Beach, an 11 km detour south. This is an area of sandstone cliffs and black sands swept by the sea.

The road drops to cross the Patea River just before Patea (pop. 1,568) another small market town, once a minor port. There is a hotel in Patea, and a motorcamp at the mouth of the river nearby. In front of Patea town hall stands an interesting memorial: a concrete model of the Aotea canoe which brought the first Maori to the area many centuries ago. Patea also has a local historical museum.

For much of the last 28 km to Hawera, the road is up and down,

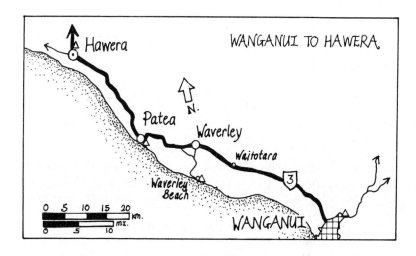

but gradually rising overall. Hawera (pop. 8,175) is a large farming centre set on a plateau above the coast. It has several hotels and motels. The motorcamp (cabins) is on Waihi Rd., adjacent to King Edward Park, which itself is off S.H. 3 as it heads northward through the town.

> ■ **Side Trip:** 2.5km northeast of the town is Turutumokai Pa, built more than 400 years ago and one of the best-preserved pa that survive from pre-European times.

An interesting and unique feature of Hawera's history is that it was once a republic, declared such briefly in 1881 by local residents who felt the Government of the time was not doing enough to defend the town against potentially hostile Maoris.

DAY 4 HAWERA TO NEW PLYMOUTH VIA STRATFORD
70 km; plus side trips to Mt Egmont: 28 km–46 km

Between Hawera and New Plymouth S.H. 3 gently crosses the lower flanks of Mt. Egmont, reaching a high point of about 350 m at Midhirst, almost exactly midway. From Midhirst to New Plymouth is mostly (not all) gently downhill, but the road dips to cross streams draining from the mountain on the way.

Between Hawera and Midhirst are the dairying towns of Eltham (pop. 2,288) and Stratford (pop. 5,528). Both have hotels, motels and a motorcamp; the Stratford motorcamp has cabins. Just south of Stratford is a replica pioneer village. Between Midhirst and New Plymouth is Inglewood (pop. 3,191), another dairying town, also with a hotel and motel.

■ **Side Trip:** You may wish to climb Mt. Egmont. If so, set aside the whole of a day. There are several roads up the mountain climbing to about 1,000 m; the remaining distance to the top is a 4 to 5 hour hike.

Just south of Stratford, you can turn off to Dawson Falls, 25 km away. The road first skirts the mountain for 14 km, then turns north and climbs steeply for 9 km to 911 m. There is a lodge, a campground and an information centre at Dawson Falls.

From Stratford itself you can head to Stratford Mountain House, 14 km away and 850 m up the mountain (a rough gravel road actually continues several kilometres beyond to a winter skifield). The Mountain House is in fact a lodge; there is also a campground nearby.

A short distance beyond Inglewood, you can turn up the mountain to North Egmont, 17 km off the main road. There is a motel here, a community cabin, a campground, and an information centre.

Besides the summit walks, there are numerous other walks in Egmont National Park. The lower slopes of the mountain are covered in bush. The upper slopes are an alpine zone where snowgrass predominates; above is bare scoria, then snow.

Wherever you decide to go, beware of sudden changes of weather. Take warm clothing and waterproofs, and food and water. The mountain has killed people who underestimated it.

New Plymouth (pop. 36,865) was founded, as mentioned above, in 1841, in an area that had once supported a dense Maori population but that had been devastated by tribal wars in the early 19th century. It is an attractive city, sloping down gentle hillsides to the sea.

Perhaps its best known feature is Pukekura Park, an area with bush-walks, ferneries, artificial lakes, plant-houses and fountains. Nearby are the "Bowl of Brooklands", a soundshell used for open-air concerts, and the Gables, an old cottage hospital (1848).

Other sights to see include the Taranaki Museum, which has one of the country's best collections of Maori artifacts, the Govett-Brewster Art Gallery, St. Marys Church (1842), and the stone-built

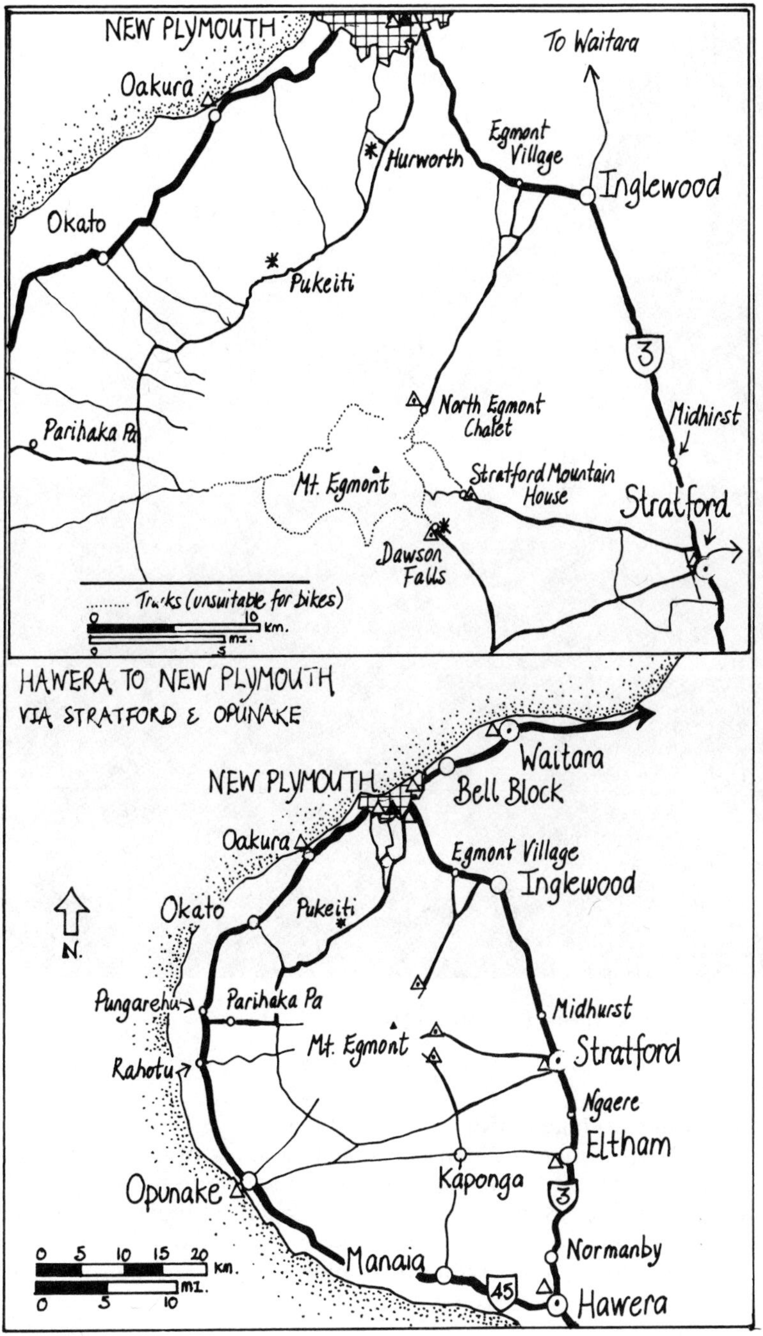

NEW PLYMOUTH

Oakura

Hurworth

Egmont Village

To Waitara

Inglewood

Okato

Pukeiti

3

Midhirst

North Egmont Chalet

Parihaka Pa

Mt. Egmont

Stratford Mountain House

Stratford

Dawson Falls

······· Tracks (unsuitable for bikes)

0   10 km.
0   5   mi.

HAWERA TO NEW PLYMOUTH
VIA STRATFORD & OPUNAKE

Waitara

NEW PLYMOUTH   Bell Block

Oakura

Egmont Village
Inglewood

Okato   Pukeiti

N.

Pungarehu   Parihaka Pa

Midhurst

Mt. Egmont

Stratford

Rahotu

Ngaere

Eltham

Opunake

Kaponga

3

Manaia

Normanby

0 5 10 15 20 km.
0   5   10 mi.

45

Hawera

Mount Egmont (Photo by Richard Oddy)

Richmond Cottage (1853).

A proud symbol of Taranaki's vast reserves of oil and natural gas is the gas-fired power station on the western end of the city's waterfront. Its 198 m smokestack is visible from most parts of the city.

New Plymouth has numerous hotels, motels and guesthouses,

also a Youth Hostel. There is a motorcamp (cabins) just off S.H. 3, 3 km before reaching town, and others in Belt Rd., overlooking the port, and in Fitzroy, towards the eastern end of town.

■ *ALTERNATIVE DAY 4A HAWERA TO NEW PLYMOUTH VIA OPUNAKE*
106 km

This road is sealed, well-kept, generally quiet. It circles the mountain at a distance, a few kilometres inland from the sea, passing through rich and fertile farmlands. It dips frequently to cross streams, but rarely rises or falls more than 100 m, except between Okato and Oakura, on the last stretch to New Plymouth, where it passes the flanks of the Kaitake Range.

Manaia (pop. 1,016), 15 km from Hawera, is a farming centre. Two blockhouses built by the Armed Constabulary in 1880 are preserved here, on the golf-course, a short detour from the main road. The Kapuni natural gas field is 10 km further north. Manaia has a hotel. There is a motorcamp at Kaupokonui Beach 7km west and south.

Opunake (pop. 1,616), 29 km beyond Manaia, is another farming centre, but set right on the coast. There is a hotel here, and a motel, and a motorcamp beside the black-sand beach.

The Taranaki Coast is interesting: a long stretch of high sandstone cliffs washed by the sea at their foot and cut at intervals by streams and rivers escaping to the sea.

At 36 km from Opunake is Okato (pop. 463), and 12 km beyond that Oakura (pop. 969), a small holiday settlement. There is a motel and motorcamp here. At 4km before New Plymouth is Omata, where there are the remains of a military stockade.

■ **ALTERNATIVE ROUTE:** A strenuous but interesting alternative to the route through Okato and Oakura is via Parihaka and Pukeiti. Rahotu is a village 16 km north of Opunake. Take the second road right after Rahotu in the direction of the mountain. Three kilometres along, this passes Parihaka Pa, the former home of the Maori prophets, Te Whiti and Tohu, apostles of non-violence, who taught their people to passively resist the pakeha and all their ways. They tore up surveyors' pegs and fenced roads, and interfered with the process of settlement. In 1881 the pa was sacked by Government troops, who met no active resistance from the inhabitants, and Te Whiti and Tohu were arrested and held without trial for more than a year. Te Whiti died in 1907. His tomb stands on the marae.

Continue inland up the Parihaka road. After about 6 km turn left up Wiremu Rd, heading north around the mountain. After 7.5km, at the end of Wiremu Rd, turn right into Saunders Rd, and 1.5km along, left into Carrington Rd. This climbs to 460 m over 8 km, crossing over the saddle between the Pouakai and Kaitake Ranges. Near the top is the Pukeiti Rhododendron Trust, a 360 hectare reserve and bird sanctuary, famous for its rhododendrons and azaleas.

From Pukeiti, the road gradually drops down into New Plymouth, 29 km away. If you keep to Carrington Rd you will pass Hurworth 8 km from New Plymouth, where is preserved the charming and historic Hurworth homestead (1855–1856), built by the noted 19th century politician, Sir Harry Atkinson. ■

DAY 5 NEW PLYMOUTH TO AWAKINO ——————
90 km

Leave New Plymouth via Fitzroy St (S.H. 3) which runs slightly north of east from town. The road passes through the eastern suburbs of the city, and continues through the dormitory town of Bell Block (pop. 3,732), into Waitara (pop. 6,482), an industrial town 16 km from New Plymouth central.

Waitara was the site of the disputed purchase that was the initial spark of the Taranaki War. The first engagement in this war took place in March 1860 when British troops besieged Te Kohia Pa 3 km west of the present town.

Overlooking Waitara on the eastern side of the Waitara River is Manukorihi Pa, which has a fine carved meeting-house and a statue commemorating Sir Maui Pomare (1876–1930), a Maori politician and statesman, founder of the Young Maori Party in the early years of this century.

Waitara has several hotels and motels and a motorcamp (cabins). From Waitara, the road crosses a coastal plain for another 16 km to Urenui (pop. 391), a small town with a hotel and a motorcamp. There is another motorcamp (cabins) at Wai-iti Beach, a 7 km detour to the northeast off S.H. 3 on the Pukearuhe road.

Beyond Urenui, you will see a representation in concrete of the prow of a canoe, set in the fields to the right of the road. This is a memorial to Sir Peter Buck (Te Rangihiroa), a great scholar and ethnologist.

The road then turns inland, climbing slightly through the gorge of the Mimi River, and entering its long gentle valley. At 29 km beyond Urenui, a steep 3 km climb begins as the road climbs Mt. Messenger.

The road here reaches 189 m at the highest point, passes through a narrow tunnel, and winds steeply down to Ahititi. From Ahititi there is a gentler run down to the Tongaporutu River where it reaches the coast.

For much of the last 20 km to Awakino, the road runs inland from the sea, with only a few mild ups and downs.

At Mokau, 5 km from Awakino there is a store, a motel and a motorcamp (cabins). There is another motorcamp (cabins) 2 km before Awakino. At Awakino, a small holiday settlement near the mouth of its namesake river, is a store and a hotel.

DAY 6 AWAKINO TO THE WAITOMO CAVES VIA TE KUITI
93 km

This is perhaps the most difficult day of this particular itinerary, crossing as it does the King Country hills. If you have time, you might consider aiming for Te Kuiti (74 km) instead, and putting aside the next day to visit the Waitomo Caves.

Inland from Awakino, S.H. 3 skirts the Awakino River and enters the steep-sided and scenic Awakino Gorge. For most of the first 22 km from Awakino to Mahoenui, the road gradually rises, with short climbs and descents where it briefly leaves the river.

Beyond Mahoenui, a farming locality, there is a steep climb to 200 m, then the road descends to the Mangaotaki River, follows it briefly, and climbs two more sets of hills before Piopio, 20 km away. Piopio (pop. 492) is a small farming town set deep in the hills. There is a hotel here.

A relatively gentle stretch of road follows outside Piopio, after which there are two further steep saddles to cross before Te Kuiti.

Te Kuiti (pop. 4,787) was the headquarters of the Maori King from 1864 to 1881. After the King Country was opened up to pakeha, Te Kuiti became a railway construction camp as the Main Trunk Line was pushed through the central North Island. On the way into town, you will pass the ornately carved Tokanganui-a-noho meeting-house, built in 1878 by the followers of the Maori prophet and guerilla leader, Te Kooti Rikirangi (ca. 1830–1893).

Te Kuiti has hotels, motels and a motorcamp (cabins).

The Waitomo Caves are now 19 km away. Continue along S.H. 3 for another 10 km north of Te Kuiti to Hangatiki. Turn west here towards the caves.

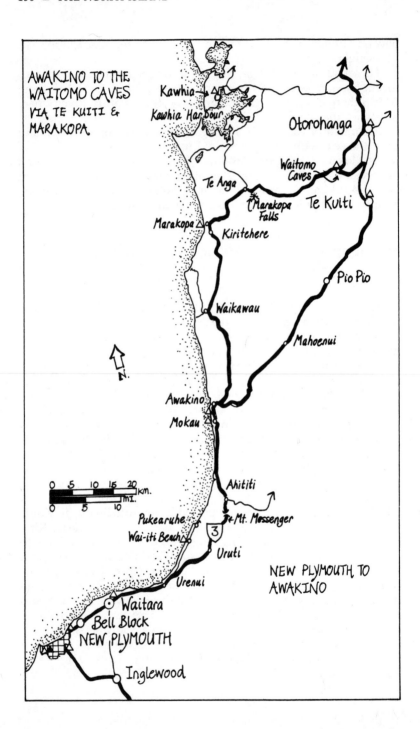

AWAKINO TO THE
WAITOMO CAVES
VIA TE KUITI &
MARAKOPA

Kawhia
Kawhia Harbour
Otorohanga
Te Anga
Waitomo Caves
Marakopa Falls
Te Kuiti
Marakopa
Kiritehere
Pio Pio
Waikawau
Mahoenui
N.
Awakino
Mokau
Ahititi
Mt. Messenger
Pukearuhe
Wai-iti Beach
Uruti
Urenui
NEW PLYMOUTH TO
AWAKINO
Waitara
Bell Block
NEW PLYMOUTH
Inglewood

0 5 10 15 20 km.
0 5 10 mi.

The Waitomo Caves have been carved out of limestone rock by underground streams and water seepage over the ages. They are famous for their naturally sculpted stalactites and stalagmites, and for their glow-worms.

The caves have been known to the Maori for centuries. They were first explored by a pakeha in 1887, and rapidly became a leading tourist attraction. Not all the caves have been surveyed, but tours of the best-known ones take place several times a day. The tours last about an hour.

There are further caves, Ruakuri and Aranui, 2 km west of Waitomo. Near Waitomo village is Ohaki, a replica of a pre-European fortified pa. Waitomo village has a hotel, a motel and a motorcamp (cabins).

■ *ALTERNATIVE DAY 6A* AWAKINO TO THE *WAITOMO CAVES VIA MARAKOPA*
108 km

This is a longer and more strenuous route than the one given above, and involves a considerable distance on gravel. However, the road is quieter and, in my opinion, more beautiful. You may care to split the distance in two and spend some time at Marakopa 56 km north of Awakino.

Turn off S.H. 3 across a bridge over the Awakino River 2 km inland from Awakino. A gravel road ascends the valley of the Manganui River, gradually climbing through the bush to 245 m over about 25 km. It then crosses a watershed and descends into Waikawau, an isolated farming valley.

> ■ **Side Trip:** a 4 km detour to the west brings you to the coast. Waikawau Beach is reached via a tunnel cut through a cliff. Before roads were put through to this region all goods had to be shipped in and out by sea, and this tunnel enabled carts carrying wool to reach the beach.

North of Waikawau, the road again climbs into the hills, reaching 300 m over 7 km before descending down the valley of the Kiritehere Stream. There is a short steep climb outside Kiritihere (you can avoid this if the tide is low by detouring seaward to Kiritehere Beach and walking up the coast) then an equally steep descent into Marokopa. From Kiritehere onwards, the road is sealed.

Marokopa is a tiny holiday settlement at the mouth of the Marakopa River. There is a store here, and a motorcamp.

At low tide, you can ford the Marokopa River below the village and walk for miles northwards along a lonely black-sand beach, your only company an occasional fisherman and the raucous seagulls.

At Marokopa, the road turns inland again, and there is a fairly gentle 14 km stretch to Te Anga, where there is a roadside tavern. At Te Anga the road forks. Take the southern fork (right), which shortly turns eastward.

A short walk from the road just beyond Te Anga are the spectacular Marokopa Falls, the four successive cascades of which drop a total of 60 m altogether.

From Te Anga to the Waitomo Caves is 34 km. The road ascends the Marokopa River much of the way, rising to 368 m to cross a watershed not far from Waitomo.

DAY 7 WAITOMO CAVES TO HUNTLY ——————
102–103km

Rather than return to S.H. 3, and if you do not mind gravel, take the Waitomo Valley Rd. northeast from Waitomo village. After 16 km this emerges onto S.H. 31 just west of Otorohanga. Turn left.

> ■ **Side Trip:** Alternatively, you might care for a detour to Otorohanga (pop. 2,747). The main attraction of this small market town is its kiwi house, where you can sometimes see these nocturnal birds in a simulated natural environment. Otorohanga has a hotel, a motel, an associate Youth Hostel and a motorcamp.

Twelve kilometres after joining S.H. 31, turn right (north) onto Syme Rd. towards Pirongia. This gradually turns west; 4 km along, you turn right (north) again.

You are now in gently rolling country, passing the lower slopes of Mt. Pirongia (959 m) on its eastern side. The small township of Pirongia due east of the main peak was the site of a redoubt during the latter stages of the Land Wars; this is still preserved on the western edge of the town. At Pirongia in 1881, the Maori King, Te Wherowhero Tawhiao, laid down his arms, bringing the wars to their close.

From Pirongia onwards the terrain is flat to gently undulating. You initially take the Hamilton road northward from town, through Te Rore, Ngahinapouri and Tuhikaramea. Just north of Tuhikaramea, which is 19 km from Pirongia, turn north to Whatawhata rather than west to Temple View and Hamilton.

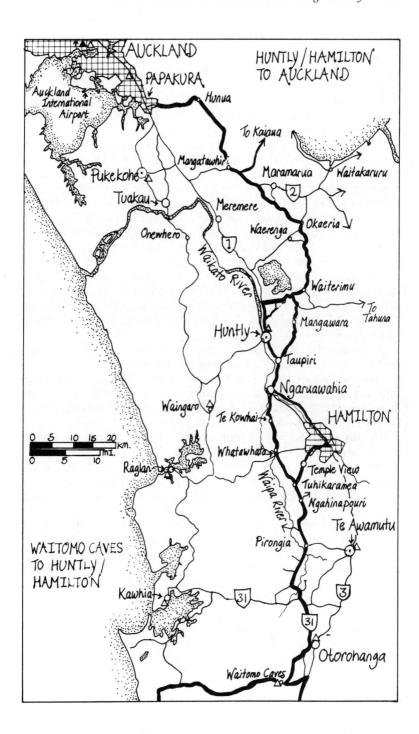

HUNTLY / HAMILTON
TO AUCKLAND

WAITOMO CAVES
TO HUNTLY/
HAMILTON

Whatawhata is a roadside village (store) on S.H. 23, 10 km from Tuhikaramea. Cross S.H. 23 and continue north to Te Kowhai, and from Te Kowhai to Ngaruawahia, entering the town from the south.

Ngaruawahia (pop. 4,369) is notable for being the headquarters of the King movement. The official residence of the Maori Queen is at Turangawaewae Marae, on the northern side of town.

Ngaruawahia has long been an important Maori settlement, situated as it is on the confluence of the Waikato and Waipa Rivers—before roads and rail these were the principal transport routes. At Ngaruawahia in 1858, with the accession of Te Wherowhero, King Potautau I, the institution of the Maori kingship was established. This was a protest against the encroachment of pakeha on Maori lands, and a symbol of Maori mistrust of pakeha motives.

War broke out in the Waikato in 1863. The Kingite forces built a great pa at Ngarauwahia, but it was taken by the British in 1863 and used as an encampment. The turret of one of the British gunboats used at the time still sits on the riverbank near the centre of town. Ngaruawahia is the scene of a great regatta every year, on the nearest Saturday to St. Patricks Day, among the events being canoe races.

Ngaruawahia has a motel but no motorcamp. The nearest motorcamp is at Huntly 14 km north (see below).

Between Ngaruawahia and Huntly you join S.H. 1, the main highway north. This is a very busy road, fortunately with wide shoulders much of the way. Beware, however, of a curving bridge just beyond Taupiri (pop. 439) 6 km beyond Ngaruawahia.

Huntly (pop. 6,750) is a mining town. In the vicinity are a number of opencast and underground mines, branches of which have undermined some areas of the town. On the western side of the Waikato River, slightly to the north, stands a massive coal-fired electric power station. Huntly also has a small but interesting local museum.

There is a hotel, a motel and a municipal motorcamp in the town. The motor camp is in Wright St., beside the Domain. Follow the main road through the shopping centre and take the first road that crosses the railway line to the right. Immediately across the tracks, turn right again into Hakanoa St., then first left into Park Avenue and first left again into Wright St.

■ **Side Trip:** There are few if any suitably private spots for free camping on S.H. 1 between Ngaruawahia and Huntly. If you want to camp out, you might do better by heading along the unfrequented western bank of the river. Cross the

Waipa River on the western edge of Ngaruawahia and turn
north on the other side. A gravel road leads all the way to
Huntly West.

DAY 8 HUNTLY TO AUCKLAND ——————————
97 km–115 km

Leave Huntly via S.H. 1, which runs northward along the banks
of the Waikato River, offering good views of the thermal power station opposite. Eight kilometres north of Huntly is the village of
Ohinewai. Turn right (east) here along a good sealed road
signposted to Tahuna.

At 7km out of Waiterimu, veer northeast to Waiterimu. Four
kilometres beyond Waiterimu you come to a crossroads. Turn left
(north). Ten kilometres further on is a T-intersection. Turn left
here along Waeranga Rd., and immediately right along Okaeria Rd.

Okaeria is a tiny forest settlement, no more than one or two
houses. Turn left here (west then northwest) towards Maramarua.
At 8 km from Okaeria the road forks. The right fork leads to
Maramarua; take the left fork which climbs gradually north-
westwards to emerge on S.H. 2, 13 km later.

Follow S.H. 2, (a very busy road) westward for 7 km to
Mangatawhiri, a roadside village with a store. Just beyond
Mangatawhiri turn right (northeast) towards Happy Valley and
Hunua.

For the first 2 km, the road is flat, running along the
Mangatawhiri Stream; then it climbs steeply through the hills for
another 2 km. There follows a gentle 16 km run through Happy Valley and Paparimu to Hunua.

■ **Side Trip:** Two kilometres east of Hunua are the Hunua
Falls, where there is a sheltered picnic area beside the pool
beneath the falls.

From Hunua, the 15 km to Papakura, after a small amount of
climbing, is mostly a downhill run through the picturesque Hunua
Gorge. Enter Papakura past the industrial estate at the southeastern edge of town.

Turn right from Hunua Rd. into Settlement Rd., then take the
fifth street right off Settlement Rd. for the railway station. Suburban trains depart for the city from here Monday to Friday between 5.49 A.M. and 5.35 P.M.

If cycling into the city, however, continue along Railway St. into

Broadway and turn right into Great South Rd. It is 31 km from here to the centre of Auckland (see Tour 4, Day 1).

■ ALTERNATIVE ROUTE: Waitomo Caves to Auckland via Hamilton

■ DAY 7A WAITOMO CAVES TO HAMILTON ———
74 km

Follow the instructions above to Tuhikaramea. Just north of Tuhikaramea, turn west towards Temple View and Hamilton. The road is flat to undulating the rest of the way to the city.

Temple View (pop. 1,364) is the site of New Zealand's largest Mormon temple. Hamilton's suburbs begin 3 km beyond.

At the first major intersection you come to on entering Hamilton, take the eastern fork (Killarney Rd.). After 1.5 km you will come to the western edge of Lake Hamilton. Turn left (northeast) along Domain Drive around the lakeside. Climb away from the lake via Tainui St. to the left. This leads into Ward St. which, within 0.5 km, brings you to Victoria St., the city's main commercial street.

The nearest motorcamp is the municipal campground in Ruakura Rd. Turn right (southeast) down Victoria St. Three blocks along, veer left into Grantham St. and cross the river. Beyond the bridge (which is dangerously narrow—ride far enough out from the edge to prevent traffic from trying to overtake), turn right into Grey St., then first left into Clyde St. Clyde St. continues eastward; take the third street to the left, which is Peachgrove Rd. Just over 1 km along, turn right into Ruakura Rd.

There is another motorcamp nearby, which has cabins. Instead of turning into Peachgrove Rd., continue along Clyde St. until the eighth street to the left, Cameron Rd. Turn left here.

Besides its motorcamps, Hamilton has numerous hotels and motels. The Youth Hostel is in Grantham St., beside the river.

Hamilton (pop. 94,511) is New Zealand's fourth largest city. It is a manufacturing and commercial centre, and the service town for the vast and rich Waikato lowlands. It was founded in 1864, in the aftermath of the Land Wars, when military settlers took up grants of confiscated Maori land.

The city straddles the Waikato River, with parks and pleasant walks along its banks. The Waikato Art Gallery and Museum is one of New Zealand's finest. The gunboat *Rangiriri*, the hulk of which for years rested on the riverbank, is being restored as a reminder of the past. Hamilton also has a University and a major agricultural research centre.

The Public Relations Office is in Barton St. North.

■ *DAY 8A* HAMILTON TO AUCKLAND ————————
125 km–156 km

Take River Rd. out of the city. This runs along the eastern bank of the Waikato River. It is a quiet road, mostly through gentle terrain, though dipping once or twice to cross streams.

Ngaruawahia is 19 km away. You enter town past Turangawaewae Marae. Turn left along S.H. 1 to reach the centre of town, or right to continue northwards.

Follow S.H. 1 for the 8 km to Taupiri. Just beyond the village, turn northeast along a good sealed road that runs across the plains southeast of Taupiri Mountain.

Five kilometres from Taupiri, turn left into Rutherford Rd. and continue to Mangawara. Turn left onto the Tahuna-Ohinewai road about 1.5 km beyond Mangawara, then right towards Waiterimu. From here, follow the instructions given for 7A above.

■ **ALTERNATIVE ROUTE:** you could instead head for Kaiaua instead of Hunua, stop there overnight, and continue into Auckland the next day. If you decide to take this option, turn right (northeast) towards Kaiaua, 4 km along S.H. 2 from Maramarua Mill. A gentle valley road with stretches of moderate climbing leads the 15 km to the coast. Kaiaua is only 76 km from Huntly; you may prefer to continue another 23 km to Orere Point, where there is another motorcamp. ■

SOUTH ISLAND TOURS

Takaka
Picton
Motueka
Karamea
(14) NELSON
Blenheim
Westport
St Arnaud
Reefton
(9)
Greymouth
Hanmer Springs
Springs Junction
(11)
Kaikoura
Hokitika
(9)
Arthurs Pass
Franz Josef
(14)
(11)
Fox Glacier
Rakaia Gorge
Mt Cook
(12)
CHRISTCHURCH
Haast →
(14)
Tekapo
(10)
Akaroa
Wanaka
(12)
Cromwell
Naseby
Alexandra
(13)
Te Anau
(15)
DUNEDIN
Tuatapere
(13)
(13)
INVERCARGILL

N.

50   100 Km.
0   50   mi.

Numbers refer to tours
subsequently described

PART III

THE
SOUTH
ISLAND

First World War Memorial, Picton

TOUR 9. PICTON TO CHRISTCHURCH

3–5 days: 346 km

Marlborough is the northeastern corner of the South Island, a region which consists of the drowned river valleys of the Marlborough Sounds, the wide, open plains of the Wairau Valley, and high surrounding mountains.

European settlement began in this region in 1827, with the establishment of a whaling station in Tory Channel in the Sounds. There were few other pakeha in the area, however, until after the founding of neighbouring Nelson in 1842, when land-seekers began to push through the intervening hills.

A disputed land-purchase led to a bloody clash at Tuamarina in 1843, between would-be settlers and Maoris under the Ngati Toa chief, Te Rangihatea. Twenty-two pakeha and six Maori died in that affray.

The New Zealand government subsequently purchased much of the area, largely to avoid further bloodshed. The pakeha took over, felling the bush on the river plains and in the hills, and establishing huge sheep-runs in the mountains of the interior.

Until the establishment of the Cook Strait road-rail ferry in 1962, Marlborough was an isolated and little-known region. Even today it remains sparsely populated. Blenheim (pop. 18,308) is its largest town, and Picton (pop. 3,563) and Kaikoura (pop. 2,209) its only other settlements of any size. The main wealth of Marlborough is its sheep, but tourism is important in the Sounds, and the Wairau Valley is becoming known for its quality wines.

Marlborough is one of the sunniest regions in the country, with Blenheim referring to itself as the "sunshine capital" of New Zealand. In summer, the Wairau Valley is hot and dry, although sea breezes temper the heat along the coast. The high-country inland is cooler, with permanent snow on the tallest peaks.

DAY 1 PICTON TO SEDDON
53 km

Follow Auckland St. and Wairau Rd. southward towards Blenheim. There is a gentle 1km rise on the outskirts of Picton, then a curving 1km descent to a gentle river valley. The remaining 26 km to Blenheim are mostly flat. Traffic is light, unless a car ferry has just berthed.

Nineteen kilometres south of Picton is the small township of Tuamarina. Near here, the Wairau incident (formerly known as the Wairau "massacre") took place. A signpost marks the spot.

Three kilometres further on is Spring Creek. Less than 1 km to the right is a pleasant motorcamp (cabins) that is sometimes the location an Easter cycle-touring rally.

Blenheim has a number of hotels and motels, and several motorcamps. The easiest to find is in Grove Rd., the name given to S.H. 1 on the northern approach to the town. Blenheim's attractions include Brayshaw Park, an extensive agricultural and historical museum to the west of town.

Follow Grove Rd. into the centre, veering right over a bridge just before the main shopping centre, then immediately left into Symonds St., then first left (east) along Main St. This street takes you out of town as it gradually turns southeastward.

Four kilometres outside Blenheim a restored cob cottage dating back to the early days of pakeha settlement is worth a stop. Not far beyond, you leave the Wairau Plains, with a tough, winding 5 km ascent over the Weld and Dashwood passes.

Seddon, 24 km south of Blenheim, is a village notable only for being named after one of New Zealand's best-known politicians, the Liberal Premier, Richard John Seddon (1845–1906). It is, however, a convenient stop for the night. There is a motorcamp in

Nursery Lane, off S.H. 1 immediately south of the railway bridge.
The nearest motel is at Ward, 22 km further south; there are also
cabins at Ward.

DAY 2 SEDDON TO KAIKOURA
104 km

South of Seddon, the road passes through 6 km of rolling hills
before reaching Lake Grassmere, a shallow lagoon which is the
site of New Zealand's only salt-works (The white conical piles in
the distance on the seaward side of the road are mounds of salt.)

The route from Lake Grassmere to Ward ranges from flat to undulating. Ward is a tiny roadside settlement with a motel, cabins
and tearooms. Beyond Ward comes a 1 km climb, then a long descent to meet the sea just north of Wharanui, 36 km south of Seddon. Between here and Kaikoura the road runs mostly along the
coast, and there are no further hills to climb.

For the next 26 km to Clarence the road passes between high,
eroded hills on the right, and long lonely shingle beaches on the
left. Good spots for free camping are plentiful, though in summer
there may be difficulty finding water. One possible spot is at
Kekerengu, 6 km south of Wharanui, where there are tearooms
and, behind the tearooms, a grassy flat set beside a small lagoon.
Note that swimming in the sea is dangerous here, as along much of
the Kaikoura Coast.

One peculiarity of this stretch of road is the number of fords.
These are mostly dry during the summer. During the spring melt,
these dry beds become torrents, and traffic must use the adjacent
one-lane bridges.

At Clarence, a tiny roadside settlement, S.H. 1 turns briefly inland to cross the shingle-braided Clarence River, before rejoining
the coast. There is a motorcamp at Waipapa Bay, 7 km beyond
Clarence. The next 20 km are particularly scenic, as the road and ac-
companying railway line wind along a narrow ledge between steep
cliffs and rocky coves and bays.

The last 12 km into Kaikoura are flat, as the road veers inland
again to cross the plain north of the town.

Kaikoura is set at the base of the Kaikoura Peninsula and com-
mands fine views of the Seaward Kaikoura Mountains across the
bay. It began life as a whaling settlement, and is today a fishing
port and farming and holiday centre, and offers a wide choice of
hotels and motels. These are mostly set along the Esplanade, the
waterfront road running southeast from the town centre. The
Youth Hostel is also on the Esplanade.

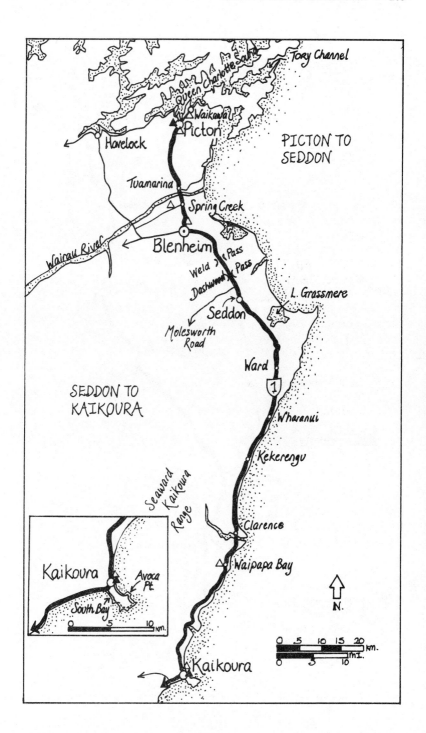

Tory Channel

Queen Charlotte Sound

Waikawa
Picton

Havelock

PICTON TO
SEDDON

Tuamarina

Spring Creek

Wairau River

Blenheim

Weld Pass
Dashwood Pass

L. Grassmere

Seddon

Molesworth
Road

Ward

1

SEDDON TO
KAIKOURA

Wharanui

Kekerengu

Seaward
Kaikoura
Range

Clarence

Waipapa Bay

Kaikoura

Avoca
Pt.

South Bay

0   5   10 km.

N.

0 5 10 15 20 km.
0   5   10 mi.

Kaikoura

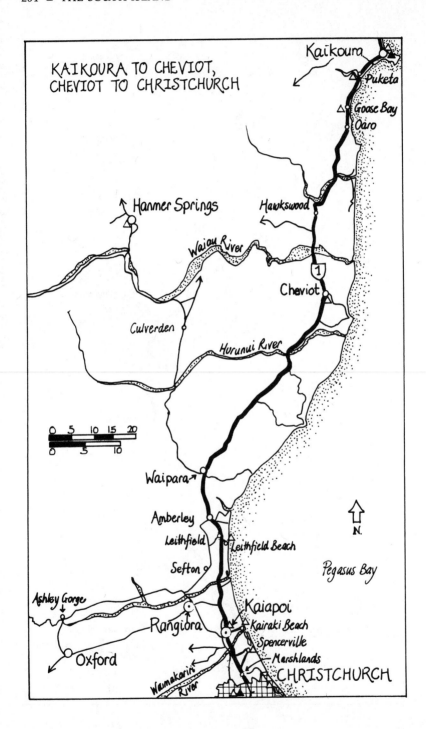

KAIKOURA TO CHEVIOT,
CHEVIOT TO CHRISTCHURCH

Nineteenth-century cob cottage outside Blenheim

There is a motorcamp (cabins) on Beach Rd., the main road into town; also a caravan park with cabins (but no tent sites) on the Esplanade. There are cabins at South Bay on the opposite side of the Peninsula, and motorcamps with cabins on S.H. 1, 7 km and 18 km south of Kaikoura.

Kaikoura's main attraction apart from its beaches is the seal colony at the eastern tip of the Peninsula. This can be reached by bike by following the Esplanade which, as it turns eastward, becomes Avoca Rd., then Fyfe Quay, before coming to an end 5 km beyond the town centre. Along the way, you pass the fishing port, also a marine laboratory run by Canterbury University, with a video display for visitors.

At the end of the road is a walkway 4km long which joins Kaka Rd. on the southern side of the Peninsula, from which you can rejoin S.H. 1. The Kaikoura Peninsula is a notable site of early Maori settlement, with numerous pa sites, some of them excavated in recent years. Fyfe House (1859), the home of one of the earliest pakeha settlers in these parts, stands on Avoca Point.

DAY 3 KAIKOURA TO CHEVIOT ———————
75km

This may not seem a long day in terms of distance, but it is in terms of effort, for there is some strenuous climbing to do.

Leave Kaikoura via S.H. 1 to the south. There is a minor rise to climb as you leave town; then the road descends again to the sea, and hugs the coast for 22 km. This is a very picturesque stretch. Just beyond Puketa, 8km south of Kaikoura (there is a motorcamp with cabins here) are two short road tunnels. Keep well to the left. At Goose Bay, 10 km beyond Puketa, is another motorcamp with cabins, also a motel and tearooms. There are cabins at Oaro, 4 km further on.

Oaro is where S.H. 1 leaves the coast, turning inland into the hills. For the first 3 km it winds gently up the valley of the Oaro River, then rises suddenly and steeply over 3 km to a height of 886 m. This is a very tough climb indeed.

A winding 1.5 km descent follows. There is a pleasant rest area beside the stream at the bottom. Then there is another 1.5 km ascent, a 2.5 km descent, a 1km ascent and—finally and thankfully—a 3.5 km descent to the Conway River.

For the next 10 km the road undulates up the river valley. There is a motorcamp at Hawkswood at the southern end of the valley. A flat 4 km stretch follows, and the last 10 km are through gently rolling country.

Cheviot is a small country town with several shops and a hotel and motel. There is a caravan park behind the hotel which also offers tent sites. Free campers who decide to carry on will find good sites along the Hurunui River 10 km further south.

DAY 4 CHEVIOT TO CHRISTCHURCH ———————
114 km

The first 10 km south of Cheviot are undulating to rolling, followed by 20 km of a gentle and almost imperceptible ascent of the Hurunui and Greta River valleys, followed in turn by the only hill of any significance during the day, at the head of the Greta Valley. Most of the last 25 km to Waipara are gently downhill or flat.

This is pleasant countryside, watered by fast-moving rivers which are fed by melting snows in the mountains, and sheltered by fine stands of willows and poplars. At Waipara (pop. 842), however, the Canterbury Plains begin, stretching from here all the way to Christchurch. In summer, the plains shimmer in the heat; in winter icy southerlies sweep across them.

Like the scenery, the small towns that stud the plain—Waipara, Amberley, Leithfield—have no great interest for the casual passerby. Traffic across the plains is fast-moving and increases in volume approaching Christchurch, but the road has wide shoulders much of the way.

35 km beyond Waipara is the entrance to the northern motorway into the city. You will have to avoid this, of course, ignoring the green signs which direct motorists to turn right, and continuing south instead along the old S.H. 1 through Kaiapoi (pop. 5,234).

Beyond Kaipoi, continue southwards across the wide Waimakariri River. Two kilometres south of the river is another motorway junction. Again, do not get confused by the signs which direct traffic to the right for Christchurch, but continue southwards instead along Marshland Rd. A long, bumpy, busy 8km straight brings you into Shirley, the northernmost of Christchurch's suburbs.

■ **ALTERNATIVE ROUTE:** If you have time to spare, you could avoid some of busy Marshland Rd. by turning right into Hawkins Rd. 4 km along the straight. This meanders southward, leading to Hills Rd., which leads to Briggs Rd., which leads to Emmett St., which leads to Shirley Rd. Turn right into Shirley Rd. and see the instructions below. ■

Marshland Rd. finishes at an intersection opposite a school (Shirley Intermediate). The city centre is now 3.5 km to the southwest. Perhaps the quickest way there is to turn right along Shirley Rd. (which shortly becomes Warrington St.), then take the tenth road to the left, which is Barbadoes St. After six blocks, you cross the Avon River. Turn right along Kilmore St. then third left into Colombo St. for Cathedral Square.

■ **ALTERNATIVE ROUTE:** The above roads are all busy ones. A longer but more pleasant route, and one marked as a cycle route by route markers erected by the Christchurch City Council, is to continue through the Marshlands Rd./Shirley St. intersection into North Parade and follow this as it snakes southwards to become Evelyn Couzins Rd. Turn off this to the right into Swanns Rd., continuing westward along Draper St. and Heywood St., and across Fitzgerald Ave. into Cambridge Terrace. Follow this along the northern bank of the Avon River, cross the Avon at Madras Ave., and continue along the southern bank on Oxford Terrace. Two blocks along, a left turn southwards down Colombo St. will bring you to Cathedral Square. ■

Christchurch, of course, has numerous hotels and motels, also a Youth Hostel and several private budget hostels. There are several motorcamps. The nearest to the city centre is the Addington Showgrounds Camp 3km southeast of Cathedral Square (phone 3897700). To get there, continue along Colombo St. southward from the Square, take the seventh right turn into Moorhouse St., and the seventh left, into Hagley Ave. The motorcamp (cabins) is in the showground, which is 1km along Hagley Ave. It is closed during showtime in early November.

There are other motorcamps in Riccarton and on the Yaldhurst Rd. west of the city centre.

The New Zealand Tourist and Publicity Department has an office in Cathedral Square, and the Canterbury Information Centre is at 75 Worcester St. nearby (phone 799629)

Some cyclists may prefer not to arrive in a large city in the late afternoon or evening, but to stop somewhere outside the city for

Dinghy on the seashore, Kaikoura

the night. In this case there are several possibilities, as outlined below.

At Amberley, 10 km south of Waipara and 48 km from Christchurch, there is a motel and a caravan park with cabins. There is also a motel and a motorcamp at Leithfield Beach 4 km south and a 3 km detour seawards.

There is a motel and a motorcamp (cabins) on the Main North Road outside Kaiapoi, 19 km north of Christchurch, and there is also a municipal motorcamp at Kairaki Beach, 4 km due east.

There is yet another motorcamp (cabins) at Spencerville, 14 km north of Cathedral Square. Turn east for Spencerville at the Marshlands Rd. junction just south of the Waimakariri River.

Finally, there are motorcamps in New Brighton, 9 km from Cathedral Square on the city's eastern coast. 5 km along Marshland Rd., turn left (east) into Prestons Rd. At the end of Prestons Rd., turn right into Burwood Rd. and continue south for 1.5 km to Travis Rd. Turn left here and follow Travis Rd. for 2 km to a major roundabout, past Queen Elizabeth II Park. Take Leaver Terrace, which runs slightly north of east out of the roundabout. Then take the second road to the right, Shaw Avenue, which crosses Bowhill Rd. and continues through Rawhiti Domain and golf course. The Rawhiti Domain motorcamp (phone 887408) is in the Domain off Shaw Ave. This motorcamp is open summers only, from the beginning of December to the end of March. There is another motorcamp, South New Brighton Park (phone 889844) (cabins), in Halsey St 2 km further south. To get there, turn left off Shaw Avenue towards the sea, then right into Marine Parade. Halsey St. runs west from Marine Parade.

Cyclist and friend in front of Christchurch Cathedral

TOUR 10. CHRISTCHURCH

With its numerous parks and gardens, its stands of mature trees, and its fine old stone buildings, Christchurch has a mature, mellow, age-old atmosphere. In fact, less than one hundred and fifty years ago, the site where the city now stands was little more than a swampy plain. Christchurch's first permanent inhabitants were the farming brothers, William and John Deans, whose first cottage, constructed in 1843, is still preserved in Riccarton. The city really got underway, however, in 1850 with the arrival of the "first five ships" of the colonizing Canterbury Association.

The city grew rapidly in size and wealth. Settlers pushed inland, dividing the plains and mountains into great farms and sheep-runs, and exporting their wool through Christchurch and itss port of Lyttleton. Christchurch became a notably conservative city, its buildings and institutions mirroring as exactly as possible those of the England most of the first settlers left behind.

Today it is the South Island's largest city, and New Zealand's third-largest urban area (pop. 299,373). It is a manufacturing and commercial centre, also a University and a Cathedral town.

Most of the urban area is flat, although the southernmost suburbs have spread into the Port Hills. Despite its flatness, Christchurch is a lovely city, well worth an extended visit. Its main drawback perhaps is its weather. In summer the city is often beset by the strong and enervating nor'wester wind (more of this later), and in winter by icy southerlies.

Notable sites in or near the centre of Christchurch include the Victorian Gothic Christ Church (1864) in Cathedral Square, the High Renaissance Roman Catholic Basilica (1905), the Provincial Council Buildings (1859–1865), and the new Town Hall (1972). To the west of Cathedral Square and at the entrance to Hagley Park are the Canterbury Museum, the Robert McDougall Art Gallery, and Christ College buildings. Hagley Park itself is a vast expanse of lawns and playing-fields and mature trees. The Botanic Gardens are situated here.

The Canterbury Information Centre, 75 Worcester Square, will provide maps and other information. There is also an office of the New Zealand Tourist and Publicity Department in Cathedral Square.

Excursions from Christchurch

If you intend spending much time in the city or vicinity, I recommend getting hold of Helen Crabb's book *Cycling in Christchurch and Canterbury* (1983). While it remains in print, this is available from the Canterbury Cyclists Association, P.O. Box 2547, Christchurch, and from some bike shops. You could have a look at it in the City Library instead. The Christchurch City Council has also produced the *Christchurch Cycle Map,* a multi-coloured guide to suitable roads for cycling and cycle tracks in the urban area. This is available from the Canterbury Information Centre or from the City Council Traffic Division, 163 Tuam St.

Two interesting excursions outside the city are also described below. The first takes you into the Port Hills, along a steep ridge which separates Christchurch from Lyttleton Harbour. The second is a two- or three-day excursion to Akaroa, a town founded by French settlers, and nestled in the rugged hills of Banks Peninsula beside the Akaroa Harbour.

The uplands of Banks Peninsula are a striking contrast to the Canterbury Plains below. Some millennia ago, the peninsula was a volcanic island. Its two harbours, Lyttleton and Akaroa, are drowned craters, that is, volcanic craters which have been invaded by the sea.

Banks Peninsula is a farming area, but also a holiday playground for Christchurch. Yachtsmen appreciate its deep coves and bays, and holiday houses line its more accessible beaches.

EXCURSION 10A Summit Road

1. NORTHERN SUMMIT ROAD
39 km

The Summit Road wanders along the high ridge of the Port Hills, offering magnificent views over both Christchurch to the north and Lyttleton and the Banks Peninsula to the south. The road was planned by Harry Ell (1862–1934), who also built several mock-Tudor roadhouses or refreshment stops along its route, of which two, the Sign of the Takahe and the Sign of the Kiwi, are in use today.

Take Colombo St. due south from Cathedral Square. It crosses the Heathcote River 3 km from the square and, shortly afterward, leads into the Dyers Pass Rd. A steep 2km climb to the Sign of the Takahe (tearooms and restaurant) at 193 m follows. The next 4 km are a somewhat gentler climb to the Sign of the Kiwi (refreshments) at 332 m.

Turn left (east) along Summit Rd, which meanders along the ridge. It can be exposed and windy, but is very scenic. Watch out for ice in winter.

Seven kilometres from the Sign of the Kiwi, Summit Rd. crosses the Bridle Path. This was, at the time of first settlement, the principle route by land between Christchurch and Lyttleton. Seven kilometres further along is Evans Pass (193 m). From here the road drops 3 km to Sumner, a seaside suburb to the east of Christchurch city.

From Sumner, detour further around the coast to Taylor's Mistake. This is a rocky little cove with colourful little baches built right into the cliffs. Or return the 12 km to Christchurch central direct. Follow Main Rd. along the harbour's edge to the mouth of

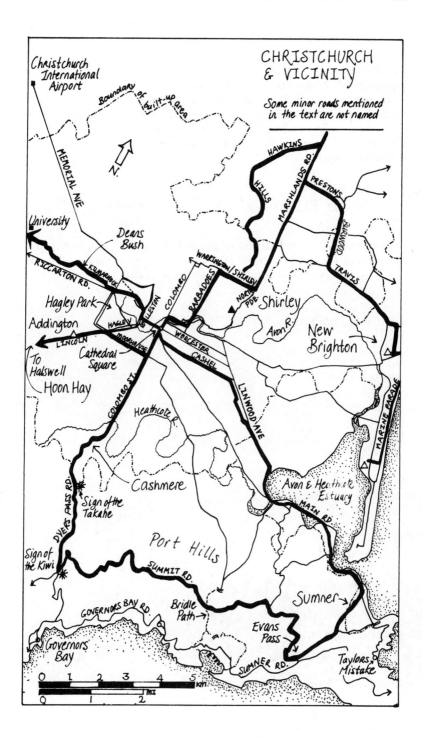

the Heathcote River. Across the river, turn right into Humphreys Dr. An official cycle route begins here—follow the signs along Humphreys Dr., which veers northwest into Linwood Ave. One and one-half kilometre along Linwood Ave., a short stretch of cycle path begins, which turns northward across a small park. On the eastern boundary of the park, cross Aldwins Rd. into Marlborough St., take the first right into Havelock St., and first left into Cashel St. The cycle route ends in Manchester St., one block southeast of Cathedral Square.

2. SUMMIT ROAD AND LYTTLETON ─────────────
50 km

Lyttleton is easily reached by car or bus via the Lyttleton Tunnel (opened in 1961) through the Port Hills. This option is forbidden to cyclists, however, who must make the steep climb over the hills.

Lyttleton Harbour from the Port Hills (Photo by Mark Lawson)

Follow the instructions given above as far as Evans Pass. At Evans Pass, turn south to Lyttleton, rather than north to Sumner. The road drops steeply for 3 km, entering Lyttleton to the east above the wharves.

Lyttleton (pop. 3,200) is a minor borough but a major port, with a container terminal and roll-on/roll-off facilities, and factories and warehouses spreading along reclaimed land on the foreshore.

Sights to see include the Timeball Station (1876), which is set in the hills at the eastern edge of town. This was once used to signal ships, but is now preserved by the New Zealand Historic Places Trust as a historic monument. Lyttleton also has a historical museum, and several old churches.

Sumner St. leads into London St., which passes through the centre of town in a northwesterly direction. Turn left off London St. down Dublin St., then veer gradually right along Simeon Quay above the wharves. The Governors Bay Rd. is the second road to the left off Simeon Quay.

Continue around the harbour westward from the town. The road hugs the coast, climbing over several ridges on its way to Governors Bay, a small holiday village, 9 km away. Turn north here up Dyers Pass Rd. A steep and strenuous 4 km climb will bring you to the Sign of the Kiwi. From here, you retrace your route, downhill this time, from the city.

EXCURSION 10B Akaroa

149 km–165 km

Allow at least two days and possible three—this is quite a strenuous trip.

DAY 1 CHRISTCHURCH TO AKAROA
83 km

There are several alternative routes out of town, but the following is an official cycle route and marked as such. Take Worcester St. west from Cathedral Square to the edge of Hagley Park. Turn left (south) down Rolleston Ave. and cross the Avon River past Christchurch Hospital into Antigua St. One and one-half kilometres south of the river, veer right into Bletsoe Rd. At the end of Bletsoe Rd., cross a small park and Barrington St. into Wychbury Rd. Turn right into Glynne Rd., which leads into Domain Terrace leading northeastward. Turn left (southwest) off Domain Terrace into Lincoln Rd., which shortly becomes Halswell Rd. (S.H. 75).

This leads through the suburbs of Hoon Hay, Oaklands and Halswell into the open country. Taitapu, a wayside village with a general store, is 12 km south of Halswell. The road is straight and flat all the way, but a more pleasant alternative is to turn onto the old Taitapu road just south of Halswell. This meanders along the Halswell River at the western edge of the Port Hills, and adds only 2 km to the faster alternative of S.H. 75.

The next 35 km range from flat to gently undulating as the road turns southeastward along the northern shores of Lake Ellesmere, then northeastward from Birdlings Flat towards Little River.

There are tearooms and a store at Motukarara, 9 km beyond Taitapu. Lake Ellesmere is a large but shallow lake (it covers an area of 276 square kilometres but has an average depth of only 3 m) which is a notable breeding ground and sanctuary for waterfowl: duck, swan, pukeko and other wading birds. Birdlings Flat, a slight detour from the main road, is an untidy huddle of coastal baches on the barren Kaitorete Spit, which separates Lake Ellesmere from the sea. This area is notorious for its high winds.

Not far beyond Little River (store, hotel), the climbing starts. You wind your way upwards for 8 km to Hill Top (457 m). There is a pub here. The road then drops 5 km to Barrys Bay on the northern shores of the Akaroa Harbour.

Akaroa is now only 14 km away in distance, but quite a way in effort. The harbourside road is a pleasant one, but strenuous, since it climbs over four headlands in quick succession, past Duvauchelle (motorcamp, hotel), Robinson Bay and Takamatua.

Akaroa (pop. 722) is a pretty town set on the sunny western slopes of the harbour. It was settled by French colonists sponsored by the Nanto-Bordelaise Company in 1840. They had set out hoping to play a part in establishing a new French colony in the South Pacific, but were disappointed to find the British flag already planted by the time of their arrival.

The street names of Akaroa and some features of its architecture still bear witness to the town's origins. A small monument on the foreshore marks the landing place of the French. There is a museum in the Langlos-Éteveneaux house (1841), an old customhouse (1852), and several old churches. Many of the town's cottages preserve their colonial style, and much of Akaroa is now a conservation area: new buildings and additions must fit the existing character of the town.

Akaroa has several hotels and motels, also a motorcamp (cabins).

The motorcamp is in Rue Balqueri. S.H. 75 turns into Rue Levaud which runs southeastward through the bottom of town. Turn left onto Rue Balqueri above the wharf.

DAY 2 *AKAROA TO DIAMOND HARBOUR*
48 km

You can, of course, return to Christchurch the way you came. A far more difficult, but more interesting, alternative is to return via Pigeon Bay, Port Levy and Diamond Harbour.

Follow S.H. 75 back as far as Robinson Bay. At the top of the headland past the bay, turn right along the Okains Bay Rd. This climbs steeply for the next 4 km to more than 500 m.

You are now on Summit Rd. Turn left (west). Summit Rd. wanders along a high ridge with magnificent views to north and south. At 13 km, turn right down Kukupa Rd., and drop the 6 km to Pigeon Bay on the northern side of the Peninsula. Pigeon Bay has a general store, a Youth Hostel and a campground.

The seal ends here. The next few kilometres to Port Levy are gravel, rough, dusty and difficult. There is a tough 4 km climb out of Pigeon Bay to a height of 460 km, then a 5 km drop to Port Levy. Turn inland at the foot of the bay to Purau and Diamond Harbour.

Another tough 3 km climb to 400 m follows. The road then drops to Purau and follows the coast to Diamond Harbour.

Diamond Harbour is a small coastal town and maritime suburb of Lyttleton. It has a hotel. There is a motorcamp (cabins) at Purau Bay.

The stretch of road between Diamond Harbour and Pigeon Bay is due for upgrading. When this is completed (date unknown) it will become an easier ride—but traffic, at present light, will increase.

DAY 3 DIAMOND HARBOUR TO CHRISTCHURCH —
18–34 km

You can return via Lyttleton or via Governors Bay. A launch runs between Diamond Harbour and Lyttleton several times a day between November 1 and Easter, and weekdays only between Easter and October 31. From Lyttleton to Christchurch via Evans Pass (see above) is 18 km.

Alternatively, head southeast along the harbour's edge from Diamond Harbour. There is one climb to do before Teddington, where the road turns north, and two more minor climbs over headlands, before reaching Governors Bay. This is a holiday and retirement settlement, an especially pretty place in autumn. There is an interesting church here, St. Cuthberts (1862), with cob walls; also a shop and a hotel.

From Governors Bay, return to Christchurch via Dyers Pass (see above).

▪ **ALTERNATIVE ROUTE: BYPASSING CHRISTCHURCH** If you want to head south instead of returning all the way to Christchurch, you can save some distance by heading straight to the Rakaia Gorge.

If returning from Akaroa via S.H. 75, the distance from Akaroa to the Rakaia Gorge is 144 km. The nearest formal campground is at Alford Forest, 18 km further south. This is perhaps too long a distance for one day. You could consider leaving Akaroa lateish, and camping overnight somewhere around Little River.

Follow S.H. 75 as far as Taitapu, then turn left (west) towards Lincoln. Lincoln (pop. 1,872), 8 km away, is a university town, the base of Lincoln College, a university specializing in agriculture. Lincoln has a hotel and several motels. There is a motorcamp (cabins) at Prebbleton, a 9 km detour northward.

From Lincoln, head northwest to Rolleston, 15 km away on S.H. 1. Cross S.H. 1 and the railway line, and continue northwest to Charing Cross. From here, see Tour 11, Day 1.

If returning from Akaroa via Diamond Harbour, the Rakaia Gorge is 101 km from Diamond Harbour. At Teddington, 10 km west of Diamond Harbour, instead of turning north towards Governors Bay, turn southwest up the Gebbies Pass road. A 4 km climb brings you to the top of this relatively low pass (150 m). Continue downhill to Motukarara from here, and turn north to Taitapu, then west to Lincoln (see above). ■

TOUR 11. SOUTHERN ALPS CIRCUIT

7–8 days: 573 km–736 km

Some would call this tour an itinerary for masochists, crossing the Southern Alps as it does both from east to west and west to east, and including three mountain passes higher than 850 m. Nonetheless, ambitious cycle-tourists will find it an interesting challenge, and the route described does pass through mountain landscapes of a rare grandeur and beauty.

You could of course, reduce the effort considerably by taking the *Tranzalpine Express* from Christchurch to Arthurs Pass or to the West Coast. It leaves Christchurch daily at 7.30 A.M. and arrives in Greymouth at 12.45 P.M. Stops en route are made in Rolleston, Darfield, Springfield, Arthurs Pass (10.28 A.M.), Otira (10.47 A.M.), Moana (11.43 A.M.) and Stillwater. (The return trip leaves Greymouth at 1.15 P.M. and arrives back in Christchurch at 6.40 P.M.).

Some words of warning: if cycling, do not leave Christchurch against a nor'wester. This is a strong, dry foehn wind (called a chinook in North America) which sweeps across the plain from the mountains for days on end. It is virtually impossible to cycle against. If a nor'wester is predicted, postpone your departure until it has blown out, or take the train.

Also, be sure to take adequate clothing. Weather in the Southern Alps can be very unpredictable. Snow and sleet are common in winter and by no means unknown even in summer. The crossing can be done in winter only by the most dedicated cyclists; the passes are sometimes blocked by snow and the days are short. Expect rain over the divide of the Alps into the West Coast, especially in summer.

Perils of camping in the Southern Alps include sandflies and keas. You will already be familiar with the first. The second are pesky little birds which steal anything bright which is not actually tied down, such as teaspoons and compasses and bike tools.

The stages described below are most suitable for free campers. Cyclists relying on formal accommodation will find it more difficult to divide the trip into relatively even stages.

There are two alternative routes on the first part of the trip. One is the direct route via S.H. 73 through Darfield and Springfield and across Porters Pass. This is a scenic route, but carries most direct east-west traffic through the mountains. I prefer the longer and quieter but more rugged route via Lake Coleridge. This involves some distance on gravel, but does avoid a stiff climb over Porters Pass. However, it is not a viable route in winter. Both routes are described below.

DAY 1 *CHRISTCHURCH TO LAKE COLERIDGE* ──────
102 km

The route out of town described below is a complex one, but avoids the frantic traffic of the main road around Hagley Park and through Riccarton. It is signposted for bikes most of the way.

From Cathedral Square, take Worcester St. westward. Turn right into Rolleston Ave. Follow this past Christs College, then left into Hagley Park.

Turn right immediately within the park and proceed north-westward. Just before reaching the far side of the park, veer left. You will emerge on Deans Ave. Cross directly into Kilmarnock St. Follow Kilmarnock St. across the railway line and Straven Rd.

Turn left through Deans Bush (nearby is Deans Cottage) into Ngahaere St., left again into Totara St., right into Miro St. and left

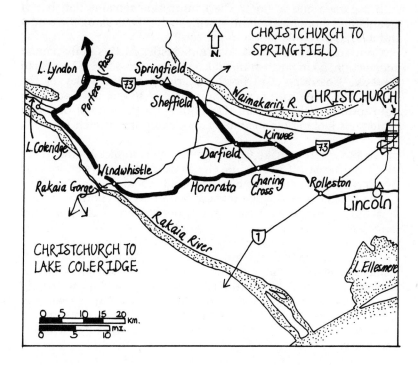

into Hinau St. This brings you out onto Clyde St. Turn right here, then the first left along University Drive. Then turn left into Ilam Rd., right into Homestead St., then cross Waimairi Rd. into Athol Terrace.

Athol Terrace leads northeastward into Parkstone St. Turn right into Avonhead St., left into Stavely St., which leads into Woodbury St., left into Penwood St., right into Bentley St., and left into Russley Rd. This brings you out onto busy Yaldhurst Rd. (S.H. 73). Follow this northwestward.

Yaldhurst Rd. takes you beyond the city limits. Eleven kilometres from the city centre you come to a major roundabout. Veer left here along the Darfield Rd. The suburban traffic now begins to thin out.

What traffic remains tends to be fast-moving, but there is a narrow shoulder to ride on, just wide enough for one bicycle. This is a relatively dull stretch of road, of long straights which lead past stony fields of sparse grass burnt brown by the summer sun and wind.

Thirty kilometres from Cathedral Square, veer left off S.H. 73 towards Charing Cross. This is a lonely intersection in the middle of the plains from which the roads radiate like spokes across the plains. Continue southwestward towards Hororata, a tiny village with a garage and a store. The countryside remains flat, but is greener and more pleasant now, with shelter-belts along the roads, and a large pine plantation to the south.

Continue from Hororata to Windwhistle. At this aptly-named intersection, 5 km north of the Rakaia Gorge, cross S.H. 72 and take the Lake Coleridge road northeast, rising up the valley of the Rakaia River. The road is sealed for the first 16 km, until you turn right towards Lake Lyndon. (Depending on the time of day, you could start looking for a camping spot along this stretch.)

> ■ **Side Trip:** Lake Coleridge Village is in fact another 6 km northeast off your route. Its associated power station, several kilometres further on, built about 1914, was New Zealand's first state-owned hydro-electric power station. There is a picnic area by the power station where you could set up your tent.

A 7 km stretch of rough gravel road through rolling hill country brings you within 1 km of the southern end of Lake Coleridge (the nearest you actually get to the lake, unless you detour to the village). The road then turns northwest up the Coleridge Stream and then the Acheron River. This is bare country, parched in summer, and often covered in snow in winter, but it is inspiringly isolated and lonely.

DAY 2 LAKE COLERIDGE TO ARTHURS PASS ─────
76 km

Another 14 km of gravel brings you along the shores of Lake Lyndon to S.H. 73. The road gradually rises for the first 7 km, but is comparatively level for the same distance thereafter.

From Lake Lyndon to Arthurs Pass is 62 km. The road is sealed, and runs through tussock-country, with sheep-runs on the river flats, and gaunt, eroded mountains behind. The route you follow retraces the steps of Maoris who crossed to the West Coast in search of greenstone (jade) in centuries past; and of pakeha gold-miners who made the same journey in search of gold just over a century ago. The road was completed in 1866. Stage-coaches then made the traverse of the Alps until 1923, when the railway finally went through. The stretch between Lake Lyndon and Arthurs Pass is less strenuous than you might fear. Lake Lyndon (843 m), in fact, is higher than Arthurs Pass township (745 m). There is, however, a minor saddle to cross between Lake Lyndon and Lake Pearson, 20 km north.

Beyond Lake Pearson the road turns westward up the Waimakariri River and enters Arthurs Pass National Park. From

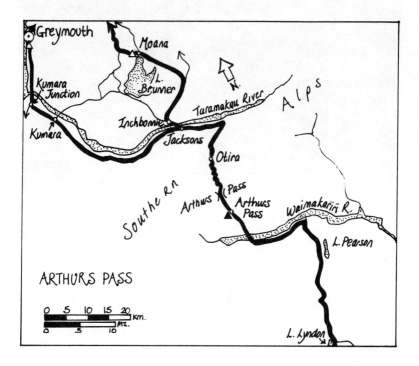

Devil's Punchbowl, Arthurs Pass (Photo by Richard Oddy)

here on, the hills are less eroded; in some parts, their flanks are clothed by beech forests.

Arthurs Pass township is a railway junction and a winter sports centre. It has a motel, a bed-and-breakfast, a Youth Hostel, a store and a restaurant. There is a small local museum, also the head-quarters of the National Park, when you can find information on hikes in the area.

■ ALTERNATIVE ROUTE: Christchurch to Arthurs Pass via Springfield

■ *DAY 1A* CHRISTCHURCH TO SPRINGFIELD ——
67 km

Unless a nor'wester is blowing, this is an easy stretch, a mere afternoon's trip. The road seems flat but actually rises gradually from just above sea-level at Christchurch, to 385 m at Springfield. Spread over 67 km, the difference becomes imperceptible.

Leave Christchurch by the same route as described for Lake Coleridge above. Instead of turning off S.H. 73 for Charing Cross and Hororata, however, stay on S.H. 73 through Darfield and Sheffield. This is all quite boring cycling—you may wish you had taken the train instead.

■ **ALTERNATIVE ROUTE:** At Kirwee, 9 km before Darfield, S.H. 73 veers left. You can avoid some of the traffic for a while by continuing due west into Sheffield instead, along Tramway Rd. This route saves 3km in distance. ■

Springfield is a small town that originated as a staging-post for the coach services which used to operate between Christchurch and the West Coast. It has a hotel. There is also a campsite on the eastern approach to the town.

■ *DAY 2A* SPRINGFIELD TO ARTHURS PASS ——
83 km

The first part of the day is the toughest. The road heads into the mountains from Springfield along the Waimakariri Valley. The first 11km are relatively gentle, but a tough climb follows over the notorious Porters Pass. The road over the pass rises from 600 m to 944 m in little more than 5 km, the last 2 km being the steepest. Beyond the summit there is a steep 2.5 km descent to the northern end of Lake Lyndon. The road from here to Arthurs Pass is described above.

DAY 3 ARTHURS PASS TO MOANA ——
62km

Arthurs Pass itself is actually 5 km north of the township, the road rising another 199 m to a peak of 920 m over that distance.

(This is a stretch you would not see by train; the railway line enters an 8 km tunnel just north of the village.) Once over the Pass, there is a formidable descent to the gorge of the Otira River. In less than 5 km the road drops more than 400 m, with tight curves and hairpin bends. Watch for ice.

The names on this stretch recall the hardships gold-miners and road-builders had to face before the road went through in 1866: Lake Misery, Death Corner, Windy Point, Starvation Point.

Otira (pop. 146) is a small railway town 15 km north of Arthurs Pass. It is also a base for mountaineering and winter sports, and has a store, tearooms and a hotel. Beyond Otira the road drops more gradually down to the wide valley of the Otira River, and turns westward along the Taramakau Valley. At Jacksons, a small farming centre 19 km from Otira, turn right, leaving S.H. 73 for Inchbonnie and Moana.

Inchbonnie is 3 km from Jacksons; 2 km beyond, turn right (northeast) along Rotomanu Rd., climbing gently. Another 12 km on, turn left (northwest) along Crooked River Rd., through Rotomanu and on to Moana, descending gently.

This road is a minor one but mostly sealed, except for a stretch between Rotomanu and Moana, and is very quiet. The countryside is a mixture of bush and swamp and scrub and abandoned farms. There are good informal camping sites at Iveagh Bay before reaching Moana. You will be plagued by sandflies, however.

Moana (pop. 87) is a farming, sawmilling and holiday village set on the northern shore of Lake Brunner. It has a store, hotel and a motorcamp. There is fishing in the lake (trout) and some good tramping in the vicinity.

DAY 4 MOANA TO REEFTON
86 km

From Moana, head northwest to Stillwater, 24 km away. The road is sealed and, except for a short rolling stretch outside Moana, gently downhill.

At Stillwater, a wayside village with a railway station and a hotel, turn northeast along S.H. 7. This follows the Grey River Valley much of the way to Reefton. Although a major highway, it is generally a relatively quiet road, with few towns in the area to generate traffic.

The first 40 km up the valley are largely undemanding. A narrow stretch of farmland has been won from the bush along the valley; behind rise the Paparoa Ranges, an untouched wilderness

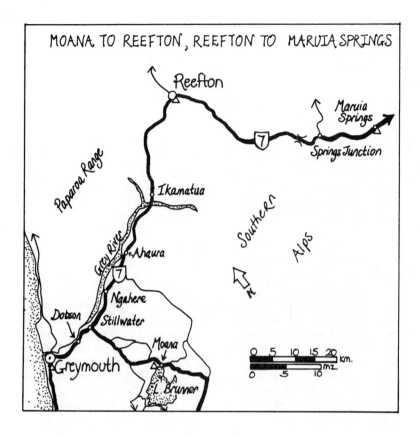

MOANA TO REEFTON, REEFTON TO MARUIA SPRINGS

stretching to the coast. There are hotels at Ahaura and Ikamatua, respectively 20 km and 39 km from Stillwater, and a store at Ahaura.

At Ikamatua, the road veers northward, leaving the Grey River for its tributary, the Mawheraiti. The terrain gradually steepens, and you must climb over the Reefton Saddle (251 m) before descending steeply into its namesake town.

Reefton (pop. 1,224) was once a wealthy gold-mining metropolis, proud enough to call itself "Quartzopolis". Today it is a coal-mining and farming centre. The hills around are littered with abandoned gold-mines. Reminders of the past in the town itself include the School of Mines building (1886), and a small museum in a former church.

Reefton has several hotels and motels, and a motorcamp (cabins) in Main St.

■ ALTERNATIVE ROUTE: Arthurs Pass to Reefton via Greymouth

■ DAY 3A *ARTHURS PASS TO GREYMOUTH* ———
99 km

This adds 43 km to the Moana route described above, but you should be able to cover the distance in two days.

Instead of turning off for Moana at Jacksons, continue on S.H. 73 down the Taramakau Valley. The road levels out in the lower reaches of the valley as it approaches the coast. There is a hotel and motel at Kumara (pop. 370), 71 km from Arthurs Pass.

At Kumara Junction, turn north along S.H. 6. The same bridge here serves for trains and for road vehicles; fortunately the trains are few and far between. The last 18 km to Greymouth along the littoral are mostly flat.

Greymouth (pop. 7,624) is the largest town on the West Coast. It was once the site of a substantial Maori pa, but became a boomtown when gold was discovered in the vicinity in 1864. It survived the end of the gold-mining era as a river port active in the timber and coal trade but, like most West Coast towns, is now slowly declining. "Shanty Town", an imaginative re-creation of a gold-mining town of Victorian times, is 3 km off S.H. 6 to the south of town.

Greymouth has several hotels and motels, and two motorcamps (cabins), both off the main road into town from the south.

■ DAY 4A *GREYMOUTH TO REEFTON* ———
92 km

S.H. 7 heads up the Grey River Valley from the centre of Greymouth to Stillwater, 15 km northeast, passing the straggling coal-mining village of Dobson along the way. From Stillwater, follow the route described in Day 4 to Reefton. ■

DAY 5 REEFTON TO MARUIA SPRINGS ———
59 km

S.H. 7 leaves town to the east, along the northern bank of the Inangahua River. Shortly outside Reefton, it enters the Inangahua Gorge, then undulates along the riverside between steep, bush-clad hills. Fifteen kilometres beyond Reefton, a long gradual climb to the Rahu Saddle (685 m) begins. The last 5 km to Springs Junction (426 m) are mostly downhill, steeply so in parts.

Springs Junction is little more than an intersection in a narrow valley set deep in the mountains. It does have a store, however, and a tourist lodge.

Turn southeast here for Maruia Springs, 15 km away, the road climbing moderately most of the way. There is a hotel at Maruia Springs, with mineral hot pools. Camping-sites are available here.

DAY 6 *MAURIA SPRINGS TO HANMER SPRINGS* ——
80 km

The only really difficult stretch of the day comes first: a 5 km climb over the bare hills before Lewis Pass to 865 m. The road then turns south beyond the Pass, dropping down the Lewis and Boyle rivers for 25 km, before joining the great Waiau River, flowing eastwards.

There are several short climbs along the Waiau River Valley, but nothing overly demanding. The trend is downhill. There are numerous good sites for free camping along the way.

Seventy kilometres from Maruia Springs, turn northeast off S.H. 7 for Hanmer Springs (pop. 1,238). This is a 10 km detour across the Hanmer Plain, but the leafy little spa town and health resort is well worth the effort.

Since Hanmer Springs is set amongst groves of deciduous trees, it is at its best in autumn. The town is set at 366 m, and at all times of year the air is fresh and clear and invigorating. There are public thermal pools used both for bathing and for health therapy.

Hanmer Springs has several hotels, motels and guesthouses. There are four motorcamps (cabins) in the town or near vicinity. The most conveniently located is in Bath St., just off the main road into town from the south.

If setting off on excursions in the area in autumn and winter, be careful about the weather. In early 1989, an incautious cycle-tourist had to be rescued by helicopter from snowdrifts on the Jacks Pass road north of town.

DAY 7 *HANMER SPRINGS TO RANGIORA* ——
102 km

At Hanmer Springs, or some way south, you can make the decision whether to return to Christchurch or to bypass it by taking the

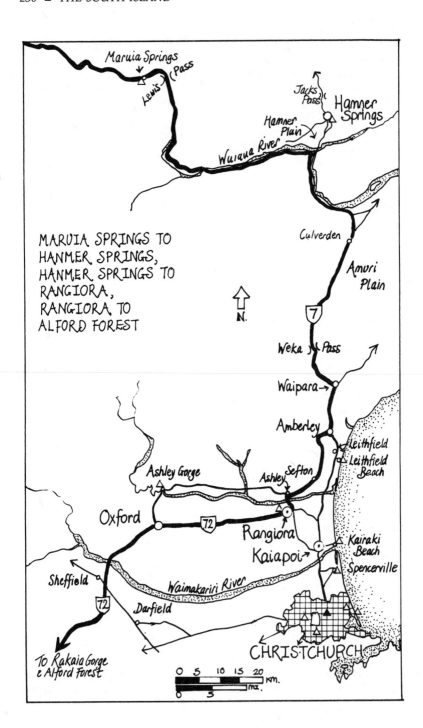

MARUIA SPRINGS TO
HANMER SPRINGS,
HANMER SPRINGS TO
RANGIORA,
RANGIORA TO
ALFORD FOREST

inland route through Oxford direct to the Rakaia Gorge.

Return to S.H. 7 across the Hanmer Plain and continue southwards. For 15 km the road runs alongside the Waiau River as it cuts through the barren hills of the Amuri Range, then emerges into the wide Amuri Plain. Continue southwest through Culverden, a village (store, motel) 34 km beyond Hanmer Springs.

Fifteen kilometres beyond Culverden, S.H. 7 enters the hills again, climbing gradually and intermittently for 12 km to the Weka Pass (247 m). From here, it descends to the North Canterbury Plains, joining S.H. 1 at Waipara, 44 km beyond Culverden. From Waipara, follow S.H. 1 south to Amberley. At Amberley, turn southwest towards Sefton, Ashley and Rangiora.

■ **ALTERNATIVE ROUTE:** You could, of course, follow S.H. 1 direct to Christchurch, as described in the last stage of the Kaikoura route (Tour 9, Day 3). Via this route, Hanmer Springs to Christchurch is 136 km. If you feel this is too far for one day, stop for the night in Leithfield or Kaiapoi instead.

Rangiora (pop. 6,674) is a pleasant old market town, and a dormitory town for Christchurch. It has a hotel, two motels, and a motorcamp (cabins). The motorcamp is in Lehmans Rd., off S.H. 72 to the west. ■

DAY 8 RANGIORA TO ALFORD FOREST —————
117 km; via the Ashley Gorge: 126 km

Take S.H. 72 southwest from Rangiora. The small town of Oxford (pop. 1,088) is 33 km away across the plains.

■ **ALTERNATIVE ROUTE:** A far more scenic route to Oxford is via the Ashley Gorge. Cross the Ashley River to the north of Rangiora, and turn west along the northern bank. An undulating to rolling road brings you to the scenic river crossing of Ashley Gorge, 32 km from Rangiora; Oxford is a further 10 km south. There is a motorcamp at Ashley Gorge. ■

Fifteen kilometres beyond Oxford, S.H. 72 crosses the Waimakariri River and, another 6 km on, intersects with S.H. 73 just to the east of Sheffield. You will have passed this way already if you took the direct route to Arthurs Pass several days before.

Follow S.H. 73 southeast for just over 1 km, then turn due south onto S.H. 72 again. The Rakaia Gorge is an easy 44 km south, and Alford Forest (store and campground) is another 18 km beyond.

TOUR 12. LAKES AND MOUNTAINS: CHRISTCHURCH TO QUEENSTOWN

6–9 days: 484 km–634 km

The route described here is the best route south. The alternative route, via S.H. 1 across the Canterbury Plains is one of the dullest roads in the country. Far better to turn southwest towards the Rakaia Gorge, and from there skirt the foothills of the Southern Alps, turning inland at Geraldine towards the tussock-lands of the Mackenzie Basin and the interior.

Here lie the great lakes of Tekapo and Pukaki. These were formed during the ice age when advancing glaciers gouged out their beds and dammed the ends with rubble. The glaciers, now in retreat and much reduced, still lie inland in the mountains. At the head of Lake Pukaki looms Mount Cook, at 3,764 m New Zealand's highest mountain, and the grandest of the many peaks of the Southern Alps.

The interior of Canterbury through which you will pass has always been an empty land. Although known to Maori tribes of Canterbury and Otago, who traversed it in search of the greenstone deposits of the West Coast, it was virtually uninhabited. It was first settled by pakeha in the 1850s, largely by sheep-farmers, who drove their flocks across the plains and through the passes into the hidden mountain valleys.

Vast sheep-stations were established, some of which stretched literally for miles. Their owners (or lessors) made fortunes from the export of wool, built themselves large homesteads, and set themselves up in manners and influence as a colonial gentry.

The larger stations have since been split up by land reforms, and the true high country taken out of production because of overgrazing and erosion. But even today holdings of 15,000 hectares or more are common, and many of the elegant old homesteads still stand.

In recent years, inland Canterbury has been exploited for hydro-electricity as well as for wool. Dams flung across the region's fast-moving rivers have created new lakes, the largest of which is Lake Benmore, almost 8,000 hectares in extent. The new lakes, like the old, are a focus for tourism, for boating, water-skiing and fishing.

Even so, the region remains sparsely populated, sheep being far more numerous than people. Between Geraldine and Crom-

Sluice gates of Benmore Hydro (Photo by Mark Lawson)

well, a distance of 288 km, the only towns of any size are Fairlie (pop. 788) and Twizel (pop. 1,274), and the latter is a hydro town and is in decline.

DAY 1 CHRISTCHURCH TO THE RAKAIA GORGE/ALFORD FOREST
86 km–104 km

If the wind is right, this is a relatively easy day, the terrain being virtually flat, with a slight and almost imperceptible upwards trend most of the way to the Rakaia Gorge. Strong cyclists may care to put in extra distance, heading to Mount Somers (119 km), or even to the Peel Forest (155 km) or Geraldine (162 km).

For a description of the route to Windwhistle, 5 km north of the Rakaia Gorge (see Tour 11, Day 1).

Just beyond Windwhistle, the Gorge comes in sight, an area of eroded cliffs, dark pines and a milky-green braided shingle river. The road descends the final 4 km into the Gorge. Just before the

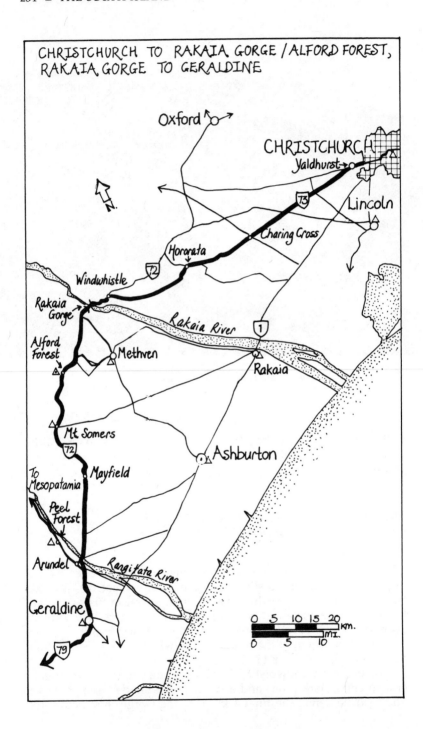

CHRISTCHURCH TO RAKAIA GORGE / ALFORD FOREST, RAKAIA GORGE TO GERALDINE

bridge which crosses the Rakaia River is a rest area on the river bank, a potential spot for free camping.

There is a 1.5 km climb out of the Gorge, then 18 km of flat to undulating country to Alford Forest. There is a campsite here (ask at the store).

■ **ALTERNATIVE ROUTE:** You can detour instead to Methven, 16 km southeast of the Rakaia Gorge. This is a small country town and winter sports centre with a number of hotels and motels, and a motorcamp (cabins) in the showgrounds. ■

DAY 2 RAKAIA GORGE/ALFORD FOREST TO GERALDINE
56 km–68 km; via Peel Forest: 70 km–82 km

This is another easy day, unless a southerly wind is blowing. You should have plenty of time for the 14 km detour to Peel Forest described below.

From Alford Forest to Mount Somers, 16 km on the way to Geraldine, the road is undulating. From Mount Somers onwards it is wholly flat, and includes one straight 14 km in length. The scenery on this particular stretch is unspectacular: wide fields bordered by long rows of trees, but with distant views of the hills to the west. Mount Somers has a motel and motorcamp. There is a small store at Mayfield, 14 km beyond Mount Somers.

■ **Side Trip:** Peel Forest is a 550-hectare preserve of native bush, one of the last remnants of the forest that once covered the entire foothills of the Southern Alps. Immediately after crossing the Rangitata River, 25 km beyond Mount Somers, turn sharp right into Arundel, then the first left, left again, then right onto the Peel Forest road.

At Peel Forest is a Department of Conservation information centre with an interesting historical display. There is also a delightful grassy campsite set amongst trees. A number of walking-tracks lead from here into the hills.

Forty-five kilometres further up the road is Mesopotamia Station. Between 1860 and 1864 this was the home of Samuel Butler (1835–1902), the English novelist and essayist, author of *Erewhon*, a satiric fantasy set in the Southern Alps.

The trip to Mesopotamia is a full day's excursion or more. Near Mount Peel (1865), a famous homestead 7 km beyond Peel Forest, the seal ends. A 4 km climb follows, after which the road rejoins and gently ascends the valley of the Rangitata River. This is a rough and dusty road, but offers the chance to see the "real" high country.

Geraldine (pop. 2,143), 23 km south of Peel Forest, is an attractive town set on the banks of the Waihi River. It has a vintage car museum and a machinery museum. There are a hotel and two motels. The motorcamp (cabins) is in Hislop St., which runs to the right off Talbot St (the main road through town) just past the main shops.

DAY 3 GERALDINE TO LAKE TEKAPO ————————
89 km

At the southeastern end of Geraldine, the main road forks. Leave S.H. 72 for S.H. 79 here, turning southwest towards Fairlie. For the first 10 km the terrain is flat to undulating. A stretch of rolling country follows, but nothing too strenuous. At 39 km from Geraldine comes a long, winding 3 km climb, then an equally long descent, then a final straight into Fairlie.

Fairlie (pop. 788) is a small country town which has several hotels and motels, and a motorcamp (cabins) just outside town on the Geraldine road. Fairlie is known as the "gateway of the Mackenzie Country." The Mackenzie Country is the vast tussock-clad basin to the south of Lakes Tekapo and Pukaki entered through the Burke Pass west of Fairlie. It takes its name from an illiterate Scots shepherd, James Mackenzie, who was caught by the law on the border of the region in 1855, driving inland a large flock of stolen sheep. Fairlie has a small historical museum.

Turn northwest along S.H. 8. There is a 7 km straight outside town (difficult in a nor'wester), then another 15 km of flat to undulating terrain to the Burke Pass township (hotel, motel). Beyond this comes a steady 4 km climb to 670 m, with the bare hills of the Tom Thumb Range to the north and the Rollesby Range to the south.

There is a monument near the top of the pass to its 19th century pakeha "discoverer", the runholder and explorer Michael John Burke. (The pass had, of course, been used by Maoris for centuries before.)

From Burke Pass to Tekapo is an easy 17 km, mostly gently downhill. Tekapo township (pop. 442) is situated at the southern end of its lake. It has a hotel and a Youth Hostel. There is also a motorcamp (cabins), and a motel, adjacent to the lake on the western side of town.

In winter, Tekapo is an outdoor sports centre; in summer there is trout-fishing in the lake and tramping and climbing in the vicinity. The stone-built Church of the Good Shepherd (1935) stands on a low promontory overlooking the lake. The window above the

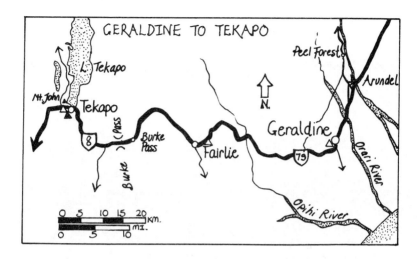

altar beautifully frames the lake and mountains beyond.

Mount John Observatory, on a peak (1,031 m) overlooking Tekapo to the northwest, is a satellite tracking station. Inaccessible to the public, it is the source of some controversy, and has been the scene of several peace demonstrations.

DAY 4 LAKE TEKAPO TO OMARAMA
86 km

From Lake Tekapo to Lake Pukaki is 47 km. The road is undulating with long flat stretches. It passes through unpopulated tussock country, with no towns or villages and few signs of habitation except for an Army camp a few kilometres outside Tekapo.

Skirt the southern end of Lake Pukaki. Its milky green waters offset the surrounding mountains, including the distant bulk of Mount Cook (3,764 m) at the northern end of the lake. At the southwestern corner of the lake, S.H. 8 turns south to Twizel. (S.H. 80 branches north to Mount Cook here; if you intend to take this road, see below.)

Twizel (pop. 1,274) was established as a service town for the great hydro schemes of the region. Now that these have mostly been completed, it is a town in decline, though retaining some prosperity as a service centre for surrounding farms and as a tourist centre. A short detour from the main road is a small shopping centre with a tourist information office. Twizel has a hotel; there is also a motorcamp (cabins) 4 km to the southwest, on the shores of Lake Ruataniwha.

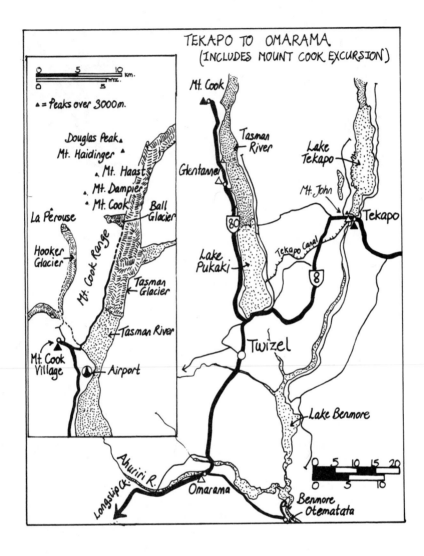

From Twizel the road is mostly flat for the next 24 km. This is an unfortunate stretch to do in the full heat of the summer sun. The last 14 km to Omarama are gently undulating. Omarama is a rather scrappy little village at the junction of S.H. 8 (to Cromwell) and S.H. 8 (to Oamaru). It has a store, tearooms, a hotel; also a motor-camp (cabins).

Free campers with a mind to continue will find good spots to pitch a tent alongside the Longslip Creek, 19 km along S.H. 8.

■ **Side Trip:** 25 km southeast of Omarama is Otematata. Another 6 km north is Benmore Hydro. This massive earth dam has formed New Zealand's largest man-made lake (approximately 8,000 hectares), and feeds New Zealand's second-largest power station (capacity 540,000 kw). There is a hotel, motel and motorcamp at Otematata.

■ *SIDE TRIP: MOUNT COOK*
Tekapo to Glentanner/Mount Cook: 83 km–106 km
Glentanner/Mount Cook to Omarama: 65 km–98 km

Allow at least two days, but preferably three, the third day leaving plenty of time for sightseeing and perhaps some hiking at Mount Cook.

At the southwestern corner of Lake Pukaki, 47 km from Tekapo, turn north onto S.H. 80, which runs along the western shores of the lake. Glentanner is 36 km away; Mount Cook village another 23 km beyond. The road undulates along the lakeside below the Ohau Range, rising gradually but steadily from 600 m at Lake Pukaki to 747 m at Mount Cook Village.

Wind may be a problem: it is funnelled down the valley in the late afternoon. The road, of course, is virtually impossible against a nor'wester, when gusts can reach 100 knots.

There is a shop, tearooms and a motorcamp (cabins) at Glentanner. This is where campers should stay, cycling on to Mount Cook as an excursion the next day.

Mount Cook village has a shop, a hotel (the Hermitage), a motel, lodges, and a Youth Hostel, but no camping facilities. There are, however, huts for trampers in the vicinity. Enquire about these at the National Park visitors centre in the village.

Mount Cook itself is 16 km north of the village but inaccessible by road. The whole area around is incorporated in the Mount Cook National Park. Within its 69,958 hectares, this encompasses 14 peaks which are higher than 3000 m and five glaciers, the largest being the Tasman Glacier, 29 km long and up to 3 km wide.

Mount Cook Village is the centre for skiing, climbing and tramping throughout the park. Scenic flights over the mountains are based on the airport, 5 km southeast. Depending on weather, it is sometimes possible to land on the Hooker Glacier, just below Mount Cook.

■ **ALTERNATIVE ROUTE:** If you feel like some challenging cycling, try the Ball Hut road. This is a rough gravel road heading 12 km or so northeast below the Mount Cook Range from the road south of the village. To reach the Ball Hut site below Tasman Glacier you must walk 4 km from the road's end. The road used to go the whole way up, but has been badly broken up by sinking and slumping. ■

Mount Cook (Photo by Richard Oddy)

DAY 5 OMARAMA TO CROMWELL
113 km

There are two main routes to Queenstown, one via Cromwell and the Kawarau Gorge, the other via Wanaka and the Crown Range (the Cardrona Road). They are of equal appeal scenically, but the Cromwell route is easier, being sealed all the way, whereas the Cardrona route involves some strenuous climbing on steep, gravel roads.

Whichever you choose, you can do the other in reverse when returning to Wanaka on your way to the Haast Pass.

Omarama to Cromwell is a longish day's cycle. There is no formal accommodation, except perhaps farmstays, between the two towns. Free campers who want to take it easy, however, can split the distance into stages, and will find a good choice of campsites in the Lindis Pass.

Take S.H. 8 southwest from Omarama. This crosses a barren plain, running alongside the Ahuriri River for the first 16 km, then turns southward into the Lindis Pass. This pass is, fortunately, much easier crossed from north to south than from south to north.

The first 3 km after leaving the Ahuriri are flat; for the next 10 km the road gradually rises up the valley of the Longslip Creek; then a steep 2 km climb to the top of the pass (970 m) follows. The next 10 km are a steep and winding descent. Watch out for the ice here if temperatures are low. A more gradual descent follows for the next 18 km, a flat 7 km stretch, a gentle 2 km ascent, an equal descent, and a 5 km flat before Tarras.

Tarras is little more than a wayside halt. There are a shop and tearooms and a service station here. Continue south along S.H. 8. The last 32 km to Cromwell range from flat to undulating.

The road runs along the eastern side of the Clutha River. Much of the valley here will gradually become a lake as water builds up behind the massive Clyde dam below Cromwell. This is part of a long-debated and highly controversial scheme to build dams for hydro-electric generation right along the Clutha. The Clyde dam is scheduled for completion in 1991; already it seems that the electricity it provides will be surplus to New Zealand's needs.

Seven kilometres north of Cromwell, S.H. 8 turns west across the river to Lowburn. Turn south again for Cromwell, on S.H. 6. This in fact bypasses the town, but the turnoff is clearly signposted to the left.

Cromwell (pop. 3,536) is the centre of a stone-fruit growing area, famous especially for its peaches and apricots. It is a town clearly divided in two: old Cromwell, the historic gold-mining town on low ground to the southeast; and new Cromwell, a

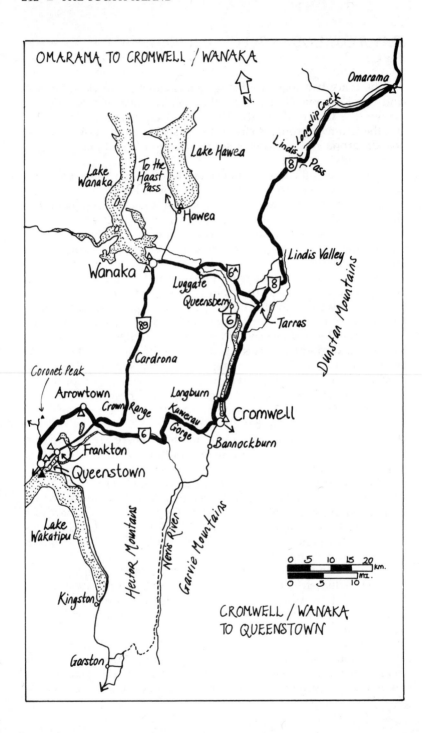

OMARAMA TO CROMWELL / WANAKA

N.

Omarama

Longslip Creek

Lindis Pass

8

Lake Hawea

Lake Wanaka

To the Haast Pass

Hawea

Lindis Valley

Wanaka

Luggate

Queensberry

6

8

Tarras

89

6

Dunstan Mountains

Cardrona

Coronet Peak

Arrowtown

Crown Range

Longburn

Kawerau Gorge

Cromwell

Frankton

6

Bannockburn

Queenstown

Lake Wakatipu

Hector Mountains

Nevis River

Garvie Mountains

Kingston

0 5 10 15 20 km.

0 5 10 mi.

CROMWELL / WANAKA
TO QUEENSTOWN

Garston

planned hydro town on high ground to the northwest.

Much of old Cromwell will disappear beneath the waters of Lake Dunstan once the Clyde dam is completed. A museum and information centre in the new town centre gives a good picture of the area as it once was.

Cromwell has a hotel, a guesthouse, and several motels. There is a motorcamp (cabins) in Alpha St.

■ **Side Trip:** 8 km due south of Cromwell, across the Kawarau River and a short climb into the hills, is Bannockburn, a former mining settlement, and now a farming and orcharding locality. In the 1860s the flats and terraces here were ravaged by hydraulic sluicing for gold and, even today, the terrain shows signs of the devastation done.

You may hear talk of the Nevis road. This is a "short-cut" from Bannockburn through the mountains to Garston, beyond Kingston at the southern end of Lake Wakatipu. It is only recommended to the hardiest—or foolhardiest—of cyclists. The gravel road is little better than a four-wheel drive track. Behind Bannockburn, it climbs steeply for most of 10 km to 1275 m, then drops into and gradually rises up the lower and upper basins of the Nevis River. There are 25 unbridged stream crossings on the way. The road then ascends the flanks of the Hector Range and drops steeply and dangerously into Garston. From Bannockburn to Garston is about 65 km. There are, of course, neither towns, nor villages, nor shops nor even habitations, except for one or two rough huts, along the way.

DAY 6 CROMWELL TO ARROWTOWN/ QUEENSTOWN
44 km–64 km

Leave Cromwell on S.H. 6 to the southwest. This passes orchards and fruit-stalls outside the town, (in season you should stop for the delicious ripe apricots and peaches), then enters the Kawarau Gorge. This has been cut deep into the hills by the Kawarau River, which flows eastward from the Frankton Arm of Lake Wakatipu.

The road winds up-and-down through the Gorge, though without any major climbs. It is sealed and usually relatively busy.

Midway through the Gorge, you will see the old Kawarau suspension bridge to the right. Built in 1880, this was replaced as recently as 1963. Still used by pedestrians, it has a 91 m span and sits 43 m above the river.

At 40 km from Cromwell, the Gorge opens out into the Kawarau Valley. Shortly afterwards, you reach the Arrow Junction. From here to Queenstown direct via S.H. 6 is 20 km through easy rolling country. I recommend, however, that you detour through Arrowtown instead.

From the Junction to Arrowtown itself is 4 km. Arrowtown (pop. 953) is a well-preserved old mining town which, despite the pressure of tourism, has managed to retain some of its original character. It has an excellent regional museum, the Lakes District Centennial Museum, and a number of old buildings, including the stone jail (1875) and a row of early miners' cottages.

Arrowtown has several motels. The municipal motorcamp (cabins) is in Suffolk St. Turn left off Memorial Drive on the way into town.

If you decide to stay in Arrowtown, you could consider walking through the hills to Macetown, 10 km further north. This was once a bustling mining town, but is now a ghost town with only traces of the old buildings and gardens left.

Otherwise, continue to Queenstown via the Shotover route. Leave Arrowtown by the main Queenstown road but turn right along the Shotover road just outside the borough boundaries. This is a narrow but sealed road running through pleasant rolling coun-

Stud rams at an agricultural show, Cromwell

try. Midway to Queenstown, you will see Coronet Peak (1651 m), Queenstown's main ski slopes, high to your right.

The road crosses the wild Shotover River 13 km from Arrowtown, climbs a short hill beyond the bridge, and enters Queenstown from the north 5 km further on.

Queenstown (pop. 3,659) is the South Island's leading tourist resort in both summer and winter, its permanent population swollen by holidaymakers all year round. Set on the northeastern shores of Lake Wakatipu, it is crammed with hotels and motels and guesthouses and lodges. There are also several motorcamps.

The nearest of these to town is the municipal motorcamp (cabins) in Man St. Turn right into Man St. from Henry St. as you enter the town centre. There is another motorcamp on the Frankton road 2 km west of town, and yet another (cabins) in Frankton itself, 7 km west.

Queenstown's sights include the Government Tourist Gardens, set on a small peninsula below the town, a motor museum, and a (declining) number of old buildings such as the Old Stone Library (1877). The tourist building boom of the last decade or so has stripped Queenstown of much of its former charm, but it retains its beautiful setting.

The New Zealand Tourist and Publicity Department has an office in 41 Shotover St. (Phone 28238).

■ ALTERNATIVE ROUTE: Omarama to Queenstown via Wanaka

■ DAY 5A OMARAMA TO WANAKA ⎯⎯⎯⎯⎯⎯
113 km

Follow the instructions above through the Lindis Pass to Tarras (Day 5). Just past Tarras, turn northwest along S.H. 8A for Wanaka. This joins S.H. 6, 21 km along. Continue westward to Wanaka. The terrain is flat to undulating.

Wanaka (pop. 1,710) is a lakeside holiday town. It offers a wide choice of hotels and motels. There are also three motorcamps (cabins) in town or the vicinity, and another 13 km westward along the lakeside road to Glendhu Bay.

To reach the most central motorcamp, entering Wanaka from the northeast, you will come to an intersection where three roads radiate southeast, south and west. Take the western road, Ardmer St., and continue along the lakefront. After just on 0.5 km, turn left into Stone St., where the camp is situated.

Suspension bridge, Kawarau Gorge

■ *DAY 6A* WANAKA TO ARROWTOWN/ QUEENSTOWN
Via the Crown Range (Cardrona Road)
73 km–77 km

This could be quite a rough trip. The Cardrona road is the highest State Highway in New Zealand, and is frequently blocked by snow in winter. It is, at the time of writing, mostly gravel, and it involves some stiff climbing. Traffic in summer is surprisingly busy for such a rough road although, fortunately, cars with caravans (mobile homes) are forbidden. There are a number of cattle-stops and one-lane bridges en route.

Take the Cardrona road due south of Wanaka. This rises gently and almost imperceptibly over the first 26 km to Cardrona (this stretch should be sealed by 1991). In the 1860s Cardrona was a gold-mining town with 5,000 inhabitants. Now there is only a restaurant, (a sophisticated place for such a rustic setting) built behind the facade of the old pub.

Beyond Cardrona, the road continues to rise, gradually steepening for 12 km. A more difficult ascent of 3 km then brings you to the top of the road at 1,120 m.

There follows a winding and risky 12 km descent, the first 9 km on gravel. The surface is usually deeply rutted, so watch your speed. The last 3 km include several hairpin bends as you descend the Crown Terrace into the Kawarau Valley. The views are glorious.

Queenstown is 21 km from the bottom of the descent direct via S.H. 6. I recommend, however, that you detour via Arrowtown, as described in 5A above.

TOUR 13. OTAGO AND SOUTH-LAND: QUEENSTOWN TO WANAKA VIA TE ANAU, INVERCARGILL AND DUNEDIN

10–15 days: 747 km–1155 km

This itinerary takes the cyclist on a great circuit of the sparsely populated countryside of the southern South Island, first skirting Fiordland, a vast area of mountains and fjords and deep, sombre lakes set in New Zealand's southwestern corner, then crossing Southland, one of New Zealand's main farming regions.

Fiordland is wet, inhospitable and almost wholly unpopulated—it is also very beautiful. Southland, by contrast to Fiordland's mountains, is largely a well-watered and fertile plain. It is more densely populated than much of the rest of the South Island, with a succession of small towns and villages. Its main centre is Invercargill (pop. 48,179).

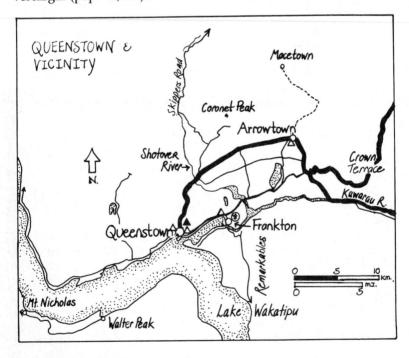

As in most of the South Island, the original Maori population was small, and mostly concentrated in settlements along the coast. The first pakeha to arrive were sealers and whalers, but organised immigration began in the 1850s. The first settlers were mostly Scots, and they have left their mark in the region's names and buildings, and even the countryside, and in the Southland accent, which retains a slight Scottish burr.

From Southland, the itinerary described below takes you up the coast to Dunedin (pop. 92,622) also originally a Scottish settlement. In the previous century this was New Zealand's largest city and its financial capital. Commercial predominance has long since shifted to Auckland. Dunedin is today, however, the South Island's second largest city, and perhaps the most civilised of New Zealand's cities in appearance and atmosphere, with any number of fine and well-preserved Victorian and Edwardian buildings.

Heading inland from Dunedin you pass through arid Central Otago, by turns the driest, hottest and coldest area of New Zealand. It is a rugged area of schist mountains separated by deep-cleft gorges and tussock-clad valleys.

Gold was discovered here in 1861 and booming shanty-towns sprang up in every likely spot. The gold ran out, however, and most workings were abandoned within less than forty years. The hills now brood over ghost towns, some of them little more than scattered humps of earth.

Stone-built shepherd's hut on the road between Mount Nicholas and the Mavora Lakes

Central Otago's wealth today lies in its vast sheep-stations and its stone-fruit orchards, its hydro-electric schemes and its undoubted tourist appeal.

Queenstown to Te Anau

There are two alternative routes between Queenstown and Te Anau. The first, via the Mavora Lakes, is the more exciting and much the preferable. It is, however, also the more difficult route, passing through isolated mountain country, and including 72 km of gravel road. It is impractical in midwinter and at times of heavy rain.

If you dislike gravel, or need to sleep in a civilised bed every night, or if the weather is unfavourable, take the Kingston route. The views at least some of the way are almost as rewarding.

DAY 1 QUEENSTOWN TO THE MAVORA LAKES ——
39 km–51 km

First, you must cross Lake Wakatipu. You have a choice of hydrofoil to Walter Peak or of steamer to Mount Nicholas.

Both depart from the quayside at Beach St. on the northeastern side of Queenstown Bay. The hydrofoil sails daily August to May (but not June and July) at 9.30 A.M. and 2.00 P.M.; the steamer departs daily August to May at 2.00 P.M. The crossing takes about an hour on the steamer. The hydrofoil is quicker, but from Walter Peak there are 12 extra kilometres to ride. The one-way fare, with bicycle, is $15.00.

I recommend taking the steamer, at least when the long days of summer give you the time to reach the Mavora Lakes. Not every day is there a chance to sail on a genuine coal-fired twin-screw steamer. The S.S. *Earnslaw* was launched on the lake in 1912 and, in its restored condition, seems as new. You can watch the coal being shovelled and the pistons thumping. There is a bar and a snackbar on board.

Mount Nicholas is a working sheep-station, founded in 1859, and today run as a tourist attraction as well. After disembarking, you can stop and watch demonstrations of mustering and shearing with the other passengers, or press on. I suggest pressing on, however, especially if the days are getting short, since it takes several hours to reach the Mavora Lakes.

There is a 2 km climb from the lakeside, then an undulating 6 km stretch alongside the Von River. The gravel road is rough and traffic is light but, if you do hear anything coming, it pays to get right off the road.

This stretch is actually private road and has gates across it. Leave the gates exactly as you find them: open if open, shut if shut.

There are several nice spots to pitch a tent along the river, particularly in the grove of trees beside an old shearer's hut 8 km from

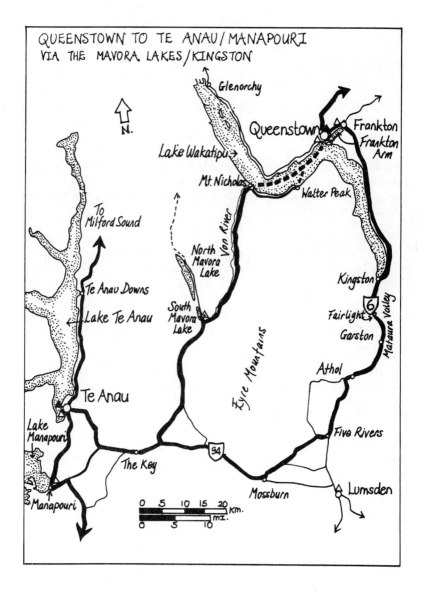

the lakeside, but camping is officially forbidden on Mount Nicholas property. If you are overtaken by night, you will have to be discreet. If the weather is bad, be on the lookout for huts west of the road at about 20 km, 25 km and 30 km from the lake.

A further 7 km stretch of river flat is followed by a demanding 4 km climb. The river gravel used on roads here makes it difficult for tires to get a purchase. Mountain bikes should manage this stretch, but touring bikes may need to be pushed.

From the top of the hill to the Mavora Lakes is mostly flat, though with short, steep dips to cross streams. These are mostly too deep to cycle across. Take your shoes off if you do not like wet feet. In spring after snowmelt, or after rain in any season, crossing may be difficult.

At 38 km from Mount Nicholas is the turnoff to the Mavora Lakes. This is not difficult to find since it is the only formed side-road for more than 20 km in either direction.

One kilometre along is a campsite set in beech forest beside the South Mavora Lake. This is very basic, with pit toilets and open fireplaces, but it is beautifully sited and is the best campsite for at least another 50 km, so resist the temptation to add any further distance to the day.

■ **Side Trip:** The Mavora Lakes road continues another 10 km up the lake, then becomes a four-wheel drive track leading another 25 km into the mountains.

DAY 2 *THE MAVORA LAKES TO TE ANAU/ MANAPOURI*
68–83 km

This is a short day over easy terrain. If you crawl out of your sleeping bag early, you could be in Te Anau well before lunch, with a leisurely afternoon before you (or a chance to begin on the Milford road).

There are 34 km of gravel between the Mavora Lakes and the main Te Anau road (S.H. 94). The first 10 km are gently downhill, the next 10 km are flat, then there are 10 km of gentle undulations, and the last 4 km are flat. There is a tearoom at the junction with S.H. 94.

Continue westward along S.H. 94 towards Te Anau. The road is flat to undulating most of the way, with the last 4 km being gently downhill. Traffic is light, except for fast-moving tour buses also heading west between early and mid-morning.

■ **ALTERNATIVE ROUTE:** If you have visited Te Anau before, you can save 20 km by heading straight to Manapouri. Turn off S.H. 94 to the southwest 12 km towards Te Anau after the Mavora Lakes junction. If you arrive in Manapouri before midday you could join the last tour departure to West Arm (see below). ■

Te Anau (pop. 2,818) is Fiordland's major—indeed its only— town. It sits on the western shores of New Zealand's second lar-

Bridge of the SS Earnslaw *(Photo by Mark Lawson)*

gest lake (34,200 hectares). Across the water are the dark and brooding mountains of the Kepler, Stuart and Murchison ranges. Fiordland National Park headquarters and information centre is on the foreshore at the southern end of town.

Te Anau is a tourist centre, the base for coach trips to Milford Sound, for launch trips across the lake, and for scenic flights over the region. If heading for Milford Sound, you may want to stay here. There is a wide choice of hotels and motels, also a Youth Hostel. There is a caravan park with cabins in Mokanui St., the second street back from the waterfront; also a motorcamp (cabins) at the southern end of town. Free campers, of course, may want to use the afternoon to make a start on the Milford road.

Otherwise, continue to Manapouri. Take the lakeshore road southwards. Manapouri is 21 km away through undulating countryside.

Manapouri village is set above the western shore of its namesake lake. There is a motorcamp (cabins) and a motel at the northern end of the village, and a shop a little further on. A further 1 km descent to the lakeside brings you to the wharf (Pearl Harbour).

Campsite, South Mavora Lake

■ **Side Trip:** Tours of the Manapouri hydro-electric power scheme, which is not accessible by road, start from Pearl Harbour. This includes a visit to the West Arm underground powerhouse, set in a vast cavern 213 m below the mountains, and a bus trip over Wilmot Pass to Doubtful Sound. The whole trip takes over 7 hours, though you can visit just the powerhouse if you wish. Tours depart daily in peak season at 8 A.M., 10 A.M. and 12 P.M., but only three days a week at 10 A.M. in the off-season. It is advisable to book ahead.

Unbelievably, given the pristine beauty of bush-clad Lake Manapouri, the Manapouri scheme included proposals to dam the lake and allow its levels to fluctuate. Massive public objections in New Zealand's first mass environmental movement forced the abandonment of this scheme in 1973. The lake is now protected by a statutory body known as the Guardians of Lake Manapouri.

■ ALTERNATIVE ROUTE: Queenstown to Te Anau/Manapouri via Kingston

■ *DAY 1A QUEENSTOWN TO KINGSTON* ————
47 km

Te Anau is too far (148 km) via Kingston for many cyclists to reach comfortably in one day, but not quite far enough to justify two. I recommend taking 1½ days, looking around Queenstown in the morning, and setting off in the early afternoon. This avoids the morning exodus of tour buses on their way to Te Anau and Milford Sound.

Alternative stages would be Queenstown to Mossburn (111 km) and Mossburn to Te Anau (58 km), allowing time perhaps to push on from Te Anau to Manapouri or Milford Sound.

Take the Frankton road from Queenstown northeast along Frankton Arm. Turn south at Frankton along S.H. 6. The road shortly dips to cross a narrow bridge across the Kawerau River, rises over 8 km, then descends 2 km to Lake Wakatipu again. From here the road passes between the lake and the Remarkable Mountains, for 30 km, continually rising and falling, usually gently, but with some short climbs.

If you have left late enough to avoid the tour buses, the main hazards are wandering stock and falling rocks. The road, of course, is sealed.

Kingston is a tiny community above the southern end of the lake. It has a shop, service station, motel, and caravan park with cabins and tent sites. It is also the base for the "Kingston Flyer," a restored steam-engine which runs along a short length of track to Fairlight 10 km south.

There are good spots for free camping along the Mataura River south of Fairlight.

■ DAY 2A KINGSTON TO TE ANAU/MANAPOURI —
101 km–122 km

There is an 8 km flat stretch south of Kingston, then the road winds gently along the Mataura Valley. At Five Rivers, 46 km south of Kingston, turn off S.H. 6 to the right towards Mossburn, 18 km away.

Three kilometres outside Mossburn is a motorcamp (cabins). In Mossburn itself, where you join S.H. 94 and turn west, is a hotel. From Mossburn the first 10 km are mostly flat, followed by rolling country for 15 km, then flat or gently undulating terrain most of the way to Te Anau, with the last 4 km gently downhill. ■

■ SIDE TRIP: MILFORD SOUND EXCURSION ———
2 days minimum: 222 km return

Most cycle tourists who visit the South Island visit Milford Sound. I must admit, however, that I wonder whether bicycle is the best way to do it. The terrain is demanding, the road is narrow and has a gravel surface for much of its length, and is busy, and the weather is almost invariably wet (unless it is snowing). This being said, I should add that the scenery is marvellous.

Also the flow of traffic is predictable and can therefore be avoided; the tour buses mostly head up the valley early to mid-morning and return at mid-afternoon.

If you prefer to take a tour bus, these leave Te Anau half-hourly or so between 8 and 10 A.M. There are various operators, and the current return fare is about $70.00. There is also an organisation based in Te Anau which supplies tourists with bicycles but transports them to the top of the pass in both directions.

As mentioned above, expect rain. Milford Sound averages more than 6,000 mm of it each year. Milford Sound itself is usually warm and muggy in summer, but the weather over the pass is change-able. Warm clothes and waterproofs are a must at any time of year. In spring and winter the road is often closed because of avalanche

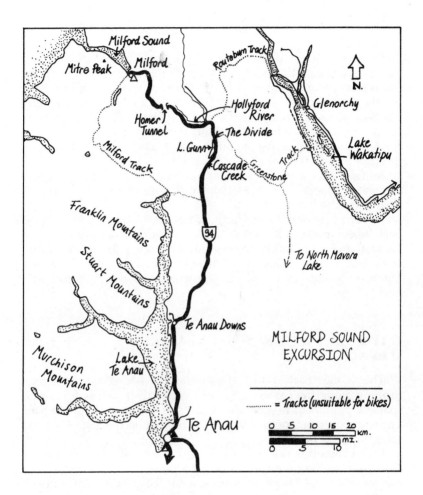

MILFORD SOUND
EXCURSION

.... = Tracks (unsuitable for bikes)

danger. No cyclists have been lost—yet.

Leave Te Anau via S.H. 9 to the north. The first 32 km along the lake to Te Anau Downs is undulating, then the road turns inland, gradually rising, dips into the Eglinton Valley, and rises gently up the valley. The seal ends 8 km beyond Te Anau Downs.

Good sites for free camping along Lake Te Anau and the Eglinton Valley are easy to find, but stock up with provisions in Te Anau, since there are no shops or settlements along the way. Take insect repellent; the sandflies are murderous.

At 43 km from Te Anau Downs, you reach Cascade Creek. There is a campground here. It is another 26 km from here to the Homer Tunnel. The road passes Lake Gunn and Lake Fergus, climbs briefly over the Divide (a watershed) and turns westward up the Hollyford River.

From the Divide to the Homer Tunnel is 15 km. More than half the distance along the Hollyford Valley is relatively gentle, then the climb to the Homer Tunnel begins. Much of this stretch is sealed, but the road's surface is often broken up by the harsh weather and the constant roadworks necessary. The Homer Tunnel is 1,219 m above sea-level, 1,200 m long, and dark and narrow. You must have lights. One cyclist recommends having a car follow you through for safety's sake.

Milford village has a hotel, and a lodge with bunkrooms and campsites. Booking is essential for the hotel and strongly advisable for the lodge.

Milford Sound is 15 km long and is 290 m deep at its deepest part. Sheer rock walls, down which waterfalls cascade, rise for 1,200 m and more out of the sea on either side. The most famous peak (but not the tallest) is wedge-shaped Mitre Peak (1,692 m). There are scenic flights and launch trips down the Sound from Milford village.

DAY 3 *MANAPOURI TO TUATAPERE*
83 km

This is the "back route" to Southland, a sealed but quiet road running along the eastern edge of Fiordland. It passes through a sparsely populated region, with no shops or towns along the way. The countryside is rough and dry at first, but becomes greener and lusher approaching the coast.

Five kilometres outside Manapouri, turn right (southeast) for Tuatapere. A 5 km flat is followed by a gentle climb above the dam and weirs of the Maroru power scheme. Undulating countryside follows for 5 km, then a 15 km plain. This is followed by the only real challenge of the day: a stiff 2 km climb up Jericho Hill. From then on the terrain is flat to gently rolling the whole way to Tuatapere.

■ **Side Trip:** At 37 km from Manapouri the road to Lake Monowai leads westward. This is sealed for the first 4 km, which brings you to Monowai power station. This was opened in 1922 and is now one of the smallest working hydro-electric power stations in the country. Lake Monowai is another 9 km west over a rough gravel road. The level of this lake was raised in 1925, drowning trees along the shore; these now stand stark and leafless above the water. It is a salutary lesson to visit Lake Monowai: this is what could

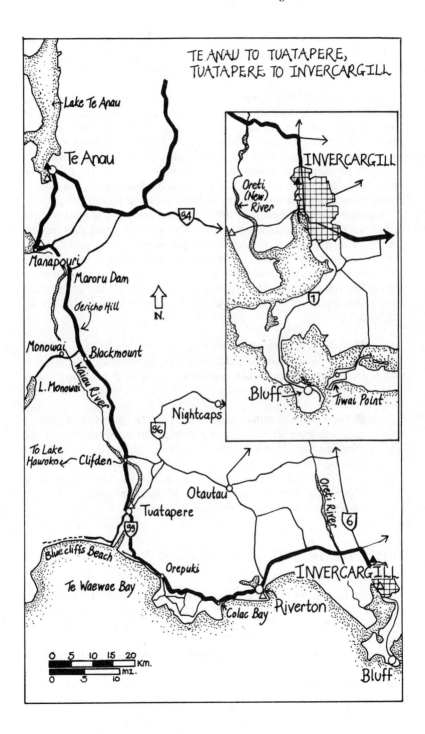

TE ANAU TO TUATAPERE,
TUATAPERE TO INVERCARGILL

have happened to Manapouri. Camping is not allowed beside the lake, but there are suitable spots along the road leading to it.

Seventy kilometres from Manapouri you come to Clifden. The old suspension bridge to the west of the main road was built in 1900, and is the largest suspension bridge in New Zealand. It is preserved by the Historic Places Trust. There is a good spot for pitching a tent below the bridge, though this is also a popular picnic spot in summer. Keep above the high-water mark, since the river level fluctuates. Clifden's other attraction is its limestone caves, which are 1.5 km along the Otautau road to the east.

Tautapere (pop. 859), formerly a timber town, is spread out on either side of the Waiau River. It has a hotel, motel and two motorcamps. The municipal motorcamp is pleasantly sited on the eastern bank of the Waiau. The other motorcamp has cabins. Tautapere is an interesting place to spend a day or two, not so much for itself as for the surrounding countryside. There is a tourist information centre in the main street which details its attractions.

■ **Side Trip:** Lake Hauroko, 32 km into the hills from Clifden, is New Zealand's deepest lake, beautifully situated between steep bush-clad mountains. There is a campground on the way to the lake.

■ **Side Trip:** Southwest of Tuatapere is Bluecliffs Beach, a vast expanse of white sand along the edge of stormy Te Waewae Bay. This is 20 km from town, half of the road being sealed, the other half being gravel and hilly, but worth the trip. Four kilometres along the beach the road ends in a wash-out, but a walking track linking Bluecliffs with Hauroko is currently being developed.

DAY 4 TUATAPERE TO INVERCARGILL ───────
85 km

Leave Tuatapere via S.H. 99 to the southeast. The first 10 km are flat to undulating; the next 30 km are through low coastal hills and are quite strenuous. The countryside is green and windswept, reminiscent of parts of Scotland.

Colac Bay, 48 km from Tuatapere, is a seaside settlement of holiday homes set on the windswept shore. There is a tavern here, but no store. The next 15 km to Riverton are flat, except for a mild

1.5 km hill just before the town. The road then drops gently down beside the Jacobs River estuary and crosses a long narrow bridge into the town.

Riverton (pop. 1,465) is a fishing-port and market town. It is the oldest settlement in Southland, dating its foundation to a whaling settlement in 1835. It is a charming town, set as it is on a sparkling estuary, with good beaches nearby. There is a small local museum, in Palmerston St., and a paua factory. Jet boat rides go upriver from the fisherman's cooperative west of the bridge into town.

Riverton has a motel and a motorcamp (cabins). The motorcamp is at Riverton Rocks southwest of town—turn right along the foreshore instead of left across the bridge when entering the township.

From Riverton to Invercargill is 38 km of flat road, rather dull, with busy and fast-moving traffic. The water in the streams across the plain is not fit for drinking and there are, therefore, few if any good spots for free camping. The best, perhaps, is at the Oreti River, halfway to Invercargill.

At 30 km from Riverton, turn south along S.H. 6 which leads into the city. This last stretch is a boring ride unless you are interested in fast-food outlets and used-car lots. Just 1 km before the city centre turn right into Victoria Ave. for the nearest motorcamp to the city centre, situated in the showgrounds.

Invercargill also has a number of hotels and motels and a Youth Hostel. There is another motorcamp (cabins) in Tay St. seven blocks south then west of Victoria Ave., and yet another at Oreti Beach, 8 km southwest of the central Post Office.

Invercargill (pop. 48,179) is Southland's largest town. It was founded in 1856 in an area that was mostly swamp and bush, but soon became prosperous as the natural outlet for Southland's wealthy farming areas.

Invercargill is a flat city with a grid layout, but it has attractive parks, of which Queens Park, near the city centre, is the largest. The Southland Centennial Museum and Art Gallery is found at the southern end of the park. The city Art Gallery is not far away, in Anderson Park.

Invercargill to Dunedin

The main route to Dunedin, the direct inland route via S.H. 1, is not an overly interesting route. If you are in a hurry, take the train instead. This departs from Invercargill at 8.55 A.M. Monday to Saturday and arrives in Dunedin at 6.20 P.M. Otherwise, take the coastal route as described below. Be warned, however, that this includes some tough cycling, including 75 km of gravel road.

The stages described below take you to Dunedin in three to four days. You could in fact do it in two if you wished but you would have to work hard. Better to set a more leisurely and more enjoyable pace.

Note that the stages described here will suit cyclists who are camping. Formal accommodation is sparse in some stretches. Cyclists who wish to stay at a hotel or motel should consider the following stages instead:

Invercargill to Chaslands: 110 km
Chaslands to Balclutha: 98 km
Balclutha to Dunedin: 77 km

The first stage can be reduced to 91 km by taking the Tokanui rather than the Otara/Curio Bay route—see below.

DAY 5 INVERCARGILL TO CURIO BAY
79 km

Leaving Invercargill, continue southward, past the city centre along Dee St. to Clyde St. Two kilometres along, Clyde St. veers left and becomes Bluff Rd., running along the harbour's edge. Turn left after seven blocks into Ohara St. Three streets along, this veers right onto Scott St. Follow Scott St. southeast. This joins S.H. 92.

The first 46 km from Invercargill lie across flat to undulating flood-plains. There is a store at Gorge Road, 31 km from Invercargill, but none at Fortrose, the tiny estuarine settlement where the Mataura River reaches the sea. At Fortrose, S.H. 9 turns northeast into the hills to Tokanui. Continue southeast instead towards Otara, 11 km away across low rolling hills. (There is a potential free camping spot at Fortrose, an open grassy space with pit toilets and open fireplaces, but no water.)

At Otara the seal ends. Just beyond Otara, turn east to Haldane. The next 12 km to Haldane are a moderately hilly stretch. Beyond Haldane is a flat 3 km stretch alongside an estuary, then 6 km of further low hills until the road reaches the coast at Porpoise Bay. At Porpoise Bay, turn left (south) for Curio Bay. The motorcamp is 1.5 km along at the end of the bay.

Curio Bay takes its name from the fossilised tree-trunks found on its rocky tidal platforms. The fossils are estimated to be 160 million years old.

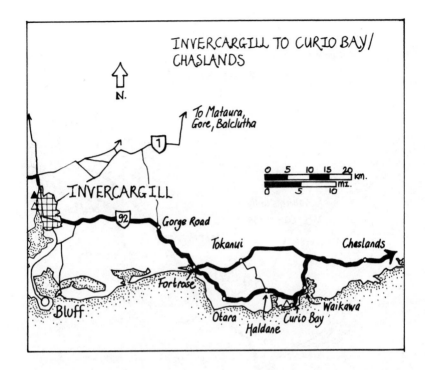

■ **ALTERNATIVE ROUTE: Invercargill to Chaslands (91 km)** At Fortrose, take S.H. 92 northeast to Tokanui. The 13 km between Fortrose and Tokanui consist of low rolling hills, quite demanding. Tokanui is a wayside settlement with a store.

A rolling to undulating 15 km stretch, follows to the Waikawa/Curio Bay intersection. Turn left here into the hills. The seal ends as the road begins to climb steeply through the bush—see below. ■

DAY 6 *CURIO BAY TO POUNAWEA* ─────────
76 km

From Curio Bay the road runs northward along the edge of the Waikawa Harbour. There is short stretch of seal before rejoining S.H. 92, 12 km from the coast. Turn right along S.H. 92. The seal ends again and a steep 3 km climb through bush-clad hills begins.

This is a particularly difficult stretch. The corners are steeply cambered and piles of loose gravel have built up. Mountain bikes

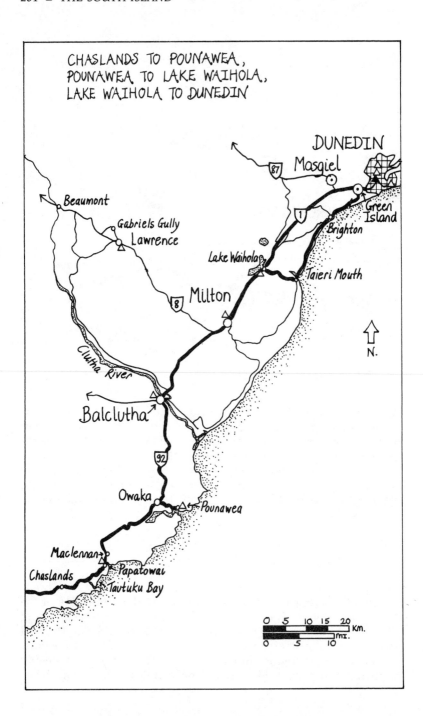

CHASLANDS TO POUNAWEA,
POUNAWEA TO LAKE WAIHOLA,
LAKE WAIHOLA TO DUNEDIN

DUNEDIN

Mosgiel

87

Beaumont

Gabriels Gully

Lawrence

Green Island

1

Brighton

Lake Waihola

Milton

Taieri Mouth

8

N.

Clutha River

Balclutha

92

Owaka

Pounawea

Maclennan

Chaslands

Papatowai

Tautuku Bay

0 5 10 15 20 Km.
0   5   10 mi.

should manage this; touring bikes may need some pushing. Fortunately, traffic is light except on holiday weekends.

After the climb there is a moderate 3 km stretch, then a 2 km descent. Seven kilometres after joining S.H. 92 you come to a lonely but idyllic camping spot—a grassy meander of the old road with a stream nearby.

A longish downhill stretch follows, then a slight climb and a descent to the Chaslands Valley. This is not a notably attractive part of the Catlins, most of its bush having been cut over. There is a farm lodge here, however, with cabins.

A climb out of Chaslands is followed by a descent to the Tautuku River, then a gentle stretch along Tautuku Bay. At the eastern end of Tautuku Bay, a 0.5 km detour will bring you to a white-sand beach that sweeps southward to the Tautuku Peninsula (accessible along the beach). There is a pleasant grassy picnic area beside the beach, but do not be tempted to set up camp here, since the sandflies are horrendous.

A steep 2 km climb up Florence Hill is followed by a descent to Papatowai. This is a harbourside settlement of holiday baches. There is a motorcamp on the far side of the settlement, and a store at McLennans 2 km beyond.

From Papatowai the next 4 km are rolling country, followed by a steep 5 km climb up Table Hill (2 km along is a pleasant roadside picnic area). A 2 km descent is followed by another 1 km hill, then a long descent to rejoin the seal 11 km from Owaka. Here the bush gives way to settled farmland.

The last 11 km to Owaka are a gentle harbourside ride. Owaka (pop. 447) is a small rural town of no great note, but it does have a tearoom and a small shopfront museum. There is a motorcamp (cabins) 4 km east, at Pounawea, on the estuary of the Catlins River.

DAY 7 *POUNAWEA TO LAKE WAIHOLA* —————————
80 km–115 km

Return to Owaka and turn northeast again along S.H. 92. The road to Balclutha, 38 km away, is quiet and sealed. There is a moderate 15 km climb 5 km outside Owaka; the rest of the distance lies through gently rolling country, with the last 2 km into Balclutha being flat.

Balclutha (pop. 4,227) is a market town near the mouth of the Clutha, New Zealand's second-longest river (338 km) and its largest in volume. Balclutha has a hotel, several motels and a motorcamp.

At Balclutha you join S.H. 1 which heads north to Dunedin. A narrow six-humped bridge crosses the river and is followed by a demanding 2 km climb, then strenuous rolling country for 16 km, and a 3 km flat into Milton. Traffic on this stretch is usually busy, S.H. 1 being the main road between Invercargill and Dunedin.

Milton (pop. 2,154) is strung out along either side of the highway. It has a woollen mill, some fine Victorian churches, a small museum. There is a motel in town and a municipal motorcamp with a swimming pool at the northern end of town.

A 7 km straight outside Milton is followed by undulating country. Seventeen kilometres north of Milton is Lake Waihola. This small lakeside settlement has a store, a tearoom, a motel and a motorcamp (cabins).

Lake Waihola is a pleasant enough place to stop for the night, though you may of course wish to continue to Dunedin, now only 35 km away along S.H. 1. The road is busy but flat to undulating, and very easy, until the outskirts of Mosgiel, 14 km outside Dunedin. There it climbs a longish hill before descending through the suburbs of Fairfield and Green Island, climbing another short hill and descending into the city itself. For further details, see below.

DAY 8 LAKE WAIHOLA TO DUNEDIN VIA TAIERI MOUTH
60 km

This is an indirect route to Dunedin, but is much more interesting than following S.H. 1.

From Lake Waihola take the Taieri Mouth road southeast. This is a gravel road which climbs steeply through the hills to 306 m, before descending equally steeply to the coast 12 km away.

At Taieri Mouth, turn northeast across the river. The seal begins again here and the road hugs the coast for the next 18 km. This is Dunedin's holiday coast, bare and often cold, but with long sandy beaches and a sprinkling of holiday baches.

Brighton, 18 km from Taieri Mouth, is the first sizeable settlement along the coast. From here to Dunedin is mostly residential. At Waldronville, 12 km south of the city centre, the road turns inland to Green Island. This is a suburb squeezed along a valley at the southeastern edge of Dunedin, separated from the city itself by a short, steep hill.

Dunedin is a strangely difficult city to find your way into. The signposting is inadequate and, because of the hills, you never quite seem to be making it. Once at the Octagon in the centre of town, however, orientation is easy.

Continue along the Main South Road through Green Island. At the eastern end of Green Island, cars turn left down a ramp onto a short stretch of motorway; cyclists will find it easiest to continue straight ahead along a stretch of footpath to rejoin Main South Road half a kilometre ahead.

There is a motorcamp (cabins) 2.5 km along the Kaikorai Valley Road which runs north of here. Otherwise, turn right (east) for the city. The road loops steeply up a hill, passes the Lookout Point firestation, and descends steeply into the city. Follow in succession, in a more-or-less northeastward direction, the Caversham Valley Rd., South Rd., and Prices St., to the Octagon.

The Octagon is, as the name suggests, an eight-sided public space right in the centre of the city. You will find the Otago Visitors Centre at its northern edge (phone 743 899). If this is closed, try the city library for information, just behind.

Dunedin has a wide choice of hotels, motels, lodges and bed-and-breakfasts. There is also a Youth Hostel.

There are two motorcamps near the city centre besides the one mentioned above. Both have cabins or on-site caravans. One is in Leith Valley 4 km north of the Octagon; the other is in St. Kilda, an equal distance south.

For Leith Valley, take George St. North from the Octagon for 1.5 km; turn left into Duke St. which passes the Woodhaugh Gardens and continue along Malvern St. to the camp.

For St. Kilda take Princes St. south, veer left onto the Andersons Bay (signposted "Andy Bay") road, then right 1.5 km along into Royal Crescent. After three blocks turn left into Marlow St. and immediately right into Culling St. The motorcamp is beside the showgrounds not far from the beach.

St. Kilda and its neighbour St. Clair are bracing, south-facing, and wind-swept beaches at the base of the Otago Peninsula.

Dunedin and Excursions

Dunedin (pop. 92,622) is certainly a town in which to spend some time. It has a number of well-preserved Victorian and Edwardian buildings, some good museums, and interesting surroundings.

The bay and peninsula on which the city stands were once densely populated by Maoris. Their numbers were much reduced by influenza and other diseases caught after contacts with visiting pakeha seamen and whalers, and their land was purchased by the Otago Association, a colonising institution associated with the

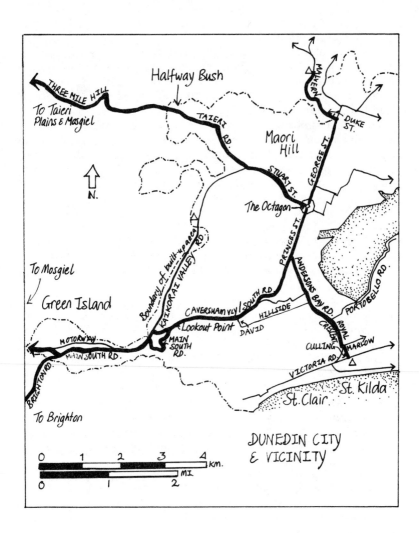

Presbyterian Free Church.

The first pakeha settlers arrived in 1847. They established what they hoped would be a just, godly and prosperous settlement. The new settlement's first years were hard ones, however, because of its isolation. Fortunately gold was discovered inland in 1861. Dunedin became rapidly less godly but substantially more prosperous as miners and diggers and their camp-followers flooded in from around the world. It became New Zealand's largest city, and the centre of its commerce and industry.

By the end of the century the gold was mostly worked out.

Dunedin gradually lost its commercial predominance to Auckland. It is now less than a tenth the size of its northern rival, little more than a provincial centre and a University town.

It retains, however, its fine old buildings and is largely unspoiled by modern development, so is a fascinating town to wander round. Its grander churches include Knox Church (1876), First Church (1873), a fine Norman-Gothic edifice behind the Octagon, St. Joseph's Roman Catholic Cathedral (1886), and All Saints Anglican Church (1875). Among the many other buildings of note are the grandiose Railway Station (1904) and Olveston (1906), a Jacobean-style merchant's home.

Museums worth a visit include the Otago Early Settler's Museum and the Otago Museum. The Dunedin City Art Gallery has an extensive collection of the works of Francis Hodgkins (1870–1947), perhaps New Zealand's best-known painter. The Hocken Library at the University is one of the country's main historical research libraries, and also has a good art collection.

A number of interesting day-trips are possible in the vicinity of Dunedin. If you have no more than a day to spare, the best choice is probably a circuit of the Otago Peninsula.

■ SIDE TRIP: *OTAGO PENINSULA CIRCUIT* ———
60 km +

The Otago Visitors Centre in the Octagon will provide brochures on the attractions of the Peninsula to study before you leave.

Take Princes St. south of the Octagon, veering left onto the Andersons Bay Rd. after 1 km, then left again into Portobello Rd. after another 1.5 km. Continue along this harbourside road which hugs the northern side of the Peninsula. At 10 km from the city you pass Glenfalloch Woodland Garden. Another 11 km on is the turn-off to Portobello Marine Laboratory (a 2 km detour) a research station run by the University.

Continue along the harbour's edge from Portobello to Taiaroa Head, 13 km away. This is a wildlife refuge, the only known mainland breeding ground of the royal albatross. Access to the albatross colony is restricted: it is forbidden during the breeding season, and you must book ahead through the Visitors Centre the rest of the year.

Other sights at the Head are the 12 m Tiri Tiri lighthouse and the Armstrong disappearing gun. This is a 150 mm cannon installed in 1886 against the imagined threat of Russian invasion. This sight is, in fact, literally out-of-sight, since the gun is situated in an excavation below the ground and only rises above the surface to fire a shot.

Across the harbour from Taiaroa Head is the Aramoana spit, an area of wild beauty once proposed as the site of an aluminium smelter.

Return from Taiaroa Head to Portobello. Turn up Highcliff Rd. behind the village. This climbs steeply to the backbone of the Peninsula. Follow the ridge southwest.

> ■ **Side Trip:** Alternatively or additionally you can turn south to Hoopers Inlet and Cape Saunders just before Portobello. This is a lonely and attractive part of the Peninsula. A hilly 12 km gravel stretch will bring you to the Cape Saunders lighthouse.

Turn off Highcliff Rd. along Camp Rd. to Larnach Castle. This is an extravagant mansion built in the Scottish baronial style in 1871 by William Larnach (1833–1898), a wealthy banker and politician. It is open to the public.

Camp Rd. drops down to the harbour's edge again at McAndrew Bay; alternatively you can return to the Highcliff road and continue westward along the ridge. At 7 km from Larnach Castle take Centre Rd. to the left, which drops steeply into Ocean Grove and continue westward again to St. Kilda.

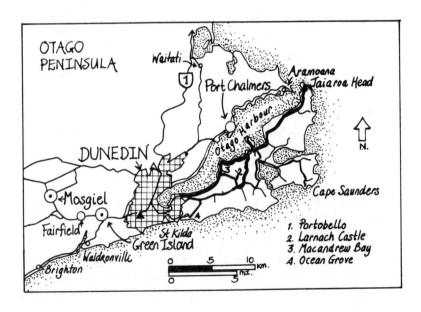

Dunedin to Queenstown/Wanaka

The alternative routes as far as Alexandra are via Roxburgh and the Clutha Valley, or via Middlemarch and the Maniototo Plains. I prefer the Middlemarch route. The countryside is starker and grander. The Roxburgh route is a pretty one and requires one day less, but it involves retracing your steps to Milton and is a much busier road that carries considerable heavy traffic. However, in winter or in bad weather, the Middlemarch road, being higher, may be impassible for cyclists, in which case you will have no option but to take the Clutha Valley route.

DAY 9 DUNEDIN TO MIDDLEMARCH ─────────
85 km

This is a moderate day in distance but a difficult one in effort. There is some tough climbing to do, that is, unless you take the train (see below).

There are two main alternative routes out of Dunedin:

A. Via Mosgiel:

Retrace your route between the city centre and Green Island via Lookout Point. Turn right at the first intersection beyond the Green Island shops and join busy S.H. 1 heading southeast.

There is a long but gradual climb between Green Island Fairfield, then a steep 1 km descent to the Mosgiel plains. It is tempting to get up speed on this stretch, but take care: there is a nasty hollow and bump on the shoulder halfway down which could end your trip prematurely if you hit it at speed.

Turn right at the bottom of the hill on S.H. 87 for Mosgiel. Mosgiel (pop. 9,063) was a prosperous woollen-milling town, but its mills have recently closed. There is a Roman Catholic seminary here (Holy Cross College), and an agricultural research centre nearby (Invermay). Mosgiel has two motels and a caravan park. From Mosgiel continue across the plains to Outram, a small farming centre 14 km away.

B. Via Abbots Hill:

This route involves more climbing, but is a quieter road, and bypasses Mosgiel to the north.

Take Stuart St. westward of the Octagon, climbing steeply. This becomes Taieri Rd. which passes through Halfway Bush, climbing to 369 m before descending to the Taieri Plains. At the beginning of the plains, you can take Dukes Rd. southwest past Invermay Agricultural Research Station, to join S.H. 87 just north of Mosgiel, or

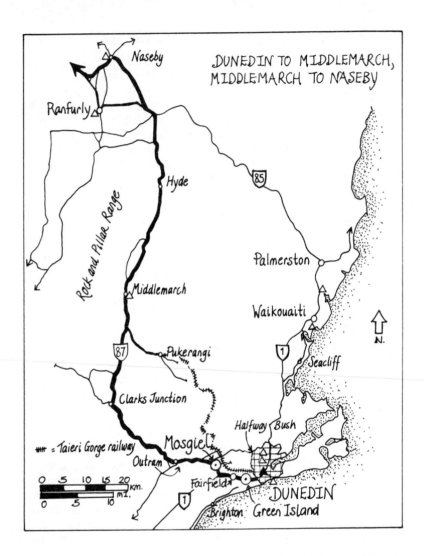

Milners Rd. northwest, to join S.H. 87 midway between Mosgiel and Outram.

Just beyond Outram, S.H. 27 turns into the hills. A stiff unrelenting 6.5 km climb follows. The road then climbs a further series of ridges, each one higher than the one before, in a seemingly never-ending succession, finally reaching 560 m.

The area is high, open farmland, green and pleasant most of the year, but cold and bleak in mid-winter, often with a dusting of snow lying on the fields.

At 15 km from Outram the road levels off for several kilometres. There is a tavern at Clark's Junction 20 km from Outram. Three kilometres beyond this comes a nasty surprise: a long, winding 2 km descent into a gully cut by a tributary of the Taieri River. Here you will curse fate as you lose much of the height you have so laboriously gained.

A long climb out of this gully is followed by another descent into another gully, fortunately less imposing than the last—and then a third! Whatever your standard of fitness, you will find this a tough stretch of road.

The compensation is, perhaps, the landscape. In these hills are seen the first of the curious rock formations that have given their name to the Rock and Pillar Range, the high hills to the west. This is a lonely region of rocks and swamp and tussock-grass, with little sign of human habitation. The water in the streams is sweet and clear. If the weather is right, you could camp out.

The last 8 km into Middlemarch are flat. Middlemarch is a tiny farming centre and winter sports centre set amongst poplars in the middle of the Lower Taieri Plain. It has a pleasant tearoom, a shop, a motel and a motorcamp (cabins).

■ **ALTERNATIVE ROUTE:** There is a much easier way to Middlemarch, via the Taieri Gorge Limited. This train runs daily between October and April up the scenic Taieri Gorge from Dunedin to Pukerangi and back. Departure time is 3.30 P.M.

The return fare is $35.00, but you can take both your bike and yourself to Pukerangi for half-fare. Pukerangi is a railway platform in the middle of nowhere, but is only 20 km southwest of Middlemarch. The first 12 km of the road from Pukerangi are gravel, the last 8 km are seal on S.H. 87.

As mentioned the train runs only between October and April. Outside these months the Middlemarch route is probably too cold for most cyclists in any case. ■

DAY 10 MIDDLEMARCH TO NASEBY ————————
65 km

Continue along S.H. 87 northwards from Middlemarch. The first 10 km are flat to undulating, then the seal ends as more difficult rolling country begins.

If you are looking for a place to camp en route, you will find that the first clear water available is from Six Mile Creek, 8 km north of the village. Most of the numerous streams from then on are clean.

There is a short stretch of seal through Hyde, a dying rural community 25 km north of Middlemarch. This is followed by 15 km of quite demanding hills, then a flat sealed stretch 5 km before joining S.H. 85 at Kyburn.

Turn west here. Turn northwest to Naseby along the second road to the right after the junction. Naseby is 18 km away. The road is unsealed and although it seems level it is in fact gradually climbing.

Naseby (pop. 133) was founded in a gold-rush in 1863. At its peak the town attracted several thousand miners but, like all mining towns, its decline was rapid. During the middle of this century it became little more than a ghost town. It has today seen a revival of prosperity as a tourist and holiday centre. In winter it is a centre for curling and for ice-skating; in summer campers congregate here.

Many of the town's old buildings have been preserved and restored. These include the Athenaeum (1865), the mud-built St. George's Anglican Church (1875) and the former County Building (1878), which now houses the Maniatoto Early Settlers Museum.

Naseby has a motorcamp (cabins) south of town towards Ranfurly, and a hotel.

■ **ALTERNATIVE ROUTE:** Instead of turning off direct towards Naseby outside Kyburn, you could continue along S.H. 85, 15 km southwestward to Ranfurly. Ranfurly (pop. 961) is the chief town of the Upper Maniototo Plain. It is a strangely empty place, its shops and houses scattered almost at random across an empty landscape. It has a tearoom, several shops, a hotel, a motel and a motorcamp (cabins). This detour adds 12 km to the day. Naseby is 15 km to the north. ■

DAY 11 NASEBY TO ALEXANDRA
92 km direct; via St. Bathans: 106 km

From Naseby it is 8 km back to S.H. 85. Take the Ranfurly-Naseby road southeast. This turns due south after 4 km: veer right here along a gravel road running southeast. This rejoins S.H. 85 northwest of Ranfurly.

S.H. 85 is a wide sealed road, usually virtually empty of traffic, except in midsummer. It continues westward through low rolling hills for 25 km, before turning south down the wide valley of the Manuherikia River towards Omakau and Alexandra.

■ **ALTERNATIVE ROUTE:** A minor road to Omakau turns off S.H. 85 to the south 16 km from Naseby. This saves 1 km on the day's total distance, but offers no other advantages. ■

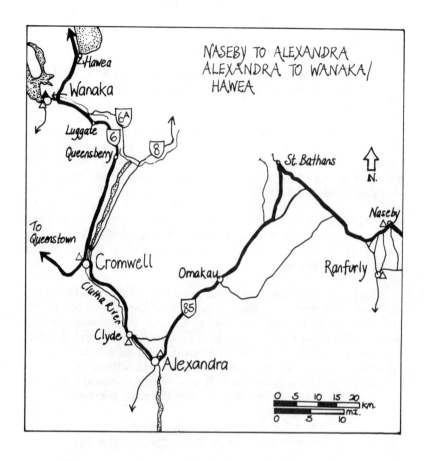

■ Side Trip: At 26 km from Naseby the St. Bathans road leaves S.H. 85. St. Bathans is 10 km of rough gravel away. The first 4 km is a gentle descent down a river valley, followed by a mild 5 km climb and a 1 km descent.

St. Bathans, charmingly situated in a small leafy valley set amidst bare hills, was also founded by gold-miners in 1863. The lake (Blue Lake) below the town is a huge crater formed by hydraulic excavations over the years.

Mining ceased here in 1934. St. Bathans today is not quite a ghost town, its permanent population of 13 being swollen by holidaymakers in midsummer. Some of its older buildings are preserved, including the pub and the old hall, which houses a historical display.

There is a hotel in St. Bathans but no other accommodation. Good spots for free camping are easy to find around Blue Lake (but keep away from the edges of the cliffs). You can swim in the lake; there are public toilets in the hall; for a small fee you can use the pub's facilities. Plans are underway to establish a formal campground.

Continue through St. Bathans and rejoin S.H. 85, 17 km south. The first 5 km beyond St. Bathans are gravel, then the seal begins again.

The road most of the length of the Manuherikia Valley is gently, almost imperceptibly, downhill, but there are several minor rises en route. The countryside is sparsely populated but fertile. The only settlement of any size en route is Omakau, which has several shops, a hotel and a motorcamp.

■ **ALTERNATIVE ROUTE:** At 9 km north of Alexandra you can save 11 km of the distance to Queenstown or Wanaka by turning southwest direct to Clyde. Clyde, 8 km away, has several motels and a motorcamp. ■

Alexandra (pop. 4,842) is a fruit-growing town and administrative centre. Founded in 1862, it sits above the confluence of the Manuherikia River with the mighty Clutha. It is surrounded by stone-fruit orchards. You can buy peaches, plums and apricots from wayside stalls as you enter town. Casual no-questions-asked jobs picking fruit are sometimes available here during the season.

There are several hotels and motels. The motorcamp (cabins) is set above the Manuherikia River beside the road into town.

■ ALTERNATIVE ROUTE: Dunedin to Alexandra via Lawrence

■ DAY 9A DUNEDIN TO LAWRENCE
92 km–104 km

Return to Milton from Dunedin, either via S.H. 1 all the way, or via the coastal road to Taieri Mouth.

Three kilometres south of Milton, turn along S.H. 8 northwest to Lawrence and Roxburgh. The first 7 km are flat to undulating, then the road passes through 19 km of rolling hill country, climbing over several low saddles before Waitahuna, a farming locality. The following 11 km to Lawrence involve more climbing, slightly more strenuous than before.

Lawrence (pop. 552) is a pretty and picturesque old town set amongst poplars and silver birch trees. It has a guesthouse and a

Blue Lake, Saint Bathans

motorcamp (cabins). Lawrence was founded in 1862, after gold had been discovered in nearby Gabriel's Gully the year before. There is a museum on the main street, and numerous sites and relics of the gold-mining days in the surrounding hills, many of them preserved as part of the Otago Goldfields Park.

> ■ **Side Trip:** An interesting excursion from Lawrence is Gabriels Gully, scene of the original strike which began Otago's gold-rushes. Cross the bridge across the river north of town. A sealed road leads 5 km into the hills to the Gully. Now uninhabited, this was, for a brief period just over a century ago, crowded with miners and covered by wall-to-wall tents and spoil-heaps. Return to S.H.8 the way you came, or take a shortcut by taking the Munro Rd. to Evans Flat 5 km northwest of Lawrence. This involves a short steep climb out of Gabriels Gully before turning southeast down a small valley towards the main road.

■ DAY 10A LAWRENCE TO ALEXANDRA —————
98 km

The first part of the day is quite demanding. The first 15 km from Lawrence are hilly, with two longish climbs, before a gentler 5 km stretch to Beaumont, a farming and fruit-growing village. Beaumont has a hotel and a caravan park with campsites.

Beyond Beaumont comes a challenging climb, the road rising to 400 m over less than 3.5 km. It then gently drops to Raes Junction. From here most of the way to Roxburgh along the Clutha Valley is flat to undulating.

Roxburgh (pop. 721) is the centre of a notable fruit-growing area, the green foliage of the trees contrasting with the dry surrounding hills. Like most towns in the area, Roxburgh had its origins in the gold-mining days. These days are long past, but there is an open-cast (open-pit) coal mine nearby and, 10 km upriver, a major hydro-electric power station, completed in 1962. Roxburgh has two motels and a motorcamp (cabins).

The road as far as Roxburgh Hydro is flat to undulating. Beyond the dam, it climbs away from the river. For the next 10 km it clings

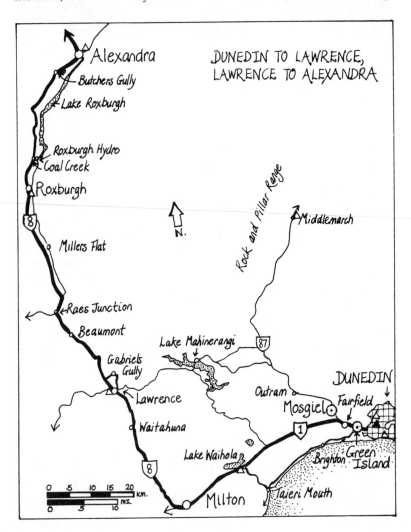

DUNEDIN TO LAWRENCE,
LAWRENCE TO ALEXANDRA

to the steep hillsides above the Clutha, usually gradually climbing, but also twice dipping in order to cross tributary gullies. It reaches a peak of 430 m just before Butchers Reservoir (25 km from Roxburgh Hydro), and drops most of the last 10 km into Alexandra.

For notes on Alexandra, see Day 11.

DAY 12 *ALEXANDRA TO QUEENSTOWN/WANAKA/ HAWEA*
93 km/86 km/97 km

Leave Alexandra on S.H. 8 to the west. The first 10 km to Clyde are flat and easy riding.

Clyde is another former gold-mining town. S.H. 8 actually bypasses the town, but Clyde is worth the effort of a short side trip. The town centre preserves many of its historic buildings, and there is a Goldfields Museum in the stone courthouse (1864). Clyde has several motels and a motorcamp.

Just above Clyde is the massive Clyde dam, begun in 1977, and due for completion in 1990 (though progress may be delayed by industrial troubles). The hydro-electric power station here, with a generating capacity of 610 megawatts, will be one of New Zealand's largest. Behind the dam, the waters of the Clutha will gradually build up, forming a lake that is anticipated to cover 25 square kilometres, filling the gorge between here and Cromwell, and drowning the old business centre of Cromwell.

You can rejoin S.H. 8 above Clyde by continuing towards the dam and climbing the steep road winding up to the lookout above. From Clyde to Cromwell is 21 km. The new road through the Gorge is well-formed and has easy gradients. There is a good view from the Dunstan Memorial at the northwestern end of the Gorge.

S.H. 8 then passes to the east of Cromwell township and crosses the Clutha to the north of town. Once across the bridge, turn south along S.H. 6 if returning to Queenstown. For a description of the route, see Tour 11, Day 6.

Otherwise, turn north for Wanaka. The next 55 km are an easy ride, mostly flat to undulating, but with some low, rolling country nearer the lake. There is a small hydro settlement, Luggate, en route, 40 km north of Cromwell.

■ **ALTERNATIVE ROUTE:** If you have already visited Wanaka, you may prefer to bypass it this time, embarking direct on the Haast Pass road. If so, turn north towards Hawea 4 km before Wanaka. Hawea, 11 km from the intersection, has a hotel, two motels, and a motorcamp (cabins). ■

TOUR 14. THE WEST COAST AND NELSON

10–12 days: 837 km–908 km
(with Golden Bay Excursion 15–16 days: 1,222 km +)

This itinerary takes you through the rugged Haast Pass into South Westland, and along the West Coast past the great glaciers of Fox and Franz Josef, and through the former mining towns of Hokitika and Greymouth.

Leaving the West Coast, you turn inland up the Buller Gorge into the high country of the Nelson Lakes region. From here, there is a choice of two routes back to Picton to meet the Cook Strait ferry: direct via the Wairau Valley to Blenheim, or via Nelson, with the added possibility of an excursion to sunny Golden Bay.

West Coasters like to regard the West Coast as a region apart from the rest of New Zealand. It is certainly set apart physically, being a narrow coastal plain hemmed in by the high Southern Alps and the wild Tasman Sea. It is also New Zealand's wettest region.

West Coasters have a reputation for being an independent and lawless people. Their lawlessness consists mostly of a certain disregard for the licensing laws (West Coast pubs traditionally stay open longer hours than most); the Coast in fact is a hospitable region with one of the lowest serious crime-rates in New Zealand.

Much of the West Coast is covered in dense bush, lush and green in appearance. Where this has been felled, however, infertile pakihi soils have formed: areas of waterlogged peat with an impermeable sub-stratum, where nothing grows but moss and rushes.

The West Coast was only sparsely populated by the Maori before pakeha settlement, but was the source of all the country's greenstone (jade), which was highly prized for making ornaments and axes.

In the 1860s, gold was discovered. A rapid influx of miners and entrepreneurs and camp-followers led to the growth of shantytowns all along the coast. After the gold-rushes were over, some of these disappeared; others survived as ports or as centres for coal-mining and timber-milling.

The West Coast has traditionally relied on its extractive industries. Today, with many coal-mines closing, and with saw-mills winding down, it is clearly a region in decline.

The most controversial issue on the Coast in recent years has been the future of its remaining native forests. The environ-

Lake Matheson (Photo by Richard Oddy)

mentalists have largely won the debate, and large areas have been preserved from milling in State or National Parks. (Consequently it is unwise to claim to be a "greenie" in many a West Coast public bar.)

As mentioned above, the West Coast has a wet climate; it is a mild one, however, since the coastal location prevents extreme cold. Once over the alpine passes, snow is all but unknown, even in mid-winter. The prevailing wind is the southwesterly, although Greymouth suffers from a curious local wind known as the "Barber", an icy breeze channelled seawards down the gorge of the Grey River. The maximum rainfall, unlike the rest of New Zealand, comes in early summer. Winter weather is often drier and more settled.

The Haast Pass

Haast Pass is the southernmost road crossing of the Southern
Alps. It follows a route known to the Maori for centuries, but first
traversed by a pakeha, the prospector Charles Cameron, in 1863. It
is named after the explorer, Julius von Haast (1822–1887), geolo-
gist to the Canterbury Provincial Council.

South Westland long remained isolated from Central Otago.
Attempts to form a road between Hawea and Haast began spasmodically in 1929, more seriously in 1956. The crossing was finally
completed in 1965.

The Haast Pass road has long been regarded as a difficult road,
with long stretches of rough gravel, and being subject to slips, particularly on the wetter western side. Today it is losing its
notoriety: seal has been laid right from Haast township on the
coast to the top of the Haast Saddle. The Pass is much easier to do
from east to west, as described here, than west to east. Wanaka is
297 m above sea-level; the Pass itself at 564 m, and Haast Junction
at 7 m.

DAY 1 WANAKA TO MAKARORA
64 km

Take S.H. 6 west from Wanaka. At 4 km from the lakeside, turn
north towards Hawea and the Haast Pass. The next 11 km to
Hawea are through dry, rolling country. The road dips 3 km along
to cross the Hawea River, then gradually rises for 8 km to Hawea, a
small holiday township at the southern end of its namesake lake.
Hawea has a shop, a hotel and a motel. There is a motorcamp (cabins) just off the main road.

From Hawea, S.H. 6 largely follows the western shores of Lake
Hawea for 22 km to the Neck, a narrow strip of land separating
Lake Hawea and Lake Wanaka. Most of the distance, it is gradually
rising, with a short, steep climb to the Hawea Lookout midway.

The road is sealed for 14 km from Hawea, but a rough stretch of
gravel follows for the next 8 km. The surface here is usually heavily
corrugated due to excessive summer traffic.

From the Neck, the road steeply descends to Lake Wanaka, then
undulates along the eastern shore of the lake and up the wide
Makarora Valley. There is a 5 km stretch of seal beyond the Neck,
followed by 11 km of gravel. This is one of the few remaining
notorious stretches of road over the Haast, winding, narrow and

rough. The seal commences again some way up the valley.

Makarora is a tiny village with a service-station, a shop, a motel and a motorcamp (cabins). It is the centre of an all but unpopulated region. It is easy to find sites where you can pitch a tent undisturbed in all parts of the valley.

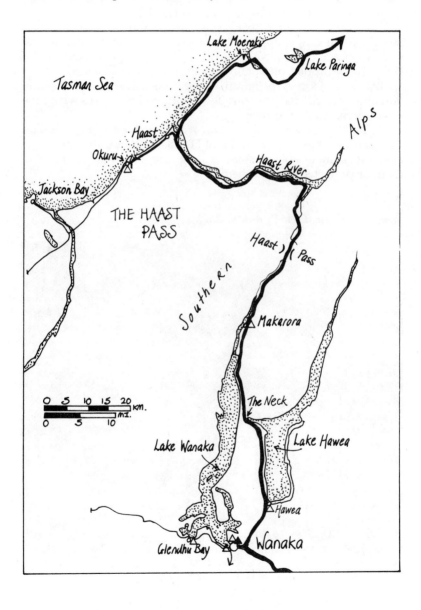

DAY 2 MAKARORA TO OKURU/LAKE MOERAKI ——
Okuru: 78 km; Lake Moeraki: 95 km

The road is sealed for 4 km beyond Makarora, then the gravel begins again. The beech forest closes in on either side as you begin the last tough climb to the Haast Saddle. Over 8 km, you climb from 350 m to 564 m, steeply over the last 2 km.

Over the Saddle, the seal begins again. You now have a curving, downhill run, dropping almost 400 m in less than 10 km. The views are glorious (if you stop to look): dark green bush on all sides, snow-capped mountains rising in the near distance.

The next 58 km to the mouth of the Haast River are more gently downhill, punctuated only by a few short moderate rises where the road briefly leaves the river.

Again, it is easy to find good off-road sites for camping. Beware the sandflies, however: as in all of South Westland, they are voracious. It is impossible to stop for long unless you are immune to them or protected against them.

Franz Josef glacier (Photo by Richard Oddy)

Just before the coast, S.H. 6 turns north across the Haast Bridge. There is a hotel on the south side of the river. Another 4 km south is Haast village, with a store, a motel, and a service-station. Another 11 km further south down the flat coastal road is a motor-camp (cabins) at Okuru.

■ **Side Trip:** The end of the road is Jackson Bay, 35 km beyond Okuru. In 1875 this was the scene of an ambitious colonising attempt; today there is nothing but a huddle of fishermen's cottages, a wharf, the beach, and the sea and bush and sky.

Lake Moeraki is 32 km to the north. The Haast Bridge is long and narrow, but has passing bays at intervals. The first 15 km after crossing the bridge are flat. Then there are some very tough hills to climb, involving three steep ascents of at least 150 m each in less than 12 km.

The last few kilometres to Lake Moeraki are more gentle. There is a motel at Lake Moeraki. If camping, you could set up your tent alongside the lake or, better, continue to Lake Paringa another 18 km upriver, where there is a lakeside rest area.

DAY 3 LAKE MOERAKI TO FOX GLACIER —————
87 km

The road initially follows the Moeraki River westward then turns northwest along the intriguingly named Windbag Stream. At Lake Paringa is a pleasant picnic area. There is a shop and takeaway bar a little further north.

From Lake Paringa to Bruce Bay, where the road briefly touches the coast again, there are 23 km of rolling to undulating country with long flat stretches. 10 km beyond Bruce Bay is a motel with cabins. This may seem to be curiously sited, in the middle of rough country in the back-of-beyond, but it is in fact only 10 km south of the entrance to the Copland Track, a major walking-track, which crosses the Alps to Mount Cook. From the entrance to this track to Fox Glacier is another 26 km, mostly flat to undulating country.

■ **Side Trip:** Fox Glacier village owes its existence almost entirely to tourism. Inland from here is the great Fox Glacier, 13 km in length (but retreating). If you want to visit the glacier, a rough gravel road leads southeastwards up the Fox River valley toward it. The glacier face is a 20-minute walk beyond the carpark. When leaving your bike, tie every-

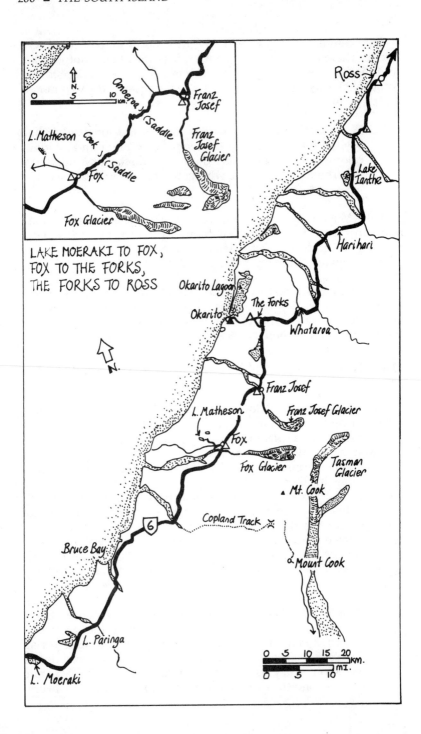

LAKE MOERAKI TO FOX,
FOX TO THE FORKS,
THE FORKS TO ROSS

thing down: the keas will steal anything loose, and probably attack at your saddle-bags. Do not venture too near the ice-face, for risk of falling blocks of ice. Information on this and other hikes in the vicinity can be found at the National Park information centre in the village.

■ **Side Trip:** Lake Matheson is another place that many visitors appreciate. On fine days, its placid surface mirrors Mount Cook. The lake is 5 km (by road) west of Fox Glacier. The walk around the lake takes 1 to 2 hours.

Fox Glacier has a store, a hotel and three motels; also a motorcamp (cabins) down the Lake Matheson road. It is usually advisable to book ahead at midsummer.

DAY 4 FOX GLACIER TO THE FORKS/OKARITO ———
39 km/47 km

This is a short stage, to allow time for sight-seeing. The area is so beautiful that few cyclists will want to hurry through it. Fox Glacier to Franz Josef Glacier, 23 km north is, however, quite a demanding stretch. The first 6 km involves a long, steady climb to the Cook Saddle (414 m), followed by a steep descent. There is a good site for free camping beside the stream at the bottom of the hill. Another stiff 3 km climb follows, another descent, then yet another ascent, only 2 km this time. A longer descent follows, and the last few kilometres into Franz Josef are flat.

Franz Josef is another tourist village. Its glacier nearby was named by von Haast in the 1860s after the Emperor of Austria-Hungary. Franz Josef has a store, tearooms, two hotels, several motels, a Youth Hostel and a motorcamp (cabins). There is also a National Park information centre in the village.

■ **Side Trip:** The tongue of Franz Josef Glacier is 7 km south of the village. A gravel no-exit road leads much of the way there, followed by a 40-minute walk across the rubble left behind as the glacier retreats. Do not attempt climbing the glacier itself without proper equipment and a guide.

From Franz Josef to the Forks are 15 km of undulating to rolling country passing Lake Mapourika en route. At 13 km from Franz Josef, turn off S.H. 6 to the Forks, a 3 km detour west. There is a motorcamp here, set in the bush.

■ **Side Trip:** Another 8 km on down a winding gravel road is the tiny beach settlement of Okarito. There is a Youth Hostel here. The beautiful Okarito lagoon to the north is the feeding and breeding ground of the white heron (kotuku).

DAY 5 THE FORKS TO ROSS ───────────────
99 km (add 8 km from Okarito)

An easy 13 km north of the Forks is Whataroa, a farming village with a crossroads tavern and a store. Another 37 km further on is Harihari, a slightly larger farming centre, with another store, and also a hotel and a motel.

The scenery along this stretch is less grand and imposing than that further south, largely consisting of stretches of farming country on the river plains, interspersed with stretches of low, bush-covered hills. But the Southern Alps form a constant and inspiring backdrop.

The terrain is mostly undemanding, with long flat to undulating stretches. There is, however, one significant climb, a 3 km ascent along the flanks of Mt. Hercules 10 km before Harihari.

From Harihari to Ross is 46 km. The first 10 km are flat; thereafter the terrain is mostly undulating, but with one mildly hilly stretch just before Ross. There is a tavern at Ianthe, a clear and beautiful lake 15 km north of Harihari, and a farmstay bed-and-breakfast with campsites 10km beyond that, but otherwise only isolated farmhouses and forest along the way.

Ross (pop. 500) is a former gold-mining town. It has a small museum, two hotels and a motel; also a motorcamp (cabins) next to one of the hotels.

DAY 6 ROSS TO GREYMOUTH/RAPAHOE ───────────
70 km/82 km

Continue northwards along S.H. 6. Hokitika is 30 km away across flat to rolling farming country.

■ **ALTERNATIVE ROUTE:** S.H. 6 runs inland the whole way. You can detour along the coast instead, if you wish. At 10 km outside Ross, turn left towards Ruatapu. The sealed road follows the coast from there. A road-cum-railway bridge crosses the Hokitika River into town. ■

Hokitika (pop. 3,414) also had its origin in the gold-rushes. It is now a market town and administrative centre. It is an interesting

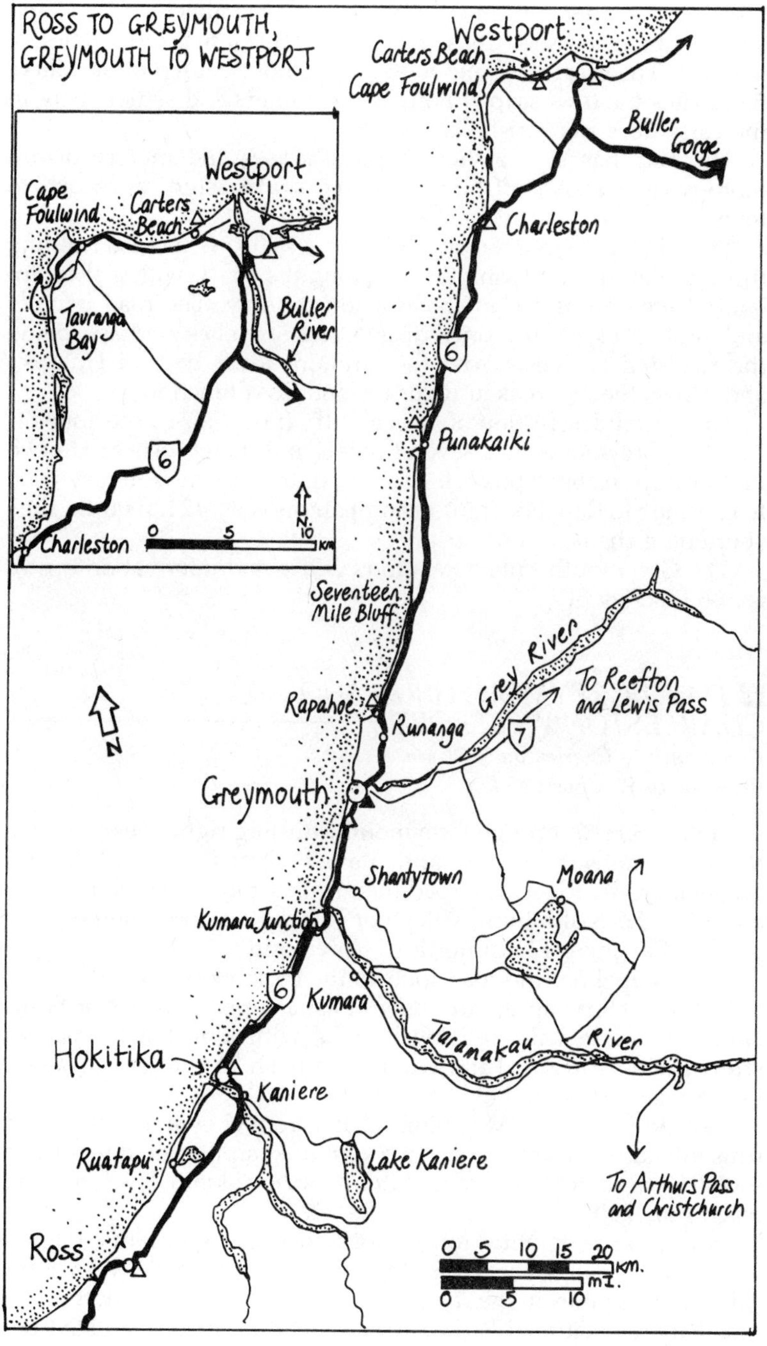
ROSS TO GREYMOUTH,
GREYMOUTH TO WESTPORT
Westport
Cape Foulwind
Carters Beach
Tauranga Bay
Buller River
Charleston
6
0 5 10 KM
N.
Westport
Carters Beach
Cape Foulwind
Buller Gorge
Charleston
6
Punakaiki
Seventeen Mile Bluff
Grey River
To Reefton and Lewis Pass
Rapahoe
Runanga
7
N
Greymouth
Shantytown
Moana
Kumara Junction
6
Kumara
Taramakau River
Hokitika
Kaniere
Ruatapu
Lake Kaniere
To Arthurs Pass and Christchurch
Ross
0 5 10 15 20 km.
mI.
0 5 10

town to wander around, with its old-fashioned shops and storefronts. The West Coast Historical Museum houses relics of the past. The great Romanesque-style Catholic church of St. Marys dominates the townscape (many of the miners and settlers here in the early days were Irish Catholics).

Hokitika has several hotels, guesthouses and motels; also a motorcamp (cabins) off S.H. 6 on the southeastern approach to town.

From Hokitika to Greymouth is an easy 40 km, the road running through flat to undulating terrain along the coast, with a short inland stretch around Kumara Junction midway. The road is quiet and well-surfaced, the only disquieting stretches perhaps being the road-rail bridges across the Arahura River beyond Hokitika and across the Taramakau River beyond Ross Junction.

For a brief description of Greymouth, (pop. 7,624), see Tour 11, Day 3A. Greymouth has several hotels and motels. There are two motorcamps (cabins) off S.H. 6 to the south of town. You may wish to continue to Rapahoe (motorcamp) on the coast 12 km north, thus shortening the next day's trip.

The Greymouth Public Relations Office and information centre is at 6 MacKay St.

■ DAY 7 GREYMOUTH/RAPAHOE TO CHARLESTON/WESTPORT
Greymouth to Charlestown: 71 km
Rapahoe to Westport: 85 km

Follow S.H. 6 through Greymouth, turning right (west) outside the main railway station, and almost immediately left (north) across the Grey River. The road then runs through a scrubby valley and past the coal-mining village of Runanga before rejoining the coast at Rapahoe, 12 km north of Greymouth.

From Rapahoe, the road follows the coast closely for 15 km or so, initially climbing up and down past a series of bluffs or headlands. This is a wild and lovely area, with long lonely beaches strewn with driftwood and windswept bush. It is often shrouded in sea mist.

Beyond Seventeen-Mile Bluff, 27 km from Greymouth, the road runs inland for 17 km, undulating past unkempt farmland which is reverting to rushes and scrub. After a further 2 km of low hills, you reach Punakaiki.

Punakaiki is famous for its rock formations—stratified limestone stacks rising sheer from the sea. These can be viewed a short side trip by foot from the road. This area is preserved as part of the new Paparoa National Park. An information centre is situated beside the road. There is also a shop and, a short distance north, at Punakaiki Beach, a motorcamp (cabins).

From here to Charleston is 31 km. For the first 16 km the road undulates along the coast, then turns inland through low scrub-covered hills. It climbs gradually for 4 km, descends for 2 km, climbs again for 2 km, descends, and so on, and so on, to Charleston.

Charleston (it will come as no surprise to find) was also once a gold-mining town. It is now a tiny, scattered village. There is a motorcamp here with cabins. The beach, once a busy but notoriously unsafe port, is just under 1 km to the west.

From Charleston, the road drops to the Nile River, passing through 8 km of low and undemanding hills, and entering a 12 km stretch of undulating plain. This is a rough-looking piece of country, mostly infertile and inhospitable pakihi swamp.

Twenty kilometres north of Charleston, S.H. 6 turns southeast up the Buller Gorge. Westport is actually a 6 km detour to the north.

Westport (pop. 4,660) began as a trading-station during the gold-rushes, and later developed as a port for the numerous coal-mining villages in its hinterland. It has a Coaltown Museum, with a representation of a working coal mine, a tribute to the source of its wealth. You can also visit working coal mines in the vicinity. Enquire at the Information Centre, 135 Palmerston St.

There are several hotels and motels in Westport; also a motor-camp (cabins), in Domett St. In the centre of town, turn right along Brougham St. (S.H. 67 to Karamea) past Victoria Square, then left (north) into Domett St. on the eastern edge of town.

There is another motorcamp (cabins) at Carters Beach nearby, but this is open only to Automobile Association members.

Excursions from Westport

EXCURSION 1 CAPE FOULWIND
40 km +

Cape Foulwind lighthouse is an easy 20 km west of town. Cross the Buller River at the southern end of town and turn right towards Carters Beach. This is a safe swimming beach. Beyond the beach lies one of New Zealand's largest cement works and, beyond that, the lighthouse itself. Five kilometres south of the lighthouse is Tauranga Bay, a lonely bay with a seal colony on a rocky islet off-shore.

EXCURSION 2 DENNISTON
48 km

In the hills northwest of Westport are a number of mining towns and villages, some of them long abandoned. Perhaps the most evocative of these is Denniston. To get there, follow S.H. 67 (the Karamea road) along the littoral northwest of Westport for 16 km, then, at Waimangaroa, turn into the hills. A steep 8 km climb from sea-level to 600 m follows.

Once a thriving town of more than 2,000 people, Denniston is now home to no more than a half-dozen. Heaps of rubble dot the bleak plateau, frequently shrouded by mist or swept by rain. Denniston was the site of the once-famous Denniston incline, the world's steepest self-acting incline railway, the remnants of which are still visible in the hills.

The road continues another 8 km into the hills beyond the derelict town, giving access to some working mines. It is sealed to Denniston, but gravel beyond.

EXCURSION 3 KARAMEA
192 km + return

This is an interesting and very scenic excursion. Its one major drawback is that the road is no-exit, and you must return the way you came. The Heaphy Track does in fact link the West Coast with Golden Bay, but this is unsuitable for bicycles. Some cyclists have crossed it, but they have had to carry both machines and luggage for about a third the distance. Not recommended.

Take the Karamea road northeastwards from Westport. This is flat to undulating for the first 43 km, as it crosses the narrow coastal plain, passing through the mining towns of Waimangaroa, Granity, Ngakawau and Hector. Eleven kilometres north of Hector, it turns inland up the Mokihinui River, but shortly leaves this to climb into the rugged and bush-clad Radiant Range.

Six kilometres after leaving the river, you reach the View Hill Saddle—at 420 m, the highest point en route. This completes the worst of the day's climbing. Although there are several further shorter rises between here and the Happy Valley 10 km north, the trend is downhill. From the Happy Valley the road descends gradually to the coast at Little Wanganui (hotel) 18 km south of Karamea. Most of the remaining distance to Karamea is flat, the road running along a swampy plain beside the sea, and turning briefly inland just before town to cross the Karamea River. A gravel road continues another 15 km further north to the Kohaihai River, where the Heaphy Track begins.

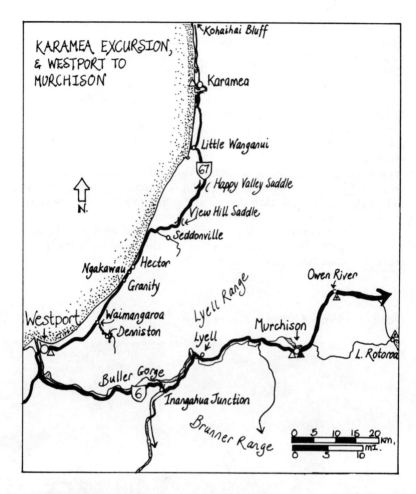

Karamea is a small (pop. 500) scattered settlement, centre of a dairying region more famous perhaps for its location than for its intrinsic interest. It has several shops, a motel, and a motorcamp (cabins.) It is also easy to find good spots for free camping in the vicinity, particularly to the north.

DAY 8 WESTPORT TO MURCHISON
98 km

Follow S.H. 67 southwards to rejoin S.H. 6 again 6 km from the town centre. Turn west here up the Buller River.

The Buller has cut its way here through the Paparoa Range on its way to the sea. The road follows its gorge closely for most of the next 40 km to Inangahua Junction. In parts it literally clings to the steep bluffs rising from the river. At Hawks Crag, 25 km from Westport, the cut rock overhangs the road.

Despite the steepness of the surrounding terrain, there is no considerable climbing to do. The road undulates through the gorge, gradually rising, but never steeply. Although this is the main road between Nelson and the West Coast, traffic is rarely a problem, but take care to keep well to the left in the winding stretches.

Inangahua Junction, a scattered village in a farming valley, is where S.H. 69 from Reefton joins S.H. 6. Turn left (southeast) just before the village. (A 1km detour along S.H. 69 leads to a service station and store, the last before Murchison.)

For 8 km beyond Inangahua Junction, the road gently undulates along an open stretch of the Buller Valley, then gradually begins to climb through bush-clad hills. At 16 km from Inangahua, it drops

Okarito Youth Hostel (Photo by Richard Oddy)

sharply but briefly downhill to cross a narrow river. Just beyond the bridge, up a side-road to the left, is the Lyell Historic Reserve. This is the site of a gold-mining town, now disappeared. There is an open-air historical display here. There is also a campground with an honesty-box for contributions. The site is beautiful, but the sandflies are terrible.

Beyond Lyell, there is some mild climbing to do over the next 23 km as the road follows the Upper Buller Gorge, but there are also long flat to undulating stretches. Three kilometres beyond Lyell you will see a massive slip in the hills: this is the result not of bush-felling but of an earthquake. This region lies along a fault-line and is notoriously unstable. The last 11 km to Murchison are through gentle terrain.

Murchison (pop. 600) is a small farming centre and service town with a small historical museum. It is a convenient place to stop, with several stores, a tearoom, two motels, a Youth Hostel (summer only); and a motorcamp (cabins) at the far end of town.

There is also a campsite at the Owens River Recreation Reserve behind the Owens River tavern 19km beyond Murchison. This is free, but the facilities are very basic unless you use the pub.

DAY 9 MURCHISON TO ST. ARNAUD
60 km

Continue northwards from Murchison, following S.H. 6 beside the Owens River, along a pleasant fertile valley set deep in the hills. The first 19 km to the Owens River Tavern are flat to undulating, with one or two gently rolling stretches. There is a 2 km hill beyond the Owens River Tavern, followed by more undulating and low rolling country.

At Kawatiri, 35 km from Murchison, is a riverside picnic area, a good spot for free camping. There is an open-air display in the reserve, a reminder of the days when this lonely spot was the terminal of a railway from Nelson, originally projected to reach Westport.

You can continue to Nelson direct from here via S.H. 6. For a longer, but far more interesting route, turn west along S.H. 63 to St. Arnaud.

St. Arnaud is 25km away. The first 8 km involve some gentle ups and downs; the rest is flat to undulating as the road passes along a wide mountain valley. This is different country compared to the bush-clad West Coast now left behind, being drier and more open. It is also cold and bleak in winter; even in summer you must be sure to have warm clothes handy.

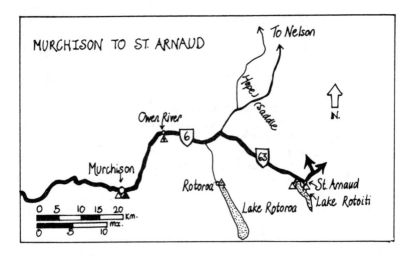

St. Arnaud is a tiny holiday village, a centre for tramping, climbing and winter sports, set at 630 m on the northern shore of Lake Rotoiti. It has a shop, a lodge, and a visitors information centre. There is a motorcamp at West Bay (turn off 2 km before the village), and a campground on the lakeside at Kerr Bay below the village itself.

St. Arnaud is where you decide whether to return direct to Picton via the Wairau Valley, or to take the longer route through Nelson.

DAY 10 ST. ARNAUD TO NELSON VIA TOPHOUSE AND GOLDEN DOWNS
90 km

Much of the route that follows has been only recently improved. Few maps yet mark the stretch between St. Arnaud and Golden Downs as a through-route. Some climbing is involved, but the road is a quiet one, and a very pretty one, and much preferable to the main road (S.H. 6).

From St. Arnaud, take the Blenheim road (S.H. 63) northeast. This rises gently through the meadows. Five kilometres from St. Arnaud, turn left (north) onto a minor road which leads to Tophouse and Kikiwa.

This road is uphill for the first 3 km, rising to 727 m. The seal ends as it begins to descend. The next 7 km are gravel, then the seal begins again.

At 23 km from St. Arnaud, turn right up the Golden Downs

road. A steepish 3 km climb through pine forests follows. The road then runs downhill for 9 km, steeply at first, but later levelling off.

At 34 km from St. Arnaud is the Golden Downs recreation area and campground. This is the centre of Golden Downs Forest, 30,000 hectares of pine and deciduous trees, the latter making a fine sight in autumn. At Golden Downs, the road forks: take the right fork for Nelson. A flat 2 km straight follows.

This is followed by a 4 km rise, steepening towards the top. From here the road drops gently down through the lovely Wai-iti Valley, joining S.H. 6 at Belgrove, 40 km from St. Arnaud. Turn right (northwest).

The last 40 km of the day into Nelson are much less scenic. The road is flat and busy, running successively through the towns of Wakefield (pop. 1,094), Brightwater (pop. 973), Hope (pop. 1,150), Richmond (pop. 7,204) and Stoke before entering Nelson itself.

There are a few items of interest along the way, however. Just before Brightwater, a monument to Sir Ernest Rutherford (Baron Rutherford) (1871–1937) stands beside the road. Rutherford, who was born here, was the first man to split the atom, and is considered the father of modern nuclear physics. In Wakefield is the church of St. Johns (1846), the oldest church in the South Island.

The last few kilometres into Nelson are through its uninteresting southwestern suburbs. There is a choice of two routes into the city centre. Just beyond Stoke, the road forks. S.H. 6 veers left here. This route leads via Annabrook Drive and Tahunanui Drive to Tahunanui Beach (there is a motorcamp down Beach Rd. to the left), and from there around the waterfront via Rocks Rd. and Wakefield Quay to the centre of the city. At the end of Wakefield Quay turn right (southeast) into Haven Rd.

Alternatively, take the right hand fork beyond Stoke into Waimea Drive. This leads via Rutherford St. direct to the city. You will pass Nelson College to your right, and shortly afterwards will see the cathedral one block away. Turn east along Hendy St. one block later.

Nelson has hotels and motels in abundance. It also has two other motorcamps besides the one in Tahunanui Beach. One is 5 km up the Brook Valley Rd. east of the city, and yet another a similar distance up the Matai River Valley. All three motorcamps have cabins.

The Regional Promotion Office, which provides tourist information, is situated on the corner of Trafalgar and Halifax Streets. (phone 82304).

Nelson (pop. 34,274) was founded in 1842, with the arrival of ships belonging to the New Zealand Company. The early settlers found the land poor and survival a struggle. For many years Nelson and Tasman Bay was an isolated and neglected region of New Zealand. In recent years, however, it has increasingly found favour as a holiday town and retirement centre. It is a civilized place to live, a sunny town with a mild climate, and a pretty town with good parks and gardens, and with a wide variety of cultural activities.

There is a good art gallery, the Bishop Suter Art Gallery, a Harbour Board Museum, the noted Nelson Provincial Museum, and any number of old buildings. The inner city and the older residential areas to the east are pleasant places to stroll in, as yet unspoiled as in larger cities by high-rise or mirror-glass buildings. Only the cathedral (1925–1967) disappoints, set prominently on a knoll above the town but of an uninspired design unworthy of the site.

■ **ALTERNATIVE ROUTE:** If taking the Golden Bay excursion, there is no need to go right into Nelson, since you will have to visit it later anyway. Head straight for Motueka instead. In Brightwater, turn off S.H. 6 northeast towards Appleby. A minor road, but a sealed one, joins S.H. 60 8 km west of Richmond. Continue to Mapua, which has a motorcamp (cabins), or carry on to Motueka. It is about the same distance between St. Arnaud and Mapua as between St. Arnaud and Nelson, but this alternative will save you doubling back over the Nelson-to-Richmond stretch of S.H. 6. ■

■ *ALTERNATIVE DAY 10A* ST ARNAUD TO PICTON VIA SPRING CREEK
129 km

This is the direct route to Picton and the Cook Strait ferry. It is a longish distance, but easy riding most of the way. If you prefer to split the distance, there is a pleasant motorcamp at Spring Creek, 107 km from St. Arnaud and 22 km from Picton.

Follow S.H. 63 northeast from St. Arnaud. This rises gently through alpine meadows for 8 km or so before crossing a watershed and entering the upper valley of the Wairau River. From here on is largely downhill as the road drops gradually from 727 m almost to sea-level down the length of the valley. In the lower reaches of the valley, the road flattens out, however, the slope becoming so slight as to be virtually imperceptible.

The first 13 km are along the northern bank of the Wairau, the rest of the distance along the southern bank. There are no towns or villages en route, only isolated farmhouses. The scenery is grand enough, with the broad, braided river on one side and the mountains on the other, but it becomes monotonous as the day goes on.

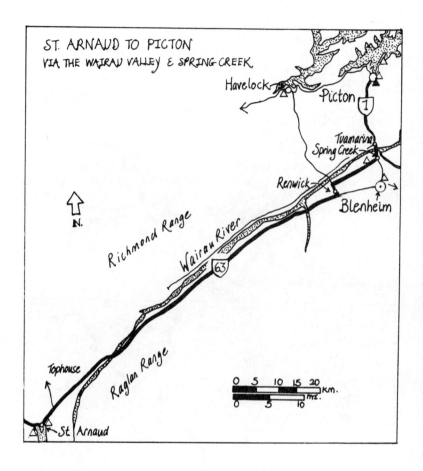

At Renwick, 92 km from St. Arnaud, turn north through the town and along S.H. 6. Another 3 km further on, turn west. At 11 km along is a motorcamp (cabins).

The Cook Strait ferries depart at 5.40 A.M. (not Mondays), 12.00 P.M. (not Mondays and Tuesdays), 2.20 P.M., 7.45 P.M. (not Mondays) and 10.20 P.M. (Mondays only). Timetables may be altered during holiday weekends.

DAY 11 NELSON TO HAVELOCK
75 km

It is 110 km from Nelson to Picton, too far for one day if you hope to catch the ferry. You could break the trip at Pelorus Bridge,

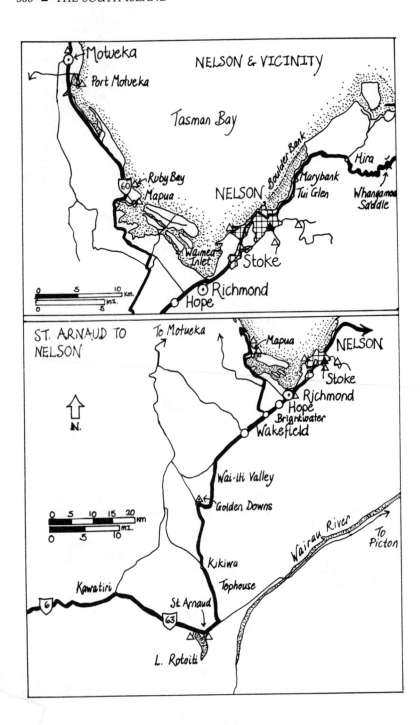

NELSON & VICINITY

Motueka

Port Motueka

Tasman Bay

Ruby Bay

Mapua

Boulder Bank

Hira

Marybank

Tui Glen

Whangamoa Saddle

NELSON

Waimea Inlet

Stoke

Richmond

Hope

0   5   10 KM.
0   5 MI.

ST. ARNAUD TO NELSON

To Motueka

Mapua

NELSON

Stoke

Richmond

Hope

Brightwater

Wakefield

N.

Wai-iti Valley

Golden Downs

0 5 10 15 20 KM
0   5   10 MI.

Kikiwa

Wairau River

To Picton

Kawatiri

Tophouse

6

St. Arnaud

63

L. Rotoiti

56 km from Nelson, if you leave late in the day; otherwise continue to Havelock.

Leave Nelson on S.H. 6 running northeast along the coast. The first 9 km are flat, then the road turns inland, gently rising for most of another 5 km up a valley, before beginning a steepish and, in parts, winding 8 km climb to the Whangamoa Saddle (357 m). A steady 12 km drop follows, 2 km of undulating country, another 2 km rise over the Rai Saddle (247 m), and a 3 km descent down the Rai Valley. There are tearooms in the Rai Valley village.

Eight kilometres beyond Rai is Pelorus Bridge, a scenic spot set in the bush, with glow-worm caves nearby. There are tearooms here, and a motorcamp (cabins).

From Pelorus Bridge to Havelock, 27 km away, is flat to undulating terrain. There is a shop and hotel and a motorcamp midway at Canvastown, scene of a gold-rush in the 1860s. There is a mural with a historical theme in the Canvastown public hall—ask for the key in the shop.

Havelock is a holiday town set at the southern end of Pelorus Sound. It has several shops, a tearoom, a summer Youth Hostel,

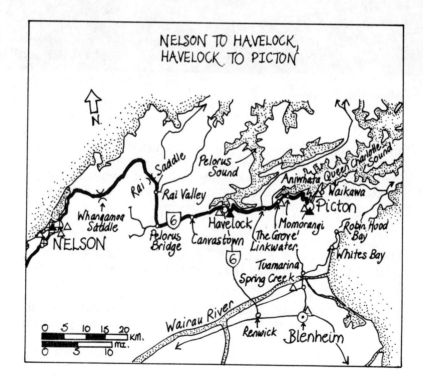

Punakaiki, looking south

and a motorcamp. The Youth Hostel is situated in the school that Lord Rutherford attended as a child. There is a museum in the old Methodist church. Havelock is the centre for exploration of the Marlborough Sounds. Launches are for hire here for day-trips or camping trips almost anywhere in the Sounds.

DAY 12 *HAVELOCK TO PICTON VIA LINKWATER AND QUEEN CHARLOTTE DRIVE*
35 km

This is a lovely scenic route. The road is narrow but sealed its whole length, and only busy, if at all, before or after ferry arrivals and departures at the Picton end.

S.H. 6 heads southward from Havelock. Just outside town, turn east onto Queen Charlotte Drive. The first 8 km are through low, gentle hills and around the southern end of the Mahakipawa Arm of Pelorus Sound. There follows a 10 km flat stretch through Linkwater to the southwestern end of Queen Charlotte Sound, and a further 17 km of low, but not necessarily gentle, hills to Picton.

There is a motel at The Grove 17 km from Havelock, and a shop and motorcamp (cabins) at Momorangi Bay, 4 km beyond.

> ∎ **Side Trip:** A short detour north of Linkwater is Anikawa. This houses New Zealand's first Outward Bound School, founded in 1962. This school runs courses designed to build people's self-reliance by training and testing them in outdoor skills.

For ferry timetables from Picton, see p. 175.

TOUR 14A Golden Bay Excursion
3–4 days: 314 km+

This is an interesting excursion into an isolated and little-travelled corner of New Zealand. Its main drawback is that there is only one road into and out of Golden Bay. The end of the road at Port Puponga is 157 km from Nelson, and to return to Nelson you must retrace each and every one of them.

DAY 1 NELSON TO TAKAKA —————————
108 km

From Nelson, return to Richmond. Just south of Richmond, turn northeast along S.H. 60 towards Motueka. The road is flat to undulating much of the way, though with some low rolling stretches, passing successively along the edge of the Waimea Inlet, Ruby Bay, and the Moutere Inlet. There is a motorcamp (cabins) at Ruby Bay, 3 km from Nelson, and another in Mapua.

Motueka (pop. 5,502) is the centre of a large arable plain where hops and tobacco and pip fruits are grown. This region is famous for its raspberries and for its apples. In summer and autumn casual work is often available harvesting and picking fruit.

Motueka has several hotels and motels. There is a motorcamp at Port Motueka south of the town (turn seaward off S.H. 60 over the causeway crossing the Moutere Inlet) and another at the northern end of town.

Follow S.H. 60 north from Motueka. This enters the Takaka

Limestone stack at Punakaiki

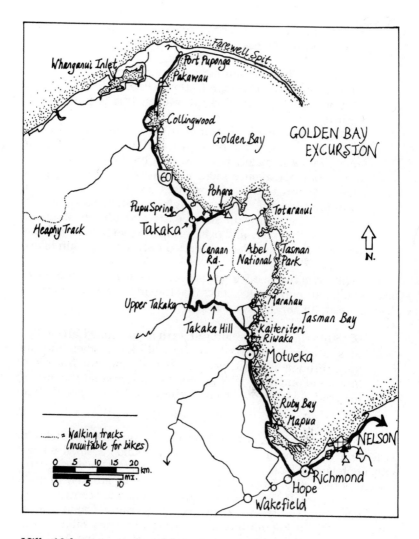

Hills 10 km across the plains. A demanding 8 km climb to 800 m follows. The Takaka Hills are the source of much of New Zealand's marble and you will pass quarries during the ascent.

■ **Side Trip:** Seven kilometres north of Motueka is the turn-off to Kaiteriteri. Another 7 km of low coastal hills brings you to this noted beauty spot famous for its golden sands and clear waters. A little too famous, perhaps: in summer, up to 5,000 visitors crowd its motorcamps. Another 9 km further north over a gravel road is Marahau, a pleasant beach and much less crowded. There is a motorcamp (cabins) here.

Marahau is at the southern end of the coastal track which runs through Abel Tasman National Park to Totaranui. Like all tracks in National Parks, however, this is forbidden to cyclists.

You can return from Marahau via a sealed road leading due south through the hills towards Riwaka and Motueka, emerging immediately to the west of the Kaiteriteri turnoff, or you can take a much more adventurous route west up the Holyoake Stream. Two kilometres southeast of Marahau, turn into Moss Rd. This is a rough road and a steep one, its surface being gravel in some parts and dirt in others. It climbs up the valley and over a ridge to join S.H. 60 halfway up the Takaka Hill. Recommended only for mountain bikes.

You will certainly need to pause for breath at the summit of Takaka Hill, and perhaps to reflect that the first wheeled vehicle to pass this way (in 1877) was a bicycle.

■ **Side Trip:** From the summit, turn north along Canaan Rd. This is a gravel road which winds 10 km further into the hills, through a landscape of dead trees and sink holes and limestone outcrops. Half an hour's walk beyond the end of the road is Harwood's Hole, a chasm 370 m deep and 50 m wide.

From the top of Takaka Hill there is a 15 km descent, steep in parts, and with hairpin bends, to Upper Takaka, a small village with a hotel in the Upper Takaka Valley. The next 20 km are a gentle descent of the valley. Good spots for free camping are easy to find.

Takaka (pop. 1,194) is a farming town and holiday centre. It has both hotels and motels. The nearest motorcamp (cabins) is at Pohara Beach, 10 km northeast. (You actually turn off towards Pohara 3 km south of Takaka.) The headquarters of the Abel Tasman National Park is in Takaka.

■ **Side Trip:** Beyond Pohara the road winds along the coast then over the hills to Totaranui, an isolated beach 33 km from Takaka. There is a National Park information centre here, and a campground. Over summer this is often crowded: if you want to stay here, you should check at the National Park office in Takaka first.

DAY 2 *TAKAKA TO COLLINGWOOD*
27 km

Follow S.H. 60 northeast from Takaka.

■ **Side Trip:** At Waitapu, 8 km northeast of Takaka, you can detour 4 km south to Waikoropupu Springs (Pupu Springs) if you wish. These are large freshwater springs set in a bush reserve. Pupu Springs was once the site of a short-lived gold rush.

Collingwood is a harbourside village, founded at the mouth of the Aorere River during a short-lived gold-rush in the 1850s. It has a motel, a guesthouse and a motorcamp (cabins). There is another motorcamp at Pakawau Beach, 14 km further on.

■ **Side Trip:** S.H. 60 ends at Collingwood, but a minor road continues around the Ruataniwha Inlet and up the coast to Port Puponga 22 km north. It is sealed most of the way, and fairly easy going.

Beyond Puponga, Farewell Spit juts eastward into Golden Bay. This is a narrow 35 km stretch of sand and marshland, unpopulated except for a lighthouse at the far end. It is not practical for cycling because of the wind and shifting sands. Four-wheel drive trips, however, depart from Collingwood to the lighthouse over the peak holiday period in summer. You need to book ahead, and to confirm the departure time which depends, of course, on the tide. The cost is $29.00 per head, and the tour takes about five hours.

■ **Side Trip:** At Pakawau, a gravel road turns west through a gap in the hills. On reaching the muddy shores of the Whanganui Inlet, it turns southwest and runs along the estuary and down the coast beyond for 41 km. This is one of the loneliest roads in New Zealand, a no-exit road petering out in the coastal hills miles from nowhere. There are no shops en route, no villages, few houses, and no way out except the way you came.

You have now come to the end of the last cycleable road described in this book, but by no means to the end of the last cycleable road in New Zealand. There is a lot more open road out there waiting for you. May the sun be on your face and the wind at your back. Good cycling!

FURTHER READING

Most of the items below can be consulted in any of New Zealand's larger city libraries. Prices are also given in New Zealand dollars for some books that are still in print. These can be purchased through any good bookstore or, in some cases, direct from the publishers.

1. Cycle Touring

One of the main sources of information on bikes and touring in New Zealand is *Southern Cyclist* (now *New Zealand Cyclist*), an Auckland-based quarterly magazine begun in 1979. *Southern Cyclist* 21 (Aug. 1984) has an Index to issues 1–20. Current subscription rates and back copies are available from Southern Cyclist Inc., PO Box 5890, Auckland, New Zealand.

The following guides together describe, albeit very briefly, most cycleable roads in New Zealand: Helen Crabb's *Cycle Touring in the South Island* (4th ed., CCA, 1989, $9.00) and J.B. Ringer's *Cycle Touring in the North Island* (3rd ed., Southern Cyclist, 1988, $13.95).

The following regional guides have been published: Helen Crabb's *Cycling in Christchurch and Canterbury* (CCA, 1986, $6.00), and Peter Satterthwaite's *Auckland Bike Rides* (ABA, 1982). The former is available from the Canterbury Cyclists Association, PO Box 2547, Christchurch; the latter is out-of-print.

There is so far only one book-length account of a cycle journey in New Zealand: Neville Peat's *Detours: a Journey through Small-town New Zealand* (Whitcoulls, 1982).

2. General Information

Useful reference sources of information on New Zealand include the *Heinemann New Zealand Atlas* (Heinemann, 1987, $75.00); the *New Zealand Atlas* (N.Z. Govt. Printer, 1976), the latest edition of the annual *New Zealand Official Yearbook* (N.Z. Govt. Printer), and *Wises New Zealand Guide: a Gazetteer of New Zealand* (8th ed., 1987)

3. General Guidebooks

Substantial background on New Zealand is provided by the *AA Atlas and Touring Guide of New Zealand* (Lansdowne, 1985, $49.95), Errol Brathwaite's *Companion Guide to the North Island* (Collins, 1970) and to the *South Island* (Collins, 1972), Diana Pope's *Mobil New Zealand Travel Guide: North Island* (5th ed, Reed, 1984, $21.95) and *South Island* (4th ed., Reed Methuen, 1986, $21.95), and Maurice Shadbolt's *Shell Guide to New Zealand* (Joseph, 1976) and *Reader's Digest Guide to New Zealand* (Reader's Digest, 1988, $44.98).

Practical travellers' guides include: John W. McDermott's *How to Get Lost and Found in Updated New Zealand* (ORAFA, 1986), the latest editions of *Fodor's Australia, New Zealand and the South Pacific* and *Frommer's New Zealand on $25 a Day*, Elizabeth Hansen's *The Woman's Travel Guide to New Zealand* (Whitcoulls, 1984, $10.95) and Tony Wheeler's *New Zealand: A Travel Survival Kit* (Lonely Planet, 1988, $14.95).

4. Specialist and Regional Guides

Cyclists also intending to travel by other means of transport will be interested in Sean Millar's *Getting Around New Zealand's North Island* (Millar, 1986, $12.95) and *South Island* (Millar, 1985, $12.95). Cyclists who are also trampers will appreciate Robbie Burton's *A Trampers Guide to New Zealand's National Parks* (Reed Methuen, 1987, $19.95), John Cobb's *The Walking Tracks of New Zealand's National Parks* (Endeavour, 1985), and Jim Du Fresne's *Tramping in New Zealand* (Lonely Planet, 1982). Lynne Alexander's *Outdoor Adventures in New Zealand* (Reed Methuen, 1986, $21.95) is also helpful, though has little specifically on cycling. The best guide to Auckland and region available is Brigid Pike's *A Guide to Auckland* (Hodder, 1987, $19.95) The Government Printer has also recently published a series of regional guides, among them Neva Clarke McKenna's *Northland* and Errol Brathwaite's *Canterbury*, both priced at $24.95.

5. Directories

Hotels and motels are listed in the Automobile Association's annual *AA Accommodation Directory: North Island* and *AA Accommodation Guide: South Island*. These are made available by the association only to members or members of associations with reciprocal rights. *Jasons Hotel Directory* and *Jasons Motels and Motel Lodges*, however, are commercially available at $5.50 and $8.80 respectively.

The NZ Tourist & Publicity Department puts out a *Guide to Country Pubs in New Zealand*, available gratis from offices of the Department and some tourist information centres. Bed-and-breakfast accommodation is covered in Janete Thomas's *The New Zealand Bed and Breakfast Book* (Moonshine, 1989, $17.95).

The Youth Hostel Association of New Zealand, of course, puts out its own annual handbook, available from any YHANZ office or hostel.

Motorcamps and campgrounds are covered in the *AA Outdoor Guide: North Island*, and in the *AA Accommodation Guide: South Island*, listed above. The most useful single directory for the cycle tourist, however, is the annual *Jason's Budget Accommodation* ($4.40). This includes motorcamps, lodges, budget bed-and-breakfasts, and moderately priced hotels throughout the country.

INDEX

THE AUTHOR

Bruce Ringer is a librarian who lives in Auckland, New Zealand. A keen cyclist who has toured extensively in New Zealand (of course) and in Europe, he commutes to work daily by bike. He has previously published a cycle tour guide to New Zealand's North Island, several books on other topics, and articles, fiction and poetry in a variety of New Zealand periodicals. He is a former editor of *Southern Cyclist* magazine. He is married, with two children.

Of *Cycle Touring in New Zealand,* Bruce Ringer says, 'the sort of cyclist I kept in mind when writing this guide was one to whom cycling is not so much an end in itself, but the best and most exciting way to see a country and appreciate its scenery and its way of life. The sort of cyclist who is able to cover long distances if the need arises, but who is also happy with a leisurely pace allowing time for sight-seeing. The sort of cyclist who likes open, un-crowded roads, and setting up camp beside isolated lakes and rivers and beaches. . . . Perhaps this means all of us!'